Diaries, Letters and

LYNETTE ROBERTS was born in Buer
1909 and died in West Wales in 1995. ~~She published two collec~~-
tions of poems in her lifetime, both from Faber and Faber: *Poems*
(1944) and *Gods with Stainless Ears* (subtitled 'A Heroic Poem';
1951). She married the Welsh writer and editor Keidrych Rhys.

PATRICK MCGUINNESS is translator of Mallarmé's *For Anatole's
Tomb* (2003) and author of a book of poems, *The Canals of Mars*
(2004), both published by Carcanet Press. His edition of Lynette
Roberts's *Collected Poems* was published by Carcanet in 2005.

Lynette Roberts in a Chinese costume from Liberty, photographed in 1953 by
Ida Kar (1908–74).

Lynette Roberts
Diaries, Letters and Recollections

Edited with an introduction by
Patrick McGuinness

First published in Great Britain in 2008 by
Carcanet Press Limited
Alliance House
Cross Street
Manchester M2 7AQ

A CIP catalogue record for this book is available from the British Library
ISBN 978 1 85754 856 3

The publisher acknowledges financial assistance from Arts Council England

Typeset by XL Publishing Services, Tiverton
Printed and bound in England by SRP Ltd, Exeter

Contents

Illustrations

Captions to most illustrations are taken from Lynette Roberts's own notes on the back of photographs and from a typed 'List of photographs suggested for my book'.

Introduction

The publication of Lynette Roberts's *Collected Poems* 2005 made her work generally available for the first time in over half a century. Those who knew it, however, were passionate and engaged, and believed in its unique place in twentieth-century poetry: experimental but in the lyric tradition, difficult yet immediate, attentive to ordinary life but also grand and heroic and full of eloquence.

Her poetry and its place in the poetic tradition are eccentric, and Roberts herself was an outsider in all sorts of ways: in terms of nationality and belonging; in terms of intellectual background; and in terms of life and location. An outsider, she was also marginal, hovering on the outskirts of the London literary scene of the 1940s and the first flowering of Welsh writing in English; she was from an expatriate family from Argentina and settled on the west coast of Wales in rented accommodation, and was even domiciled with her children, in the 1950s, in a caravan, first in Laugharne and then in Hertfordshire. Committed to mental institutions sporadically from the mid-1950s onwards, she became a Jehovah's Witness after her first mental breakdown. Falling silent as a writer, not tending to her reputation, and making no attempts to reintroduce herself into literary life, she became forgotten. Her obituaries in 1995 were, for many, the first they had heard of her for nearly fifty years.

Roberts's poems lie outside and beyond the obvious markers, but this puts them in good company. Roberts has perhaps more claim than most to that title – by which we designate writers we know are important but who don't have the readership or the reputation to prove it – of being a 'poet's poet'. T.S. Eliot published her two books at Faber, *Poems* in 1944 and, in 1951, the resonantly titled *Gods with Stainless Ears*. Over the years she developed a small cult following, often among writers on the experimental wing of the poetry 'scene'. Several critics – notably Tony Conran, John Pikoulis and Nigel Wheale – kept her achievement in view, while a *Poetry Wales* special issue in 1983 laid the groundwork for a substantial critical revaluation of her work.[1]

---

1 See especially: Tony Conran, 'Lynette Roberts: War Poet', in *The Cost of Strangeness: Essays on the English Poets of Wales* (Llandysul: Gomer, 1983); 'Lynette Roberts: The Lyric Pieces' (*Poetry Wales*, 1983 19/2); and 'Lynette Roberts', *Frontiers in Anglo-Welsh Poetry* (Cardiff: University of Wales Press,1997). John Pikoulis,

Roberts's poetry is extraordinary, and remains her central achievement. However, her prose writings have a claim on our attention too, and not just because they illuminate her vibrant, experimental poems. They are of interest because they document a particular life under extraordinary circumstances: a woman's experience of wartime and its everyday hardships, but also the imaginative life that flowers in spite of them, and the passion and imagination with which she makes a world from the material she has at hand.

I

Lynette Roberts was born Evelyn Beatrice Roberts on 4 July 1909 in Buenos Aires, of Welsh-descended parents: her father's family was originally from Ruthin in north-east Wales, and her mother's from Pembrokeshire. Her father, Cecil Arthur Roberts, trained as a railway engineer and became head of Western Railways in Argentina. Lynette had two sisters, Winifred and Rosemary, and a brother, Dymock, who was sent to school at Winchester. After a mental breakdown when he was sixteen, he was committed to a mental institution in Salisbury and remained there until his death in 1980. He is mentioned in Lynette's autobiographical notes, and in *Gods With Stainless Ears* the poem's speaker remembers 'my brother./ His Cathedral mind in Bedlam'.

Her mother, Ruby Garbutt, died of typhoid on 3 July 1923, the day before Lynette's birthday, after drinking contaminated water. In her notes for an autobiography, Lynette claims that it was she who, on her mother's instructions, fetched her the poisoned water. Soon after their mother's death, Lynette and her sisters were sent to Bournemouth for their schooling and Cecil Roberts remarried his childhood sweetheart, Nora Sloan.

In the 1930s, Lynette studied at the Central School of Arts and Crafts in London, and after travelling around Europe (notably visits to Germany, Spain and Hungary), she trained to be a florist with

---

'Lynette Roberts and Alun Lewis', (*Poetry Wales* 1983, 19/2); 'The Poetry of the Second World War', in *British Poetry 1900-50*, ed. Gary Day and Brian Docherty (London: Macmillan, 1995). Nigel Wheale, 'Lynette Roberts: Legend and Form in the 1940s', *Critical Quarterly* (1994, 36/3); '"Beyond the Trauma Stratus": Lynette Roberts' *Gods with Stainless Ears* and the Post-War Cultural Landscape', *Welsh Writing in English*, vol. 3 (1997). To this must be added a substantial review entitled 'The Brain's Tent' by John Wilkinson of Roberts's *Collected Poems*, published in *The Boston Review* in September/October 2006, and now collected in his book *The Lyric Touch* (Cambridge: Salt, 2007).

Constance Spry, before setting up a flower-arranging business called Bruska. She was briefly engaged to Merlin Minshall, intelligence officer, amateur racing driver and the man often claimed to have been the inspiration for Ian Fleming's James Bond. The engagement was broken when Lynette agreed to marry the Welsh writer and editor Keidrych Rhys, whom she first met at a *Poetry London* event in London in 1939 organised by Tambimuttu, the magazine's editor. As Lynette recalls in her autobiographical notes, Keidrych 'was charming and spoke like a prince'. His friend (and best man at their wedding), Dylan Thomas, remembered Lynette as 'A curious girl, a poet, as they say, in her own right ... with all the symptoms of hysteria'. Lynette and Keidrych married in Llansteffan (Llanstephan in English), a village on the Tywi estuary, on 4 October 1939.

They rented a cottage in the village of Llanybri, a few miles from Llansteffan, where they lived throughout the war, with frequent visits to London. As her diary and her autobiographical writings show, it was a hard life: not only in its material deprivation and isolation, but also because of Keidrych's frequent absences from home on military postings or scraping money together for his publishing projects. After a miscarriage in March 1940, Lynette gave birth to two children: Angharad, in May 1945 and Prydein, in November 1946.

In 1942, Roberts sent some poems to T.S. Eliot at Faber. A few months later she followed it up with the manuscript of what was then called *A Heroic Poem*, which in 1951 became *Gods with Stainless Ears*. Eliot found it 'stiff going' at first, but suggested she send him a volume of short poems. He liked the book, and *Poems* came out in 1944, with a generous recommendation from Eliot on the dustjacket:

> She has, first, an unusual gift for observation and evocation of scenery and place, whether it is in Wales or her native South America; second, a gift for verse construction, influenced by the Welsh tradition, which is evident in her freer verse as well as in stricter forms; and third, an original idiom and tone of speech.

The Roberts/Eliot letters are unpublished, but they reveal the extraordinary care and goodwill with which Eliot did his job: suggesting revisions, tactfully expressing bafflement at some of Roberts's more *outré* lexical choices, patient and flexible in the face of her explanations. Her account of a visit to his Faber office is published here for the first time, and is a revealing insight into the private Eliot: as the children lay waste to his office, Eliot is gracious and supportive to Lynette, and charming with them.

Initially through her husband, Roberts knew the poets associated with the 'new romantic' and 'Apocalypse' schools. She moved in the same circles as Tambimuttu, Henry Treece, George Barker, Roy Campbell, Kathleen Raine and others, and was part of the Fitzrovia scene of the 1940s. She also knew the Anglo-Welsh poets – not just Dylan Thomas, but R.S. Thomas, Glyn Jones and Vernon Watkins, and had a brief correspondence with the soldier-poet Alun Lewis, for whom she wrote one of her best-known poems, 'Poem from Llanybri'. Her diary also gives us an amusing early impression of the young R.S. Thomas, who published his first book, *The Stones of the Field*, with Keidrych's Druid Press.

In 1942, Roberts began a correspondence with Robert Graves. She helped Graves with his research into Celtic myths for *The White Goddess*, and Graves in turn read and commented on her poems. Much like Eliot, he found some of her lexical adventurousness hard to follow, but as she had been with Eliot so she was with Graves: she mostly held her ground and argued her case. Some of the letters in this volume show how Graves and his wife Beryl supported Lynette during and after her divorce, though their correspondence peters out by the early 1950s, by which time Lynette's career as a poet was effectively over.

Lynette Roberts's most significant work was done in Llanybri during the war. It was in there and in West Wales generally that she found the inspiration for her poetry, and where she developed her distinctive style. But she also wrote prose – as well as her diary, she wrote essays and articles, and pursued eclectic researches, almost always on subjects near to hand: etymology and dialect, butterflies and insects, cattle, mining, farming methods, architecture... She read voraciously but in a scattered and autodidactic way, borrowing books from libraries, sending off to the National Library of Wales in Aberystwyth for materials, even writing to the authors for copies of their books on birds or butterflies. In addition, she was reading Welsh myths and legends from the Mabinogion and elsewhere, and keeping up with contemporary poetry in English and, so far as she could, in Welsh. Among the regrettably lost work that she produced in this period – and there must be a great deal of lost material, given her itinerant and damaged life – was a novel, *Nesta*, which was read by both Graves and Eliot.

By 1948, the marriage with Keidrych had broken up, and Lynette left Llanybri and moved temporarily to a caravan in Laugharne, the village that inspired Thomas's *Under Milk Wood*. Her address for a while was 'The Caravan, The Graveyard, Laugharne'. Divorced in

1949, she returned to London before moving to another caravan in Bells Wood, Hertfordshire. In 1951, she sent *The Fifth Pillar of Song*, eighty-odd pages of new poems, to Eliot. He finally turned it down two years later, and with good reason. Though there are a few fine and unusual poems in the manuscript (these are now published in the *Collected Poems*), most of the work is too unfocused and rhetorically overloaded. Poems continued to appear in journals and magazines until 1953. In December 1952, a verse play, *O Lovers of Death*, was broadcast on the Welsh Regional Service, but no script survives and the recording is lost. In February 1953 *El Dorado*, a 'radio ballad' about Welsh colonists in Patagonia, was broadcast on the Third Programme. She proposed a few more projects to Eliot and other publishers, but they came to nothing, and in 1954 she published her last book, *The Endeavour*, a novel about Captain Cook's expedition.

In 1955–6 Roberts started the Chislehurst Caves art project, in which she planned to exhibit contemporary art in the unusual setting of the caves. The venture ended in disaster when a cave ceiling collapsed and injured one of the artists. Partly as a result of this failure, she had a mental breakdown in 1956. That same year, while she was recovering, she became a Jehovah's Witness, and remained one for the rest of her life. She returned to Llanybri in 1970. She was diagnosed as schizophrenic soon after, and was committed four times under the Mental Health Act to St David's Hospital in Carmarthen. After her first stay in hospital, she moved to Carmarthen, and then in 1989 to a residential home in Ferryside, overlooking Llansteffan. She died of heart failure on 26 September at Towy Haven, and is buried in Llanybri churchyard.

II

This volume covers the decade between 1939 – the meeting with Keidrych Rhys, the start of the war and the move to Wales – and 1949, when she divorced him and left Llanybri. It is the prose counterpart to her *Collected Poems*, covering not just the same period of her life, but often the same subjects and preoccupations that find their way into the poetry.

This book begins with Lynette's diary of her war years in Llanybri. Consisting of 157 pages of typescript with handwritten additions, it is an extraordinary document: tough-minded, optimistic and engaged, but also humorous and affectionate in its portrayal of people and place. It describes traumatic events such as

air raids and village deaths, downed planes and the arrival of evacuees, but also the less spectacular dimension of daily life: water
shortages, bad crops, boredom and solitude, even the difficulty of
getting library books .

'To the village of lace and stone/ Came strangers', she recalls in
the poem 'Lamentation', 'I was one of these/ Always observant and
slightly obscure'. Roberts retains the outsider's perspective, and
indeed thinks of herself as a perpetual outsider, but she plays her full
part of the village's daily life too: she milks the cows, digs the fields,
makes wreaths for the dead. The diary's opening entry, for 3
November 1939, less than a month after they were married, gives us
a sense of its freshness of tone, Roberts's feisty and mischievous
manner, and her restless intellect:

> Keidrych enjoyed his lunch; he looks very unpleasant today.
> Debauched, with his four-day beard, he is busy scratching behind
> me writing to Kilham Roberts asking if the Literary Society will
> grant us some money to live on. There can be no dole for us. The
> M[inistry] of L[abour] said we had no stamps. Even though we
> have both worked previously for two or three years. Neither can
> he give us a job. Then what are we to live on, Government, I ask
> you? There are always fallen apples, and the onion soup, but how
> long will that last! Today Keidrych frequently found cinders or
> grit in his stewed apples. I told him poets must always expect
> pieces of chimney in their dishes, that is their fate. He laughed
> and said what he usually does, 'You ought to be filmed.' His ears
> are scarlet and I hate him, he is always chewing humbugs.

We can imagine this strange, eccentric couple in their two-roomed
cottage, living on the breadline and arguing about poetry.

Roberts knows the conditions of life in a wartime village – she
partakes in them – but she manages to express the quiet heroism and
determination of the people around her without resorting to ideal-
ising them. Roberts may speak, in a Gravesian way, of 'true poets',
and her research into Celtic beliefs and legends certainly led her
towards some arcane material. But her own poetry and prose are
notably free of such preoccupations. In her poems she braids past
and present together: the war and the daily life of the village are
constantly mapped onto the mythical past, but never at the cost of
strangling contemporary reality, the dirt, the drudgery or the
tedium. The myths and legends she refers to are not an escape from
reality but a way into it. Roberts was most at home with the world
as it was, making a culture from what she had to hand: friends and

neighbours, their language and their habits, the village and its traditions. Her prose, like her poetry, is an extraordinary work of incorporation and inclusion, and many of the characters from the diary – John Roberts the fisherman, Rosie Davies her neighbour, the pub landlord, Keidrych himself – return in the poetry, re-imagined and transformed but still essentially themselves.

A recurrent theme in the prose is craft and craftsmanship, not just for practical and aesthetic reasons, but as a marker of continuity between the old and the new. In her poetry too, past and present are bound together like a body and its shadow. Making and cultivating and digging are important to the daily life she records, and their metaphors recur in her poems. We might even think of the patching up of old clothes, or the resourceful mixing and matching of disparate materials she describes in her diary – part of the domestic necessity of a period of shortage and rationing – as analogous to what she does in poetry with language and subject. Equally important to her – since she is no nostalgist – are the opportunities offered by the machine age: her poems are full of metals and alloys, alive to new technologies of making. By the same token, her prose is full of speculation about how new materials might improve daily life. She is always reading architectural magazines or looking out for new inventions in farming or clothesmaking or construction. When, in her diary, she writes of her belief in traditional crafts, she specifies: 'I do not mean the retention of arty crafty work of the past, but rather the modern craft that is contemporary and is required for practical use in our time.' We see what she means in her article on coracles:

> Pastoral meadows on the one bank grazing cattle and sheep; butterflies flitting among the agrimony and soft rush at the water's edge; the hard line of the Roman Hills; further distant, the limestone ridge of Llangyndeyrn, with its square-boxed chapel resting like a full-stop on the horizon. But near? What changes break before us. The Cow and Gate milk factory, railway signals. Harries' Towy works, galvanised sheds, Joseph Rank, flour merchants, the new Carmarthen bridge. Perhaps, soon, a new coracle: lighter and tougher than the pair now floating downstream, one nearer to that fashioned by Jochebed, a coracle covered with synthetic textile made from the cellulose of reeds, and machine-sprayed with ICI plastics.

Just as her poems are machine-age reworkings of the old myths, so she imagines the venerable coracle as all the better for being reinvigorated with new material. As with the instruments of daily life and survival, so with the language we use: the shape and concept are perfect but the materials are constantly updated.

Though she does occasionally idealise the old forms, as well as those she unquestioningly calls 'peasants' and 'workers', she never idealises the past. She is *modern*, and we see this for instance in her attitude to Ernest Rhys, the founder-editor of the Everyman editions and a frequent visitor to Lynette and Keidrych in Llanybri. Though she likes and respects Rhys, Lynette complains of his obsession with the Celtic twilight, and she is uninterested in its ideologically charged crepuscularity: 'He was still caught up in its aura when he met us, and, frankly, this nauseated me.' The Celtic margins Rhys and many others envisaged were relics of the past; for Lynette Roberts, her Welsh-speaking village on the edge of the water was a living, breathing microcosm. Nonetheless, it remains likely that Ernest Rhys's work on his landmark Synge edition influenced Lynette – certainly her article on dialect and her short stories bear the imprint of Synge's research on the Aran Islands as well as that other influential Celtic image-maker, Pierre Loti.

An Introduction to Village Dialect with Seven Stories was first published by Keidrych Rhys's Druid Press in 1944. The stories were intended as illustrations of Lynette's article about village dialect, in which she sought, by means of such disparate figures as Chaucer, James Joyce, Milton and Amelia Phillips, her neighbour in Llanybri, 'the essence of all languages of the soil'. It is a bold, amateurish and totalising view she takes: soil for planting, soil too producing the conditions of life, but also language and thus poetry and prose. The essay is passionate and piecemeal, and is unlikely to satisfy the scholar. No matter – from Yeats and Synge on Irish to Pound and Fenollosa on Chinese, poets have trampled over the terrain of linguistic study unhindered by their ignorance, and their insights are usually revealing even when wrong. The same is true in Roberts's case, though it is more likely to be the stories that interest us: fresh, vibrant and funny, these are modernist vignettes. 'Swansea Raid', about the devastating bombing of Swansea, in a classic piece of war writing.

In Roberts's essays on the Welsh village and on coracles, we see how she applied her intellect and her research to the everyday life she saw around her. In the essay on the Welsh village, she argues that the 'extensive peasant democratic tradition' of Welsh architecture can be made to 'harmonise with modern architecture'. She goes on:

I should like to stress that, besides upholding the best of our traditions in the main structure of peasant architecture, there are many sympathisers already interested in this subject; and I feel more strongly that the more vigorous and courageous drive should be devoted towards the younger architects. For the sake of our country in years to come, let us give our generation a chance to go forward, and experiment with the new building processes now being manufactured. Many of us can accept nylon for fishing lines and textiles, glass bricks, plastics and steel sheeting for aviation, cars and household use; but, somehow, when we hear that these materials are to be used for building in large quantities, we flinch.

Lynette Roberts's mind is shaped as much by ICI catalogues and newsreel, by Le Corbusier and Walter Gropius, as by the Mabinogion and *The Golden Bough*. It is also likely that her radical openness to the world around her, her recording of daily life and ordinary habits, her transcription of speech patterns, her sustained attentiveness to the lives of others, were influenced by the Mass Observation movement, which began in 1936, and was dedicated to creating 'a living anthropology' of ordinary life. One of its instigators, the poet Charles Madge, was the husband of Kathleen Raine, someone Roberts knew and read.

The three memoirs included in this book – of a meeting with Eliot, of tea with the Sitwells and of a visit to Federico García Lorca's birthplace – were never published in Roberts's lifetime, and were reconstructed from messy typescripts. The first two give us an insight into life in literary society in the period, and also into the difficulties faced by a young woman writer with no money and two children. In the discussion with Eliot, while Angharad and Prydein are tearing up his papers and bawling on his office floor, Lynette tries to sustain a serious conversation with her editor. This is described in her typescript, which gives a sense, however hurriedly expressed, of the choices she felt were open to her at this point (June 1948):

That of returning to the elemental words and simple voices of living – *i.e.* basic rural cultures, earth rhythms ... what we will be forced back to if that atom war arises. A cleansing purity and rebirth of sound, recreation, refolding of the world such as we had the refolding of the various strata, Icelandic stone and bronze age etc. And ... hitting against that view which is one of isolation, severe pruning, the whole discordant universe, the cutting of teeth, one rhythm grating against another, the metallic convergence of words, heavy, colourful, rich and unexplored.

What we have here is the paradox of Roberts's vision: on the one hand elemental and stripped down, and on the other hand charged and eclectic and full of disparate material. Her work is unique because these tensions are unresolved, and perhaps indeed because it shows that they may not have been so incompatible after all.

The despondency into which her afternoon with the Sitwells ('Yesterday, a wretched day of my life') throws Lynette, who begins awed and finishes up merely bored, is partly due to her failed attempts to make herself heard: she tries to interest the Sitwells and their group in Welsh poetry, and in the realities of wartime life. She also makes a suggestion about the potential for blending poetry with film (an important idea for her, given the filmic nature of *Gods with Stainless Ears*), but we sense that she is mostly ignored or patronised by her audience. Nonetheless, Edith Sitwell remained a friend, and their correspondence (also unpublished) shows how much she supported and encouraged Lynette, who in 1951 dedicated *Gods with Stainless Ears* to her. The account of her visit to Lorca's birthplace dates from the early 1950s. It is the most substantial and finished of the memoirs and must have been intended, unlike the others, as an article for one of the magazines to which she contributed.

After the letters to Robert Graves, a fuller selection of which were first published in *Poetry Wales* in 1983, edited by Joanna Lloyd, the final section of this book is the appendix in which extracts from Roberts's autobiographical notes are reproduced. Some of this was published as 'Parts of an Autobiography', in the same issue of *Poetry Wales*. The style is a mostly notational telegraphese, and towards the end Lynette merely ransacks her diary for pieces to reproduce verbatim. It would not do to consider it a coherent whole, and in any case, the circumstances under which she wrote need to be clarified: she had just been sectioned for the third time under the Mental Health Act, and many of her recollections are hazy or inaccurate, especially insofar as her childhood and adolescence are concerned. We have decided to start it just before the death of her mother in 1923 – much earlier than that and the dating is unreliable and the content, according to family and friends, frequently incorrect or misremembered. For these reasons the text has been put in as an appendix: it is partial, fragmentary, and not dependable.

A Note on the Texts

The quality and accuracy of the original texts vary greatly. Some, such as the articles and stories, could be published as they stood with a few silent corrections of typographical errors. Others, such as the diary and autobiographical notes, involved handwritten corrections and marginalia in addition to already erratically typed text. My aim as editor has been to aim above all for readability, and for this reason I have not only corrected obvious errors but, where necessary, made my own decisions where the sense is unclear or the meaning confused. Stylistic conventions in relation to punctuation and numerals have been made consistent; underlined words in the original texts have been printed as italic. Omissions are indicated by ellipses in square brackets.

Acknowledgements

I am extremely grateful once again to Angharad and Prydein Rhys for allowing me such access to their mother's papers. Angharad Rhys kept me well supplied with anecdotes and stories about Lynette, and I hope that this book expresses something of the vibrancy and humour of her mother's extraordinary character. I continue to be thankful to Judith Willson at Carcanet, who worked on this especially difficult project with remarkable good grace and a great deal of knowledge.

Patrick McGuinness

A VILLAGE IN WARTIME

Llanybri landscape, painting by Lynette Roberts. 'Llanybri landscape in rain with border of Rosie apron with the mauve violets.'

A Carmarthenshire Diary

1939

My sister's birthday, and I have celebrated it by scrubbing the floor, cleaning the grate. Keidrych says I have some funny ideas about poets. I have. I think good real living is more important than spreading yourself on paper. If only the gutless poets that abound today (and there are too many of them) lived admirably rather than preach the exact opposite to what they sing, then I am with them. But when they distort poetry and merely use it as an outlet for their worst grievances and sidewalk niggles, then please God I am not a poet. Not to be classed with these nit-wits, these perambulator bards, but to be just a normal person who can take my full share of responsibility. I have met them, many of them, and they have tried to drag-weigh-me-under with their twisted ways. But I will have none of it. If it were not for the fact that literature would suffer (so little is thought of it already) I would expose these poets; but I feel there is, unfortunately already too little interest from the public; and for me to write about it to the strain-eyed world could only lessen the little faith that the people have in dedicated writers.

Keidrych enjoyed his lunch; he looks very unpleasant today. Debauched, with his four-day beard, he is busy scratching behind me writing to Kilham Roberts asking if the Literary Society will grant us some money to live on. There can be no dole for us. The M[inistry] of L[abour] said we had no stamps. Even though we have both worked previously for two or three years. Neither can he give us a job. Then what are we to live on, Government, I ask you? There are always fallen apples, and the onion soup, but how long will that last! Today Keidrych frequently found cinders or grit in his stewed apples. I told him poets must always expect pieces of chimney in their dishes, that is their fate. He laughed and said what he usually does, 'You ought to be filmed.' His ears are scarlet and I hate him, he is always chewing humbugs.

The psychology of the Welsh people must be extraordinary. I notice that most things which are made outside their country have

Unpublished typescript.

to be labelled Welsh and preferably with an additional illustration of a Welsh high-hatted girl.

I want to write an article on Christopher Marlowe. Also one on Welsh ironwork, a poem which will, I hope, be of value to the miners since it is exclusively for them ... for their cause. They are wonderful people, and how they fight for their rights.

November 11th   *Tripe Washing, Llanstephan*

The top-hat hag wringing out the tripes and swilling them at the running pool up by the Blacksmith's shed. The sloping cottages, and the gentle way the roof is prolonged and slants low over the dairy roof, whereas the angles of the slates on the front roofs are sharp and short.

December 10th   *Tygwyn, Llanybri*

Powder shivers down the walls, grey as the cold grate. This is my own cold surroundings where green men call and death walks up the stairs. I go out stumbling to face reality. The kale roads are full of careless droppings, but this I think is a good omen. A land of plenty ... dig for Victory, back again to the soil.

Lynette Roberts, Tygwyn, Llanybri. 'When first married, in my garden, Oct. 4 1939.'

Our village is small, the cottages I have passed are not unlike Robert Burns's cottage which is illustrated in the *Encyclopaedia Britannica*. The first, two-roomed 'Tygwyn', is my own, which I wrote about in the poem 'Tygwyn'[1] and Douglas Glass photographed.[2] Alongside it is another two-roomed 'Tygwyn' and next door to that, also of the same pattern, is another 'Tygwyn'. Here an old widow of eighty-four lives. She always seems to have a pink geranium flowering at her window throughout the year. I cannot tell you more about her as I pass, as today she has fussily put up a lace curtain right across the lower window frame, drawn two citrine curtains towards the middle of the window, which she told me she had dyed with her own water. She has at the side of these two dark blue hangings of baize. Then there is as well the navy-blue blind just inside the small frame of the non-opening window. Such are the window dressings of many in the village; and now in wartime, since a great many have not bothered about buying black-out material, old blankets, coats, wood or tarpaulin are balanced again on rails or pinned in front of all the curtains and blinds.

Opposite to these three Tygwyn cottages lie the Chapel cottages known as Chapel House, Nos. 1 and 2, and the Old Chapel itself with its protecting stone wall and motionless clock. The clock is drawn on to the stone. It is always ten past two.

The cattle pass to and fro, to and fro morning and night so that no clock is required anyway. Here I wrote in 'Rhode Island Red' 'Calling cattle from celandine and clover, Song of joy I sing'.[3] Another attempt at the Welsh englyn with its intricate inner rhymes and alliteration. The poetic form itself like the village, like a piece of quartz.

December 15th   *Llanybri Vicar's Wife*

Mrs Williams, the vicar's wife, called. It was her first visit and she had already heard that I played the piano, and wanted to know if I would help them out with the organ. I managed to evade this answer and got her instead to give me a long account of the village drama.

'For seven years we have always had the drama, now in this eighth year there can be nothing. So much talent in the village. There's Mrs Rosie Davies opposite who won't act unless she is a man, to begin with. Seven years back we had no men, all the girls took their part, but the Methodist preacher was furious, mind – you know the Church on the hill there? (referring to the Methodist Chapel and their preacher). We practised in the Vicarage kitchen, but not until a boy gave me the tip and winked, saying "Get the old man out, we're too shy", could we begin.

'We strove hard, Mrs Davies always rehearsing in the vicar's trousers. Emlyn Jones and Mary Williams were to make love in a wood covered with ghosts, but they were too shy – so I rehearsed with Mary and hugged her until she got over that. The ghosts were the vicar's sheets, and I bought torch batteries for eyes as they roamed about the Kylsant Estate. Kylsant, because the boys had hacked down trees from that particular wood. Years later, these two were married, Emlyn Jones and Mary Williams, so that was a real romance.

'The other play was about Bad Jack and Good John. It was lovely. Phyllis from the Plassina Farm was the mother of Bad Jack and it was sad. At the father's dying, tears poured down his cheeks ... the people, too, cried ... it was *really* lovely. At the end when Bad Jack did take to drink and was lying in the gutter and the pals passed singing, 'Oh, it's only *Jack*!', everyone again cried, for they really thought Emlyn Jones was dying. He came and asked at the Pub for bread and water, but they refused as there was no money in it. In the end he *died*. He did refuse to drink at first, but then his older friends jibed and said why didn't he join them and have POP. He eventually succumbed and had POP, but the beer too, and got into bad ways. No longer clean and tidy, but dirty, and went about raggety. They later did this, and thatched a cottage on the stage. When they were asked to transfer the cottage and play, they took it in a van to the next village parish and performed it in the parish eight miles away. The clothes we got from the farms around. One farm sent some lovely old things. They're shy at first through their parrot teaching; as they are not taught to use their heads, and can't even understand the meaning of the words; but once they have grasped the theme they act marvellously. There's a lot of talent around here. A lot of talent in this village. The parson and vicar of Pendine came. He's a bachelor, of course, and thought it wonderful. Emlyn Jones is a real actor, there's no doubt about it. But now he's gone to the Rhondda to make quick money, and now he's quite a lad.'

1940

January 15th   *Making 'Pele'*

We make our own 'pele' and most rural villages still use this. Either by making their own, as Keidrych and I have, and these are usually the older and more traditional members of the community, or by buying a load from a 'pele' merchant. To read the *Western Mail* in the 'Day to Day' column is to feel that the journalists only consider that this happened years ago. We have used the clay brought up from Cwmcelyn and mixed one bucket of this with seven buckets of coal dust and a quantity of water. The clay, coal dust and water are worked first, some tread it in with their clogs in a circular move-ment to soften the lumps of clay. It is then lifted onto the gardening shovel and turned over in a systematic pattern, buckets of water having previously been used, if possible it is best to use not the cleanest rainwater saved in the tanks or waterbutts but some dirty or brackish water instead. A good bit of water is absorbed until the shovel when it is quickly turned over should retain the 'pele' as it is turned upside-down. Like syrup swizzled on a spoon The mixture has a distinct binding quality and is always put on the fire damp, either with the hand in the shape of hand-made balls, or with a 'pele' stamp. These ingenious gadgets are handmade, only one old man who has since given up the job could supply these to the iron-mongers. They enable the 'pele' to be formed and placed on the fire without touching it by hand. A small circle is made about the size of a large scone with a hole in the middle to aerate the flames. Such fires are warm and peaceful to sit over, keeping up a consistent level heat not unlike a brazier. These fires, once lit, need never go out. Some fires in the village have [been] alight for several years. Their defect is the fine red dust that accumulates in the ash pan and has to be lifted from day to day.

> ... flight of hovering flames
> Break fire diaphanous,
> Use discipline to feed-guide its flame;
> The hearth is yours,
> She within it with you over the pain.
>   From my poem 'In Sickness and in Health'[4]

February 2nd   *LDVs*

Mr Sid Davies said, 'Last night Major Evans came, but there were no men at their posts, on their first visit too. Many of them did not know, neither were they told, about the two previous meetings.' Mr Sid Davies went on to say that the men were reluctant to leave their homes as 'it's said that the man who goes on duty *might* get his poultry stolen.' So there were toughs at Llanybri, I said, just as the Llanstephan people say? 'Well, I wouldn't say that, but there are a good many that you couldn't call quite genuine.' 'How are they getting on?' I asked, but Mr Davies continued to answer my first question, 'Besides, the men are fond of larks and might frighten their wives.'

I returned from the Pub, and went to bed. Keidrych went up with Sid Davies to visit the LDV Brigade. He later told me that there, practically the whole manhood of the village had congregated, including Reynolds back for 48 hours' leave from the B.E.F.[5] Mr Thomas was merry and had some cute things to say for each member. He suggested that for the winter months, each person should bring along his hobby. Mr Howells, the carpenter, his fretsaw. Mr Vaughan of 'The Farmers' Arms' could count his money. Mr Sid Davies send out his accounts and Ben, the Blacksmith, shoe his horse. He, Mr Thomas, would bring two sacks of lambswool to lie on. For the present, as they had no room or hut of their own, they were using the Llanybri Social Hut, recently presented to the boys. Few ever used it anyway, they preferred instead the traditional 'stand-at-corner' attitude ... backchat ... watch and comment.

March 7th 1940   *Sarah Ann*

I feel chequered with energy. Full of positive red squares and black negative ones. What shall I do? One moment I feel I could draw the moon from its zenith and the next I am unbearably listless, can find nothing to interest me in this bare stone village. I should write to Sheila in Guatemala, I definitely should, but I can't be bothered. This is no reflection on her but it just means that I can't direct my stupid mood towards her Mexican ways. At Mariusa, yes! she would understand and allow it to pass. But what shall I say? I'll tell her that I have a great affection for Sarah Ann.

Now, Sarah Ann is the person who helps to lighten my restless life. She took from my hands Keidrych's shirts, pants and trousers, and squeezed them until I no longer held that responsibility. I do not have to wash, wring and hang things on to a line any more. I never was much good at wringing, anyhow! This solved the clothes-washing problem but – how did I wash myself? Well, Keidrych (that is my husband) and I wash once a week: we boil a bucket of water, strip-tease exposing a small bare patch of flesh, we scrub the exposed part violently, then cover the part with wool, and immediately attack another part. Soon, our whole body is cleansed from our head to toes. We work thoroughly and methodically, each bending over his or her basin sharing the soap which rests between us on the kitchen table.

> To speak of everyday things with ease
> And arrest the mind to a simpler world
> Where living tables are stripped of a cloth
>
> Of wood on which I washed, sat at peace …[6]

I have the most awful headache, I feel cramped and barred from life, imprisoned. Can it be that I dislike the ties of married life, that I resent *having* to cook four times a day, wash up, see to the kitchen fire (Keidrych does the other)? All this when I am 'with child'. All this when I am foolishly worried over lack of money, which keeps me awake at night. (Why worry, it never yet has helped anyone? I know this, yet cannot control my seething mind.) Now quick again, I feel full of bubbles in the head. Blood-pressure, perhaps?

Sarah Ann brought me an apple-pie when she came. At least, a huge portion of one. She said, 'You must eat all of this yourself, the picken is for Mr Rhys. I am always bringing him a picken and nothing for you, so you must have the apple-pie. Eat all of it mind?' Yes, of course I will. But I couldn't. I'm tired of reading the *Western Mail* every day. The only news from the outside world. I'm tired of reading the poems of puny poets and want to do something. Something, I don't know what.

March 20th   *Cold Wind*

The wind was cold. I drew my scarlet cape around me and walked leisurely, as village people do. There was Tygwyn, my home, with the hand-wrought gate made by the village blacksmith. Tygwyn belonging to Mrs Johnson, and next to it Tygwyn where Mrs Phillips lived All square, white, two-roomed cottages with grey slate roofs. On the other side of the road opposite my home lies the graveless Old Chapel with its motionless town clock painted by the mason on the stone. Above, five swallows' nests run along the rain pipe. And Rosie Davies, who lives beside this chapel, also owns the smallholding called Tygwyn. This is the road down which I am walking. It is a grey day. We expect Spring, have been expecting it for these last two months but only three sunny days have come down to us. Milk floats flash by, followed by wagons, Cow and Gate churns loose on rumbling lorries. Carts drawn by straw-harnessed horses, the yokes bursting out with straw from the frost ... for it is ploughing time and manure wanders the countryside finding fields on which to lie.

I don't know why but somehow I have become very fond of the schoolteacher, Miss Williams. I have only met her once, but her age, occupation, and ways somehow delight me. I am going to see her now, and wonder about her as I go. As the village is very small, I have to be careful not to pass through it as I wander in my step. Today nothing grows, there is a grey light hovering over all the plants, but yesterday there was joy, creeping things curved, pushed, and glistened in the sun, and the fields lay emerald. Today, all that has gone. Age and Time have dragged it back. The whole of the village is affected in fact, especially Miss Williams who sits in cinder attire, her hair like strands of Welsh wool loosely tied back with hoops of black hairpins.

It is a characteristic of this village that people often suffer from pains in the head. That is why so many wear old felt hats, or, less frequently, their 'bosses cap'. Miss Williams, I noticed, never wore one, perhaps that is why she had this headache.

March 28th   *Ernest Rhys's Visit*

Not so long ago, about three weeks from today, I had a very strong feeling that someone was coming to see us. Now, those who are Celts will understand this. Others, when I tell them that no one ever visited my cottage, may be inclined to believe me. Anyway, I was so frightened that I might receive this guest alone that I persuaded Keidrych to return as soon as possible.

It was a cold spring day when he set out and the dust whirled in circles like a waltzing skirt. Most of the hedge flowers, celandine, orchids and borage, we knew too well for we had used them, as all villagers here do in the preparation of herb ginger beer. So Keidrych walked as I knew he would, in the centre of the road, taking the clear highroad overlooking the bay. Within a short time he returned, but not by himself; with another voice younger than his. Because I was sitting by the fire, just sitting and dreaming, I had time and peace with which to consult this voice. The most

'Rosie and her family as they are. Her husband the saddler and daughter Iris. Who she offered to sleep with me for company when Keidrych went as a gunner to Yarmouth, East Anglia and later Dover during the Battle of Britain.' Note on back of photograph: 'Rosie Davies my v. dear friend in Llanybri who lived opposite to Tygwyn. Her daughter. Her husband the saddler of the village 1940–1948. Photo given me, I believe, by Douglas Glass, photographer then under contract to *The Times* "profiles" series (i.e. photo-portrait and article) when Douglas was staying with us with his wife at Tygwyn, Llanybri.'

appealing thing about it was its two-toned vibration; essentially an emotional voice, soft, young, that carried far. Imagine, to my surprise, when the door opened there stood an old old man.

He stood there awhile, just long enough for me to realise that he was used to public attention. Mr Ernest Rhys.[7] He said 'Such a strange thing occurred, I feel I was guided here, I was straining up the hill wondering where Llanybri was situated and where Keidrych Rhys lived.' But the funny part was that E.R., as we now call him, approached Keidrych and asked if *HE* knew of a poet called Keidrych Rhys and where exactly he lived!

Days passed, weeks, we met at his old Carmarthen home; at the place where his father's bookshop stood. And he in cold grey evenings would walk out to meet the tide; go up to Llanstephan Castle, or slip back to the shaded woods where he would sleep quite suddenly like a small lamb against the sheltered hedge, start up, then shake with delight at the joy of the Spring flowers or the fragrance from the trees. His clothes hung loosely on his frail form and though they might appear exaggerated or grotesque, on him they were not especially noticeable except as a part of his personality. As I think of him now, I remember his grey-felt waistcoat, his flimsy mackintosh and white green-stained tennis shoes, while on his head he either wore a Basque beret, or trilby jauntily caught with a curlew's mottled feather. He smoked herbs, wayside herbs, spoke a little Welsh. Had lived himself in a Welsh cottage in the Dee Valley: so somehow with us he found happiness, and we in return were happy to hear tales from his long adventurous life. He told us stories, fantastic wicked and daring stories, and sometimes we retaliated with better ones. Many are in his autobiography, *Wales England Wed*, just out; others were too dangerous ... at least for the present.

April 20th   *E.R.'s postcard from Llanstephan*
                                                                 posted, Carmarthen

E.R. to K.R.
Bad weather (and recurrent 'flu) kept me from climbing up to see you both. Return your coat and 'Talk over your "EL"' suggestions. Copyright wd. rule many of them out, but we might find one or two possible if the paper restriction does not prevent. Cd. you look me up one day soon? I might have to go early in May. I write at Carmarthen.

                                                                 (signed) E.R.

April 27th   *E.R's Second Visit*

Now another interval has passed during which time I have been able to read E.R.'s book. For a person in his position, and what he has done to enable a high standard of literature to reach all pockets, this book should be read by all. It may not be a great literary book. In fact it isn't. But it is human, refreshing, and interesting reading of the author's life, quite apart from its revelation of the inside struggle of Everyman's Library. Which, by the way, he still edits.

May 5th *E.R. Went Away to London*

Now that Ernest Rhys had gone I could not help remembering certain things about him. Stories or mannerisms. He would sit in the corner of a pub filling his pipe with a herbal mixture that he picked up at odd moments as he strolled through the lanes. I had learnt from him which plants were good, and vaguely recollect silverweed, pinch of wormwood, and plenty of yarrow or fennel, I can't remember which; and I distinctly remember seeing an acorn among all the other dried-up herbs. He seemed to be bubbling over with joy and carried his emotion, which was not very deep, on the surface, so that if he were not full of smiles he would, and in fact did, rest his head on your shoulder and sob. It was age. It was also, I believe, a sense of loss ... resulting from the death of his wife, and the desire, which he expressed to me, to walk in Carmarthen until he fell dead. So the human weakness was there, no resistance and the will to die.

He was working at the time on the long poem which he called 'Voyage Unending' or 'Dark Sea'. He had taken to Keidrych and me because it reminded him of his own cottage in North Wales. But we found he knew nothing whatsoever about the young contemporary writers; and like most of the older writers was apt to relate them to his own early struggle, which in his case was blind romancing. He was one of a pattern: of the rather short, bearded, charming person-alities who just didn't succeed in having enough drive or individuality to become a good writer or artist in his own sphere. He had fickle moods of melancholy which slowly absorbed his courage, that which determined the editing of Everyman's Library, and the interest in rather a mock Celtic Twilight. He was still caught up in its aura when he met us, and, frankly, this nauseated me. He told me once that he, Yeats and Ezra Pound were dining with a friend and his Irish wife, and that in the course of conversation Pound would occasionally bend forward and take a petal from one of the tulips centred in the middle of the table and then proceed to eat it. To the astonishment of all, he soon scoffed off the whole lot. Followed by a large drink of iced water. He then took his hostess's best animal rug, swirled this around him, and curled up to sleep.

Of W.H. Hudson,[8] E.R. said he was so shy when they walked together in his garden that in sheer nerves he asked Hudson to notice his Juniper tree when in reality he knew only too well that it was a Judas tree. For this blunder E.R. said for the moment W.H. Hudson gave him such a look as to say 'I believe you're false!'

On another occasion I asked him if he had ever met James Joyce, and whether he was aloof or obscure in his conversation. E.R. said he was neither of these; he was particularly interested in music and, of course, Ireland. 'We had this in common because of my Irish wife, Grace, who died ten years ago.'

One thing I noticed when I read his book of poems was that nearly every one was connected with the sun, and he carried this enthusiasm to Spain. Of all literature he loved Cervantes best. When he was sad ... or thinking of death or had nothing much to read ... he would turn to Cervantes who never left his side.

May 10th   *Meeting With E.R., London*

E.R. told me in London only a few days ago, all that enthusiasm and preparation which he had arranged for a new volume had now had to be rejected owing to the lack of paper. Even the edition on Synge, which he had edited and prepared whilst staying with us in Wales, had to be laid aside. It was his ambition to reach the thousandth volume.

E.R. deserves more recognition than he has already received. The Welsh have contributed some honour in the form of a gold medal presented by the Cymmrodorion Society, but the English, they are behindhand again and may still be too late. For E.R. is 84. He told me last time I saw him, 'I am leaving my office at Dent's on Thursday, as the doctor says if I hear a bomb my heart might give out.' And then he continued with his usual mischievous humour, 'You see, I have such an acute ear!' After we had lunched quite simply at an A.B.C., we went back early to his office, as he said he had so much to do. I was amazed when we got back to find that the work consisted of signing his name eighty times on various letters. Perhaps, as I did, you will think this at first rather amusing and sit contentedly watching his ways, but no – it was sadder than that, for his nerves were so shattered that he could only sign his name with the greatest of trouble, taking about five minutes over each signature, and this I then saw with helpless pain and understanding.

Wales England Wed is an autobiography, published by Dent. The cover scarlet is E.R's favourite colour. The print is excellent, and here and there are portraits of well known writers familiar to us all, with many quotations from various poets. The quality of style is light, also its interpretation of life. He speaks of his experience in Wales, of the casualties, but somehow the tale affects us very little emotionally. It is like an experience which has happened very long ago. But on the other hand, remembering the contacts E.R. had, he seems too much to avoid and throw aside responsibility with boyish hilarity, which he still possesses. He believes in destiny, romance, superstition.

'I am going to a farm in Exmouth, but I do not know how long I will stay there.'

June 16th   *Turning Hay*

> Who will turn the hay with me
> Before the rain comes again?
> Who will save lives on the sea
> By tossing these waves so green?

                                   Lynette Roberts[9]

We followed the cream-coloured cow that had escaped out of the shed. It was slow going as she kept stopping to twist and pull the grass from the banks of the hedge. Strawberries, pink and white orchids and the golden shine of celandine were all growing profusely. Finally, straight in front of us we saw a row of hay-makers returning from the field in their gay coloured aprons. Working the hay had added colour to their cheeks and pieces of straw caught in their hair, clogs and aprons gave them an air of joy and recklessness. 'We've just been turning. Do you want some tea, come back with us.' 'No, but we'll continue to turn while you are away if you will lend us your wooden rakes.' They did and Keidrych and I worked on and on thinking they would never return. Soon however, the gambo arrived with beer, cider, and tea and sandwiches for those or all who preferred it.

As I was the amateur I was given the inner circle to turn. Each person took a row and worked rhythmically until he or she had finished their particular round. They then started immediately on the next, for the cutting in the Welsh fields is arranged in a maze-like fashion on and on and on, and blisters rise up for those who are out of practice, and there is much shortage of breath. All this was most irritating to one like myself as I had all the willingness and energy to continue and keep up with the rest but could not.

Before sundown we managed to take in 3½ gambos of hay, and then after another highspirited harvest meal, witty remarks, chases, and scrambles among the soft mounds of hay, we were gently coaxed and led to another big field to start turning all over again. By now several other friends from the village had come along to give a hand. The field was harder than the last as it had a tremendous dip. Rosie Davies picked up a small herb and told me that this particular weed – called in Welsh, the Lamb's tongue – heated up quickly and was the worst thing out for putting a rick on fire.

I looked forward to leaving at the end of turning this field. It was getting dark and I wanted a rest. My back was aching and the handkerchief I had been given for my blisters wasn't much good. But no, no sooner had we finished when somehow or other without any forced persuasion, we found ourselves guided into the next field, larger than either of the two previous ones. After fifteen minutes rest we were ready to start again. Of course, the ex-collier, farmlabourers, and strong farm-bred women like Rosie, kept well up with this work: but I noticed soon, even Keidrych was lagging behind, in fact he was a whole round behind the rest. As for me, I gave up before a third of the field was turned. Why I was so praised I can't imagine; unless it was because I made such a bold attempt to keep up. We rushed to finish for the news, but failed and returned home about 9.40 p.m. For the next two days I could help no one: I had no less than fourteen blisters on my hands and feet.

We had used wooden rakes. And some of the straight prongs had just been put in. I remarked about this to Keidrych, and said how much I liked these wooden implements but he replied that he much preferred the Llandeilo rake, which had its prongs set vertically to the handle so when in use the prongs lay flat to the ground. Keidrych and I turned a great deal of that field …

June 17th   *The Fall of France*

Again it is clear and hot and there has been no rain. This is good for the hay cutting: many farmers have still several fields to cut. But for the vegetables and small plants which are transplanted in preparation for the winter, it is disheartening.

I did not wash up for Rosie last night as she had finished cutting sooner than she had expected.

Tomorrow, Thursday, I will naturally help her with the turning … perhaps this time with greater success. 'Well, you see, it's like this, Mrs Rhys' … and Rosie stands on one foot with her hand on her hip, she licks around her mouth, then begins talking again, and it is always the same, 'Well, you see, it's like this, Mrs Rhys. I can't imagine the war or fighting at all, I've never travelled at all, only to go to Cardiff, so I can't imagine this war at all. She's very wrong mind you (meaning the WAR), and what I feel is they're all flesh and blood like you or I, Mrs Rhys, aren't they? If you were to be stabbed you would feel it just as much as they, wouldn't you? WAR there's no sense in it. We're simple people we all get on. War there's no sense in it'.[10]

I continued my journey down to the Shop as I was anxious to

find out the 10 o'clock news. Mrs Sid Davies, petite, with a crop of red curls, looked worried ... but then she often did. I asked her the usual question, 'What's the news?' 'FRANCE HAS GIVEN IN.' ... Will England also accept peace, or fight on, I wondered. I knew Hitler wanted peace with England from the strategy recommended by the Banse plan published in a Penguin edition, but would he get it? Indeed, I felt so much for the French and their suffering that I was ashamed to be in the British Isles. I wept. I was ashamed to think that I formed part of the community who had so desperately let her down. I felt like running off to France and selling my British status. And I could do this, since I held an Argentine Passport and could demand protection from the Argentine Embassy. If it were not for the understanding and knowledge of most of the people here in Llanybri, there, and everywhere, I would REBEL and mightily. The villagers are superb in thought and action, and strangely enough there is considerable unity in their thoughts and approach to the war. They are far more intelligent and efficient than most of the ways and means of Parliament. If the leading M.O.I. officials, jour-nalists, or MPs could see the faces or hear the remarks of these folk when their own high educational voices are broadcast, it would do them a world of good, for the officials speak at their own low level, and do not understand the wise and simple minds of the agricultural community. And if we do not listen to the rural wisdom of the common man we shall be a lost Nation. See my poem 'House of Commons'[11] [illegible] tradition and false promises of fear.

The tragedy and immediate fault is that the Government fills the agriculturalist with false beliefs. And as these officials have such a detachment from the soil, the effect is one of enforcing a corrupt set of laws and splitting the Nation in two. In fact, both Communism and Socialism are examples of this. It is the imposition of a bour-geois and shallow town culture forced on their wholesome ways. That is why I have such an interest in the village of Llanybri. I see that in the future it will be forced to change for the worse.

The dignity and pride of the craftsmen and farm labourers should be permitted to prevail, and let me say at once that by craftsmen I do not mean the retention of any arty crafty work of the past, but rather the modern craft which is contemporary and is required for practical use in our time, even if it is making plastic electrical wires, or elec-tric stoppers that lock and cannot endanger the life of a child. The people I have met here in Llanybri seem to me to retain all the natural and true qualities of an aristocrat.

And I found the same throughout the provinces of France, where so many women are seen working out in the fields.

As for equality, I do not believe in it. If you have any sense of justice then there can be no such thing as equality. It is an absurd solution based on the deformity of the avaricious mind. Socialism should be a natural result of the people's everyday life ... and not a forced movement ... only then will it become beneficial. A village such as this, is not conscious of its everyday socialism. If it were it would cease to exist.

I write here, apart from the educational side, of which I absolutely disapprove, since reason and curiosity are the basis of a good education and both are everyday stamped out. In years to come, they will, if they are wise, *uneducate*, and teach the children to reason: to develop for themselves. They will give them good roots from which to work: Astronomy, Mechanics, Geology, Ornithology, Poetry and all that is related to the spiritual side of man. *Not religion*. But the development of the spiritual qualities which are inherent in every child. Religion again is a supplanted dogma and out of date. Another spiritual form of expression will have to take its place.

June 21st

The shortage of water during these last few days has been a continual source of worry. The only reliable spring has been tapped by the County Council; tapped to such an extent that water will only drip out of it if a brass button is continually pushed. I have seen this type of tap used in large towns and in railway trains, but never in a village where the people are taxed every year for its use. What would happen if Llanybri were bombed by mistake, as the BBC often implies most villages are, I don't know. There is, of course, the possibility that it will be mistaken for Pembrey, since both lie opposite to one another in the Bay. If it were bombed then surely the whole village would burn outright ... the water takes too long to draw, and it is too far away to reach. Outside the village down a steep hill about 600 yards away there is a trickle of water, but we never had a pump except to look at! No remarks will be made about this; for those in a position to complain have their own private pumps and remain immune from discomfort. Though these last few days ... the third week without rain ... did threaten those further afield. So I wrote about meeting '"Death that Monster" down at the well' and was the questioning Water-Carrier.[12]

Last night I lay alone. It was strange. I thought I should feel free, released somewhat from the responsible but small thoughts that crowd out my day when Keidrych is around. But I was mistaken,

'Photo I believe by Douglas Glass which he gave me when staying with us at Tygwyn, Llanybri, Carmarthenshire, South Wales. This family consists of the publican at the Black Horse Inn and his daughter, her husband and two daughters. The old man would be reading his large weighty Bible, with his thin steel-rimmed spectacles and every now and then get up and serve his customers (village friends) with a pint (there were no bars), just all sat by the kitchen log together.'

for, if anything, his absence made me even more alert. I was out of milk and had to visit at least three farms before I could get a small supply. Most of them had already cooled, checked, and labelled their milk for the morning's delivery. I called at the Farmer's Arms, for as it was only just after closing time I thought they might still be up. But no one answered. A girl with a baby hung out of the window and said, 'Mr and Mrs Vaughan have gone out to the fields again to finish their work.'

I passed Rosie Davies's house and I looked up; there was a light in the top window so I naturally thought she had turned in. I walked to the top of the road by the Vicarage but there my way was blocked by a whole track of cows turning down the road. There were two boys standing at the useless village pump where they always gathered. I tried to appear indifferent to those cows but failed; but one boy, to show off, slapped a passing cow on its back, a good slap. The grey-limbed girl turned swiftly and slashed the cowstick hard on the boy's back. It pained him. He flushed but remained silent. She turned and in Welsh said, 'That will teach you to play with my animals.' I followed her slowly up to the farm. I had to, she was like Cinderella, besides, I wanted milk.

The following day I went with Keidrych to hear the news at the pub, as we had no wireless. I asked Mrs Vaughan who this girl was. She said, 'She's a wonderful worker,' and I believed her. 'In fact, a slave to their right hand?' She continued, 'She works much too hard and never seems to have any time off at all. She is rough, of course, and quick, but that may have been her upbringing, since she came from a Home in Llanelli where the best working and toughest men and women in the world seem to exist.' All the boys, though they admired her looks and spirit, were frightened of her and not one, though there were many who had fallen in love with her, had yet succeeded in courting her.

When I got back I made some tea and put it in the thermos as I had arranged; then prepared some farmers' sandwiches so that Keidrych could have them when he returned off duty in the early hours of the morning. Of course, I didn't sleep, scarcely at all ... or was always gliding on the surface of sleep.

At about 2 a.m. I distinctly heard church bells ringing against a background of wailing sirens. Next morning when Keidrych returned I asked how he got on. Whether he had heard anything. He said that about 2.30 he heard church bells ringing and mentioned the fact to the rest of the LDVs, but none of them bothered. I think both Keidrych and I were right, and that the church bells *did* ring. We both thought it very far distant and probably Llanelli or Swansea.

There have been, and are of course, far more raids than the BBC acknowledges. Neither do they tell us the truth. They can't, of course ... it would be too revealing for the enemy ... and demoralising for our people. One is aware so strongly that the lives of the people, that is, civilians, are of little importance compared with the ammunition factories. And the sad part about it is, that it is *TRUE*. For ammunition is vital in war ... France has learnt this only too well! And what is the result of all this broadcasting blackout, tact, and evasiveness? The British Public – a great many of them – listen instead to Haw-haw, and though they are intelligent enough to realise that he also conceals, tells lies, or exaggerates, but combining and sifting the two broadcasts something nearer the truth can be grasped. Haw-haw for instance, told us when Pembrey had been hit – which we knew to be true – when the BBC said nothing.

The trouble with this modern world is this: THE PEOPLE ARE TOO INTELLIGENT FOR THEIR GOVERNMENT. Both Broadcasting House and the Government are speaking below the standard of the people, consequently most of their statements are jeered at. The people want action, the best resources of manpower used and evenly distributed, but what happens? Social contacts, nepotism, personal introductions win every time to the detriment of the State.

June 23rd   Rain

Yesterday it rained, so I spent most of the time transplanting in the garden. The parsnips, beetroot, leeks, onions, are all thinned out. I experimented with a poem on Rain by using all words which had long thin letters so that even the print of the page would look like thin lines of rain. The poem called 'Rainshiver' looks like it.[13] Rain

> Chills the air and stills the billing birds
> To shrill not trill as they should in
> This daffodil spring

June 24th   Evacuees

Today it did not rain so my plants which have been transplanted are beginning to look very flat. Gardening is a disheartening job as the work relies too much on the good-will of God, and He is not always cooperating.

I can hear the thin-lipped spinsters rasping their teeth, saying 'Ah,' (they always say 'Ah') 'Ah, perhaps He is anxious to punish someone who may have done something wrong.' Maybe? But this time the answer is 'NO'. That's what infuriates me. My small garden is too big for me, too big even to look after properly, but I still fill it with every bit of energy that I have, and with every plant that is seasonable. I realise too well that it will be WE who will starve first, not Hitler's regime. They have their stores put away – but we, why, all the farmers round here say the same, 'We are not storing this year's crops but eating them right away.' So, as I said before, I grow for Llanybri, for Llanybri that I love and that has given me so much.

Late last night I heard young voices, strange voices, which I gathered must have come from the evacuees. I was already in bed, and was surprised that they should arrive so late. Early this morning I was anxious to see what they were like. We had heard so much on paper about the evacuees spoiling Welsh culture!

They passed the window as I was lighting the fire. Five strong little boys. At least that was my first impression. Probably because they had an air of self-confidence and independence; and also because they were wearing khaki shirts and shorts like the Hitler children. I was amazed and drew my curtain even further aside, as all villagers do, who continue to gaze. I heard a woman shouting out to the 'adopted' village parents who escorted them, 'OH POOR THINGS!' The boys had more sense, and merely pointed up to the window to the woman who was shouting. Later, as I went to the post office to fetch *The Western Mail*, I saw several other groups of 'strangers', again all boys. I naturally concluded that the village of Llanstephan had divided the children up, and had carefully kept the pretty girls, and sent the tough boys to Llanybri. I was right, as I found out a few hours later.

At first there was great difficulty in finding foster parents for them, but as nearby villagers heard they had arrived, a few, especially the sons and daughters of the various farmers, came to see what they were like. Out of fifty-four children sent, three were girls. The smaller ones, after the strain of the long journey from Sussex, had started to cry, there was confusion, rudeness between the adults, and a final quarrel arose in front of everyone, between Mrs Williams of the Vicarage and Miss Williams, the Schoolteacher of Llanybri. Apparently the vicar's wife who is in charge of the evacuees department in Llanybri has seven bedrooms at the vicarage, a maid, no work, no one but herself and her husband, and is paid a salary by the Crown as a result of land left for the privilege of the residing clergy. Room could not be found for three of the evacuated teachers who had arrived with the children, and Mrs Williams was asked by the Llanybri teacher to put them up. She refused. Yet she forced evacuees on homes of poverty where they hadn't even beds for the children to sleep in. Sarah Ann, Mrs Rollands, was one. Although Mrs Rollands refused. She was definitely told she must take one. Now, Sarah Ann has two children. One her own, a boy of eight, and an illegitimate child of her sister's who was five. These two children were entirely dependant on their mother whose husband was dead; and her only means of income was the 10/6 from the widow's pension. She got no allowance from the Government for her sister's child, so that her life was hard, extremely so. I have visited Sarah Ann and had tea with her more than once, and on the first occasion she took me upstairs I saw her two bedrooms. Her father was staying with her at the time in one bedroom, so there remained only the second small bedroom. In it were the medium-sized bed and washstand. Each night in this bed lay the boy, Sarah Ann herself, and the girl on the other side of her. The father does not sleep at the cottage anymore, so I presume the evacuee will sleep in that second bedroom. Now, today, her sister has rushed down the hill to see if she can't catch Sarah Ann before she goes out on the fields to tell her that she must immediately prepare another bed.

Mrs Williams's name is pretty well mud, and the religion she represents goes with it. What person can willingly, lovingly go to church, just to hear a raucous voice drumming out the amens with a military precision. No God ever enters that church. If He were human at all he'd put a bomb under it, but He is not human. Anyway, most of the villagers are Chapel-goers, and the few that used to go to the Church have declined and reverted to the Yellow Building. Myself, I prefer the old towered Chapel opposite my cottage, Tygwyn. This used to be a Roman Catholic chapel, whose simple history dates back to the fourteenth century. No one in the locality knows anything about it. Anyway, I myself use the path through the Old Chapel every morning and never fail to pray, just a word or two, as I pass. It is the least I can do. I wanted to attend the Chapel when they had a Welsh service, but shyness and inability to sing in Welsh or understand the language prevented my going, so instead I had to be content with listening to the hymns and voices vibrating through the air between the Chapel door and the kitchen door which I had left open. A 'hwyl' arose, the first I had heard, and I was glad of it, though more seriously I felt the act rather spectacular and not to be repeated. The singing, too, was dreary and drawn out   a melancholy dirge.

At 1 o'clock Keidrych and I went to the Farmers' Arms to have a drink and hear the news. Mr Thomas was there lying in great pain. His knee was worse, and inflammation had set in just below the knee-cap. He was a brave person, and proved it when the horse kicked him and he lay without a murmur on the field. There was no brandy in the pub, so whiskey was rushed to him instead.

We spoke a great deal, chiefly about farms. He told us two interesting things. One, that last year if any farmer attempted to grow more potatoes on his land than that which he already wanted for his family, he was to pay eight shillings a ton extra as duty. This year they want them to grow as many potatoes as possible, and of course, as is only natural, the farmers are not so keen. The Union is valueless as they have continually let down the farmers right and left. In much the same way as Sir Reginald Dorman-Smith, who immediately sold his farm when he became Minister for Agriculture, for he had so little faith in farming. The corn too, our country burnt tons of it, when Germany *at the same time* was busy paying and saving to make conditional storage units for under or on top of the soil. And then again, with the milk control. Most of the milk from Llanybri is sent direct to the Cow and Gate Factory just outside Carmarthen. The receipts of each customer are then sent and registered at the Milk Marketing Board. For these small accounts and attentions alone, Mr Thomas has had £12 deducted from his monthly milk profit bill. Is this right? Even the Banks do not ask for such a high percentage of money for keeping their clients' accounts. Other farmers around here who have larger farms naturally have to pay more each month, some £23. Keidrych maintains that the money of this country should be invested in the land and not invested in places abroad or in shipping etc. etc. In this way the possessors of large incomes would not be so ready to ship the money abroad in a crisis, or be so eager to lend it to other countries, whether Allies or not. If it were in the land, he thinks the Government would not be so ready to waste their time asking questions concerning these foreign countries, but instead would be concerned about the farmers and thereby encourage agricultural growth and maintenance of the land.

June 26th   *Hayrick and Rushes*

They had just finished their hay-rick in time; and as the rain fell in heavy jerks, they managed to run to the bottom of the field and cut ten bundles of reeds. These they placed over the top of the rick so that it might be protected until a permanent covering of thatched straw had been prepared to cover the whole area. On this occasion there was only one man to stack the rick-builders so that the rick was inclined to fall and had to be supported by four wooden props. The hens and ducks waddled in and out with wisps of fallen hay clinging to their feet. Meanwhile a cock and goose had mounted a roost pole and fought over a small red worm. The cows grazed slowly to the top of the meadow and were beginning to stand around the cowsheds waiting to be milked. A child scratched a pig's back until it sat down in ecstasy, whilst another child set a trap to catch a goldfinch. The child with the wire cage interested me so I walked up to her. She had long fair hair which had been bound in flannel ringlets and had yet to be combed out. Her knickers were made of black cretonne and her dress was dust-powdered white. I asked her if she had ever caught any other birds in it, but she merely sucked three fingers and turned away. The boy standing three yards off answered for her, and said at once, 'Sure, missy, we caught a field mouse and a toad. I seen them myself.'

He was an evacuee, one of the favourites among the farmers as they heard he could milk four cows. To me he looked like a young Indian. His skin was dark, and his large brown eyes softly shaded with lashes. He had confidence in himself and the ability to back up that confidence. Only last night as late as 11.15 p.m. a group of us had heard him sing like a golden-crested bird as often as we pleased.

Twice running he sang Mendelssohn's 'March of Saul' before we would let him rest; and then he ran into plainsong he had learnt at Chiddington Church, Sussex, followed by Kyrie Eleison. His skin was now as sunburnt as all the other evacuees from Sussex, but there was something distinctive in the pigment of his skin, a shadow that suggested that he was not altogether English. Most orientals have it – it's paintable but elusive – it's as though they appeared slightly chilled under the Western skies – green-shadowed. I wrote a poem about the 'Displaced Persons' in Europe, likening them to birds without winter food and dying of starvation.[14]

The vegetables I transplanted the other day have failed to survive so that I am beginning to feel very despondent about gardening. The more I strive the less do I succeed. In the front garden I have had greater success as many of the flowers are already in bloom, but somehow they, too, have a peculiar characteristic of most of the plants this season – though perfect, they are considerably dwarfed. As it is the general effect is rather like a wild rock garden after about three weeks' neglect, where groups of grass and weeds have suddenly towered into flower and covered the cultured plants from the glare of the sun. The neglect of weeds to our garden-peas has proved a blessing in this long drought, as where other gardens are superfluously clean the stems of these plants have become so exposed to the hot dry sun, that they have withered at the base and dried up the roots. On the other hand, although our peas are perhaps rather choked, the moisture and shade from the weeds have helped to protect them. That is why we have been able to gather and cook our peas before anyone else.

There is a grey wind this afternoon that seems to wander about and visit us at unexpected intervals. I find it refreshing to my general mood of disturbance which occurs just before the birds' first migratory flight. But the question arises, where shall I go and when? For instinct cannot altogether guide those who are caught in the chains of culture and a barbaric civilisation. A conflicting problem for peace-dwellers. But we are at war so there remains only 'chance' or fate to guide our footsteps.

July 1st

Letter to Lynette from E[rnest] R[hys]
Wilsham,
Brendon,
N. Devon
1.7.40

Dear Lynette, (or Eiluned?),[15]
I wonder how you are – you two, and Llanybri, and if my book ever

reached Keidrych? (Some Welsh reviews came, but none by him.)

I've been a month now in this Exmoor farm – lonelier then Llanybri – with plenty of work for my slow pen, articles for USA.

Now I want to consult you about two little Llanstephan girls, to whom I promised to send 'Fairy Gold' then lost their addresses. Joan Price one was called, the other – ? Connor – an Irish kid. Could you trace them for me – or shall I send you the book to give them for me? Which wd. be the less bother?

Anyhow it serves to keep us in touch. The War makes one anxious, but air-raids will hardly reach at Ty Gwyn. Weather has been superb, but rain's wanted.

Gyda chofion caredicaf,[16]

ER.

Rush Thatching

The most unusual thing today is the gentle movement of the wind; never have I felt it so soft and fresh to the face, even the most dreary tasks take on an ethereal quality. Unfortunately Rosie Davies could not obtain any wheat stalks for the covering for her rick; so she has had to be content with rushes. They were cut and collected early this morning, and then stacked in bundles to facilitate the carrying and handling of these reeds up to the ricks. Bill Rogers had just started when I came along, and had cornered the first side, leaving a magnificent tuft mounted on a pole which finished one end of the rick. I watched him make this tuft. He took a small bundle of selected rushes, placed them round the pole, and then bound them down for about eight inches with string. The final appearance was smart, a labour of pride, not unlike a fair-horse's dressing. Bill took the ladder for a guide and as he required the rushes I took a fork and pitched them up to him. He usually liked two large bundles to work with at a time. These he placed beside him, and raised a kind of manger by leaning the bundles against another fork which he had dug into the rick. He took enough rushes to fill one hand, drew out a few odd strands that hung longer than the rest, then bound the small handful of rushes by twisting these odd strands around it. The bundles were then tucked slightly under the hay, so that when they were laid side by side the knot of these strands remained covered. The bales of cord were kept parallel with the work and each bundle pegged smaller at the top, and wider at the bottom as the rick grew wider in shape. The sticks, to my amazement, were two feet in length. But even these were short for the strong winds of Llanybri.

'It's a pity we haven't the wheat stalks this year, they're much better.' I found this hard to understand as I imagined the waterproof rushes would make a much better covering.

As it was Iris's birthday, Keidrych and I felt we would like to buy her some sweets. It seemed stupid to buy any variety so I asked her mother Rosie. She either purposely evaded the answer or forgot to reply. By talking about Iris's tenth birthday she started to tell me how she had saved her daughter's life when she had the bronchitis by keeping her in an even temperature which the doctor had recommended. 'You may not believe it, Mrs Rhys, but I had my apron on for ten day – days and nights – I didn't sleep a wink, and had to sit always forwards otherwise the child got pain in her chest if I should lie back. On the eleventh day Doctor Phillips came. But it saved her life I can tell you, I was always sitting by the kitchen fire.'

'As for me, I'm a bugger for sweets,' said Mr Davies the saddler and Rosie's husband when I appealed to him to let me know which sweets Iris preferred. Eventually, receiving no satisfactory answer from either, I bought ¾ lb of satin-cushioned sweets. These looked more festive so I put them in a tall pickle jar, I cleaned the metal top with Brasso, then tied the whole together with pale-blue ribbon. Iris was shy and completely overcome by this gift. I really doubt if she had had any other present at all, for Mrs Davies had said to me only a few hours ago, 'Iris said to me this morning, "Mam, it's my birthday today you must make me some pancakes for my tea." And truly I had quite forgotten it was the child's birthday.'

Last night at the Farmers' Arms, Mr Thomas said, 'I have complained to one of the councillors I met in Carmarthen, and hope shortly there will be some improvement in the water supply.' He cleverly used the evacuees as an excuse. 'Fancy sending evacuees to a village that had no water supply; all the wells were dry except one, and that was the one at the bottom of a hill outside a village and controlled by a push-button pressure similar to those on trains and no bigger, and with no greater amount of water. What were they thinking by sending fifty more evacuees to the village too, to add to this grave water shortage.' Myself, I felt that the greater need was as a preventive of fire, to prevent the danger of typhus or any other germs breeding when the water was down to its lowest ebb. My mother had died from drinking contaminated well water.

The Sunday newspapers had been effectively dealt with by Keidrych who typed out a statement asking for the deliveries to be sent to the villagers who had registered, and also to the additional ones who had added their names to his list. Quite a number signed. It really did seem too bad the way people, who had taken the trouble to register, to be sure of securing a Sunday Paper, were let down, Sunday after Sunday.

July 12th   *Keidrych Called Up*

When Keidrych was called up. He tried to enter the Army at an earlier date in December, and went to a recruiting office; but they told him they already had too many, so when June came the villagers looked towards us. Here, when there is any distressed condition in the village they all show their kindness by the small and big gestures which are natural to them. Rosie offered me her daughter, Iris, to sleep with me when Keidrych was 'called up'. This seems to be customary around here. Mrs Rollands, i.e. Sarah Ann, has also offered me her sister's love child who was six years old. But naturally I refused. Though she persisted more than once and said she could manage without because she had John, her son, for company, aged nine. I stayed alone and wrote 'Low Tide'.[17] If anyone is ill, the village soon gets to know, for trays of food, plate of tart, or bowls of 'cawl' carried as gifts to the ailing person are soon noticed, however hard anyone tries to disguise the food with a draped apron. It is quite biblical in the sense that the neighbour is usually the most helping friend: but if I am truthful, as I must be, it is also partly because the neighbour sees that she, too, might have a 'turn' and require help.

July 31st   *P.C. from E.R. to Keidrych*
                                              Wilsham,
                                              Brendon,
                                              N. Devon.

E.R. to K.R.
Pray forgive this sluggish pen. It is writing to K.R. but has little news to send a poet in war-array, that is likely to *cheer* him up, and quicken the Celtic Muse. A letter to the lonely lady of Llanybri will follow soon. *Her* letter was as good as a play.

                                              (signed) E.R.

August 1st   *Letter to Lynette from E.R.*
                                              Wilsham,
                                              Brendon,
                                              N. Devon.

Dear Lynette,
I've only heard from Dent this morning that Keidrych has 'joined

the Forces' and I hasten to send you a word of sympathy. Dear girl, you must miss him woefully in your solitude; I'm sorry I bothered you about those two little schoolgirls at Llanstephan, and 'Fairy Gold'! Do you manage to do any writing – or reviewing? I'd have been proud to hear your verdict on my old book? ... My brain pan is very rusty these days, and this babble of folk in the garden, i.e. of townsfolk staying here! – makes it hard to write anything at all. I'd be *very* grateful even for a postcard! My love to you both, so far as it can carry –

E.R.

Drawing of Keidrych Rhys by Lynette Roberts. By permission of the Harry Ransom Humanities Research Center, The University of Texas at Austin.

August 10th   *Cowpat Poultices*

How good Rosie is to me, twice she has called to ask if she could
help in some way. I remember when her finger was poisoned from
cutting rushes. She comforted it last night by holding her hand
against her breast … 'like a baby,' she said. Later when she tired of
this, she wrapped her bloomers around it to keep in the warmth. I
was more anxious, I remember, than sympathetic, as I thought she
might get blood poisoning. Now I have a similar gathering and
realise how disturbing it all is.

Later in the day: She told me her mother would use cowpats for
poultices: 'she would wait to get the mixture hot from the cow'.
Somehow I could not do this. Though I believe strongly in some of
the local cures. Mrs Jones, my neighbour living to the right of me,
told me that wild sage was wonderful for drawing out pain, and
using it as a poultice.

August 18th   *Letter to Keidrych from E.R.*
                                                    Wilsham,
                                                    Brendon,
                                                    N. Devon.

E.R. to K.R.
In a letter, merry and sad by turns, Lynette sends me your address,
and I write to wish you soldier's luck in your regiment – so far from
the 'hen wlad'.[18] I wonder if you will find a lyric stimulus like
Edward Thomas in the last war (but without his ill-fate) and give us
a new note in 'poetry' – that would help Lynette in her solitude at
Llanybri. I am a solitary myself today on Exmoor for Stella went
back to London last week, and I sorely miss her. My old pen is
turned rusty down here, without my books and papers: and I feel
cut off from 'Everyman', whom the paper-shortage has hit badly.
The *Synge* Vol. has not yet gone to press. Let us keep 'calon cryf'
and pray for the day that can record *Exit Hitler*!

Gyda chofion caredicaf.[19]

September 2nd   *Accepting People*

I am beginning to accept people as they are. I love Rosie for her
untidiness; for her dark-grey blouse and coarse woven skirts that she
sleeps in; for her pots and pans littered about the garden yard, and all
the old clothes bought from the various sales, hanging in the tool
shed so that they look like pawn droppings. Mrs Webb and her
precise neatness … the way she polishes her spectacles slowly and

continually ... knocks the newly-baked bread to see if it is cooked, or wipes the shining oilcloth table. There is no weed or herb to be seen around her cottage. I wrote about Rosie and used her idioms in the poem called after her childhood farm 'Plasnewydd'.

WAR there's no sense in it
WAR there's no sense in it
For us simple people
We all get on so well.[20]

September 3rd   *Letter to Lynette from E.R.*
                                                        Wisham,
                                                        Brendon,
                                                        N. Devon.

Eiluned anwyl – dear Lynette,
What a pleasant epistle. It brings Llanybri back so clearly, for I wish it was nearer and its roads not so steep! Even so, I'd be but a gruesome guest, and *bad gardener*.

You'd laugh to see the mellay of papers where I write! Horrid arrears of letters to authors who want books published – from a Chief Rabbi (tact!) to a Welsh rabbit who writes bad English. They accumulated while I was on the sick list lately – a foul *gastritis* from drinking some cider (not like that at the Swan Inn – to whose old landlady give my Cofion Caredig i gyd.) Also I've got a brief *cofiadur* of E.R. to write for a USA publisher and sundry other dockyments. So, the game goes on, and there's no rest for the wicked or Mr Rhys. Would I had a sect. in a red cloak to type this MSS and pay his a/cs for him, *dyn tlawd*![21]

BBC war news! Exit King Carol. Raids pretty bad in Kent –

Here I must pause – good letter last week from Keidrych! (Just as well Censor didn't open it for gunner's satirical 'asides'.)

Influx of town refugees here, have spoilt the farm quiet – may have to retreat further. Love and good luck to you both.

                                                        (signed)
                                                        E.R.

                                            I'll probably go to
                                            Exmoor Forest Hotel
                                            Simonsbath
                                            Somerset, on the 16th.

1941

January 3rd   *Gas Masks*

The threat with so many of the children is not the old theme 'I'll give you to the gypsies' but 'I'll put you in the baby's gas mask.' Even when they arrived in the village some children were terrified at the sight of them and started to cry.

January 18th   *Manoeuvres*

Every now and then there are tremendous outbursts of motorcycle engines dashing through the village. The soldiers are on manoeuvres. Why don't they explore the short cuts? The enemy would be sure to use the main roads. Where was their knowledge of the smaller, but quite good intricate lanes, which could block an enemy approach in any direction.

February 2nd   *Evacuee's Report*

A grown-up evacuee called on me this morning and wanted to talk. She really liked the village, and was grateful at the time, to come away from her bombed house. I gave her a cup of coffee and let her talk, and this was roughly her opinion and the opinion of many of the other adult evacuees at the time. One point I should like to make quite clear, is, that although all this may be said to contain a great deal of truth; spoken by itself, it did tend to stand as a momentary and biassed opinion. Here it is: 'They're wicked in a sly way. Nearly every person you meet is a bastard. What could they have talked about before we came? Have you heard I sit on my ass all day and smoke? (In Llanybri no woman smokes.) They've never lived the up and up, as we do in London. Mrs Reynolds has never been outside Llanybri. They say London is being bombed because it is so wicked. They all seem to think London is terribly wicked ... wish I could take lots of them there.'

Following a village death when an evacuee helped me make a wreath for the funeral I wrote 'Earthbound'.[22]

Another evacuee called and said: 'My three children, except the baby, all remember it ... when the man almost pushed me down to the basement shelter. He was the warden, but I had to go up and out, as I felt something was wrong at home, and found when I got there my mother was bombed out. One of my husband's first jobs in the First Aid was to find a mother halfway up the stairs trying to reach her baby. He found her hanging over the banisters ... her head out open with her brains hanging out ... children next door with no arms or legs, the dustbins collected hundreds of them, they were taken away ... when he came here before the weekend he vomited and vomited. Could not eat with the horror of what he had seen ... now he's better and can accept things more easily.'

What a statement of truth. And what a contrast with the ways of the village. 'They haven't even got an iron here, no lights and no water.' But we lost quite a few men in one village. My friend Phil Davies. He came on leave after a baptism of fire over Germany with the RAF. He was the gunner and he was NEVER the same after that. He told me. He said he dare not tell his mother Mrs Syd Davies. Not long after he was missing. Then there was my friend who knew he would die. With him it was a presentiment. 'I know nothing Mrs Rhys. I haven't even lived yet.' He used to call with the other son of Mrs Syd Davies, his friend Arthur Davies. He was the one who was so sensitive when that cow girl hit him on the back as she passed with her herd.

Then there was dear Mrs Rogers and her fair eyed fair-haired daughters and sons. Her husband was also killed. He was the only one in the village that could do the thatching. I helped and learned so much about thatching from him.

Then there was the young airman who was killed as his plane crashed into the meadow behind my cottage. And Alun Lewis, the poet who had spent days with us and his girl Gwyn in our village.[23] He too died in Burma. Not one of these were suited to the climate of war. Some men are suited. These were not.

March 6th   *Frost Discovery*

Because of the bad frost I have made a discovery. Through the thick pieces of lime falling off the stone walls, I am able to discover many of the previous colour washes of the village. A predominant one throughout seems to have been pink. This colour having covered farms, the 'Farmer's Arms' and some of the cottages. This gave me courage, and this year Keidrych and I limed our cottage pink. Using for this process terracotta and a pleasing proportion of white lime. A favoured wash is yellow ochre mixed with white lime for the farms and houses, and the outbuildings and stone walls are then limed white. The general pigment for paintwork is a dark brown-red. Not quite maroon, because the colour contains a large proportion of red. For the front door, a special effort is sometimes made on the larger houses and farms, which consists of light scrabbling. An undercoat of biscuit with a transparent golden varnish on top, combed or drawn-in with a fine brush to resemble light oak – which of course it never does. The 'Farmers' Arms' had all the interior woodwork done up in this 'posh' style ... it is bizarre, but then so are many of the things in this village. Mr Howells, for instance, has very success-fully painted the frame of his front door a deep carnation red suggesting two pillars with capitals in imitation marble, using silver, grey, green and white paint. Like Stilton, I thought, and liked it very much.

When Mr Howells called with some carpentry he had made for us, probably the bookcase, and used the blow-lamp to take off the first coat of paint on the front door, I remembered the visits to London in the raids. It was not on this exact visit but it was the use of the blow-lamp that started off this connection. 'The Blow-lamp', the air raid that ended with the smell of burnt paint at the Temple and the East End.[24]

April 1st   *Report, RAF*

There was a report some time ago of some of our pilot officers visiting German prisoners of war in Hospital and offering them ciga-rettes. The newspapers put this down to our great qualities of sportsmanship: but surely it was far more a feeling of guilt and humility.

April 15th   *Apron Design*

'Will you lend me your apron, Mrs Davies? The one you wore two days ago, with the mauve violets. I want to put the design round one of my paintings of Llanybri.' 'O, it's very old, Mrs Rhys.' Everything was old that Rosie wore; no one could ever guess where she got all her clothes. From sales perhaps; some suggest she buys bundles at a time. Her farm hats are shapeless, but they have a quality and shape which is not of this generation. Her black crochet shawl, high-heeled suede boots lined with lamb and voluminous heavy tweed skirts. On the whole there is not much vanity in her dress apart from the metallic pricked designs of her aprons. These are worn all day, even for feast days; and for rougher work a further canvas, homemade sack, or Welsh flannel apron is tied to cover just the front of the one underneath. The sleeveless closed apron which

Llanybri old chapel, painting by Lynette Roberts. 'Rosie wearing her best harvest apron when I painted her as an angel. This painting also shows how the manure is laid methodically in the fields and later on when it is mature i.e. weathered and cool, it is scattered over the whole field with even distribution. The same method is used with the lime which is frequently laid into pointed clumps of chalk and left awhile until it is cooled when again it is scattered evenly over the fields.'

draws over the head is the most popular where all–over designs are used. The variety of design is limited, as there are only the rolls of blue print or ready-mades at the local Post Office; or one chosen from a pile of aprons off a passing van. Nearly all have a dark background, favourable black or navy-blue with a small geometric or natural design pricked in white. These prints are excellent as they do not show the dirt, improve with washing, and when they do tend to fade after many years of use, they look better still as they tone in with the austerity of the buildings and brilliant green of the surrounding fields. For this reason I decided to use in my painting a blue print apron for the whole background of our cottage, 'Tygwyn.'[25] The apron which Rosie wears in my painting as an angel with flying goosewings is also traditional, since it is one she has had for years and happened to wear it one harvest when I remarked on the design.

There seem to be three or four distinct styles of clothes worn for the winter. The elder Llanybri women, who wear flannel shawls and no overcoats; the London evacuees; and some of their children who wear fishnet headscarves and gloves; the poorer evacuated children with the schools, sometimes with toes sticking out of their boots – who would go through a pair in one week – who wear no hats, but often carry very gay scarves which Mr Hudson had encouraged them to knit themselves. The local children wear no top-coat, and copied their friends by also wearing gay-coloured scarves, some even gloves. These were often odd, as the oddments of bright coloured wool had run out.

May 6th   *Vicar's Newspaper Report*

A vicar wrote in the newspaper today complaining that he was poor on £1000 per annum. His parish consisted of two cottages and the Church, but he explained that he had three children and that two of these were boys attending public schools. Keidrych at the same time got eight shillings a week as a gunner, and I 17/6 per week. It is a pity that there are so few vicars aware of these social conditions; there is, at present, a great deal of attention given by the press to the poverty of the clergy and their large unwanted houses.

May 22nd   *Peasticks*

'I'll be away a minute, I'm going to fetch some peasticks from the hedgerow. A short hazel we'll fetch, with spreading side branches and leaves attached. William tells me they're the best for drawing up the pea ... There's something in them that attracts the pea to the sticks.' This is what dear Rosie said to me and she left.

July 13th   *Bernard's Voice*

Bernard, the evacuee's conversation with me on music and about his masters. His voice. Bone or slate jazz-rattlers. They all had them.

Mr Vaughan's great passion for scent. Bought most of the PO scent. Muriel and her fiancé, Ken Lewis, nearly drowned. LCC tarring roads through the village, not particularly necessary, far better to see to the water supply. The water problem is evasive.

Keidrych's mother visits us. Manners wanting. She suggests Keidrych washes his face, shaves, and that I should put boiling water and salt on the weeds in the back yard. Liked vicarage church; because no weeds were on the path. It was well kept, whereas I prefer the old fourteenth-century chapel; one of the reasons for this is because there is a certain look of wildness about it! No graveyard, just tall hay ... grass grown to seed, in great variety. I like the sound of cinders being riddled, sticks cracking. Goat chase. The typewriter is much better now that I have put in a new ribbon. When I go out in the morning I often wonder if it will rain as it did once in Buenos Aires when all the roots and underground animals were drawn well above the ground. When the rooftops looked like rafts, and a washing line of clothes a bait for fish. Tree tops floated out their branches like pools of seaweed.

All Welsh homes seem to have a harmonium. I played on Rosie Davies's opposite though I wasn't very successful as I kept repeating the same notes too often. Here are cucumbers in flower, tomatoes and sweet corn, but in my home – my South American home – we have bee-like humming-birds, flamingos wandering in the paddock, white peacocks, and the sun's resilient rays.

I was lonely and homesick for the Argentine. I wrote the succession of my S. American poems: about the Pampas 'The New World', about the Incas' mountain grave, 'Xaquixaguana'; about my father, 'Argentine Railways'; about the 'River Plate'; about Mechita where I was born, 'Blood and Scarlet Thorns'; about the convent 'Canzone Benedicto'; about Sao Paolo Brazil which I called 'Royal Mail'. I had the strong desire to leave the village and go to S. America.[26]

July 15th   *Bird Notes*

Today's moorhen. There was an agreement between us that if every Arthur Davies shot any out-of-the-way birds by mistake, he would first bring it to me, so that I might make a study of the bird's plumage and characteristics at close quarters. This has been invaluable to me, for not only have I been able to study the change of plumage at different times of the year, but equally important to me, to know the taste of its flesh. I daresay some naturalists would squirm at this, but I believe them to be wrong in their judgement.

Take, for instance, the pigeon I plucked and drew myself. I found a full crop, not of grain, when grain was so plentiful, but a mixture of green celandine, clover and trefoil. There were small pieces of grit in the gizzard with chopped heather sticks and powder. As the pigeon lay in my hand I was able to feel the loose setting of the breast feathers. Iridescent mauve and emerald feathers. Delicate gradings of grey, almost bronzed or tarnished on the uppermost layers. The strange and unusual colour of its insides: and when cooked, its very good flesh. But the dark and full breast of the Moorhen is even better to eat. Here are the notes as I jotted them down on the various days that they came in. And the black and white ducks with rust colours on their feathers.

Moorhen   Poem on moorhen and its scarlet garters.
The dull slate ostrich texture of its breast feathers. The sheen of rust or parmel lichen on its back – the brown yellow-gold of ginger-nuts. The two scarlet garters above the shining and rather large-scaled legs whose vivid colouring was lime green, as fresh as the inner barks of trees. Enamelled or lacquered beak, scarlet with a bright yellow or orange tip. Brown eyes, with a red-purple sheen when caught in the sun's rays. With this bird you SKIN it, not feather it. The flesh is very delicate. [Illegible] certain sharpness to the polished beak.

Curlew
Legs, the grey shagreen of shark, small-netted, thin and firm. The curlew is also skinned, not feathered.

Oyster-catcher
Not black and white at all, but nigger brown and white. Very definite and clear division of pattern and colour. A dumpy little fellow. Legs not pink or red but a murky pale grey with vague pink tinge.

Rosie taught me how to skin and clean these birds. Later I used these observations in poems 'Curlew', 'Seagull', 'Moorhen', 'Woodpecker', 'Robin' and two others.[27]
    For instance because I had noticed a scarlet ring round the leg of the 'Moorhen' I wrote 'scarlet bill and garter'. I also observed the legs and the colour of elms and that they were webbed slightly so I wrote 'elm webbed stretch'. With the poem 'Curlew' I wrote concerning its voice. The four short bleats running into the final fluid warble. The ever hammering of the 'Woodpecker' in the poem was contrasted with the mechanical hammering in the war

factories. 'Poem'[28] mocked war and spoke of the birds and need to arise out of the misery we found ourselves in.

July 16th *Flower List*

Vervain
Bittersweet (*Solanum dulcamara*)
Common Comfrey
Centaury
Pimpernel (the scarlet and yellow variety)
Lousewort
Ivy-leaved Toadflax
Knotgrass
Wild Thyme
Meadow Cranesbill

July 17th *Keidrych and Lynette*

Tonight, Keidrych and I went to the Farmers' pub as usual. Mr Vaughan, large as ever, told us about the breakfast he had had. 'Bacon as much as you liked and fried potatoes all for 6d. There were thousands there eating, so let me see, more than that.' Poor Mr Vaughan and his accounts, the whole village teased him about them. But he always smiled very simply. As he reached for a large scarlet box, his wife shouted at him, 'Now, Jack Vaughan, you leave that alone, that's Muriel's. Oh, he's a terror for scent, Mrs Rhys. Always going at Muriel's bottles and shaking it over himself before he takes out the cows. Lavender is what he likes best or Carnation. I'm sure it's he that's bought most of those bottles at the PO. It's getting scarce now, but they are very good, and still only 7d a bottle. Perhaps you've noticed that the Sweet Pea, Carnation, Lavender and Violet have all gone, and maybe tomorrow someone will buy the Rose. Under his arm-pits and all.'

If I write a Welsh play founded on my observation of Llanybri, I must remember to introduce the Welsh people talking about the English in contrast with their own simple realities of life.

Mr Vaughan on the Pendine Sands: 'All I want, Mrs Rhys, is to have a Pub in Laugharne, there's nothing I'd like better. Oh, I love Laugharne, Mrs Rhys.'

David Johnson, my neighbour, holy terror and devil of the village! has just been made drunk by his father and uncle. He has rolled up and down the road to the shrieks and delight of many. Poor David! His language is frightful, but then not speaking Welsh I do not understand the terrible things he says, so I merely smile, hoping that at the moment he won't slash at me with the butcher's knife in his hand, or throw the nearest stone at me within his reach. He has done this so many times with the village children who have attempted to play with him that now he has no one. Poor David. Two nights ago, his mother, shawled and looking like the Virgin Mary, sat on her wooden chair comforting her young baby. David took this quiet opportunity to creep behind his mother's back and after a lot of unobserved manoeuvres set light to his mother's chair and shawl so that soon she was in flames. Being a calm person, she soon put this out and just said, 'Isn't he a terror!' This is only one terrifying incident. And yet there seems no cure for his wildness. He has let out the new pig, just bought with their savings so that it can no longer be found and tortured the pig two days previously. Set light to his cottage by collecting a huge dump of paper and dry sticks and lighting the bonfire in the middle of the kitchen floor. On this occasion a chair was burnt out and the leg of a table, but nothing more. He will call people frightful names when he cannot get his way. For instance, he said to Keidrych yesterday when his mother chased him out of the house like a partridge, 'Dirty old bull-shit.' His mother's sister, when he went down to Hatchy Hill to tea, refused to have him to sleep the night. He had got it into his head that he wanted to sleep with his Aunt Sarah Ann, in her bed, and not go back to Gwen's as he calls his mother. She refused because he was a nuisance, and because she already had too many people sleeping in her bed. So, David in his customary way, swore at her, 'You bloody shit.' All this, and David is only three years old in April.

David and his father, Harry, sleep together, and Gwen in the second bed with the baby. Two beds in the one room so that there is scarcely any floor-space left at all. Harry, when he had returned from the Sunday 11 o'clock church service, took off his starched collar and proceeded to lie back in bed with the young baby in his arms. He lay there uncomfortably for a long while, until we entered at 1 p.m. to hear the news. He then got up, and put on his old working-day clothes and appeared a relaxed and happier man.

1942

January 3rd   *Snow Walk*

A quiet fall of snow drifts from the sky. It is the first this season so I decide to go out and look at the view which changes here each day. My dog, his coat curled with the frost, in excitement tosses up the snow, then sometimes prances 'up and up' to catch the flakes as they fall.

We choose the lane overlooking the valley; nearly all the other roads radiating from the village are too steep. There are six different ways out. By the Moche Farm; Llanstephan Bay; Coombe; Chapel Road; the Laugharne field and Cwmcelyn Bay and the water-mill where we wanted to go. The lane was warm, and sheltered by an enormous quantity of sticks which ran sparingly up towards the light. I still could not see the valley, only the full sky overhead and smooth white path. The change of warm air between the interlacing hedge and sticks and the sudden chill of air rushing over the field-gate so overpowered me that in defence my breath arose like a mythical beast's and rose like smoke over the hill. There was not much to see, but for a day like this, the peace, cold-shouldered by the earth, gave great comfort. The cry of a passing curlew as the only sound, and the hardier cattle grouped under the hedge were the only animals in sight.

The bleached valley shone with its own springing light and the brown line of the hedges strongly edged the field patterns of snow. My dog and I continued over the brow of the hill. I was still fascinated by the clear footprints as they sealed the whiteness of the snow. Paws first to one side, and then to the other, then a small print of bird's feet marked the way. Their bardic symbol keeping me snowbound until I reached the marshes, where I rested under the salt spray of the trees. Here the clear outline of birds was belling the air, sail-snatching at the slightest movement from the bread-hand of man. The black round ones still swollen with feathers, seeped in clusters on the tips of the trees. Beside a stream, a wagtail flittered among the stones; and fussing around it lay yellow threads of last summer's grass, bracken, and blackberry bleeding wild. Here to Cwmcelyn I walked so many times. Nearly always in my scarlet cloak. I wrote 'I walk to Cwmcelyn ask prophets the way'.[29]

On my way back I continued over to the Chapel road.

Today its hideous shape standing bleak among the chessmen graves looked more like an ammunition dump than ever. The black and white polished gravestones gilded and machine-turned. And the rough grey of the older stones of granite; the slate slabs hand-moulded and so deeply cut so as to catch the slanting rays of the sun. As I returned to the village into my cottage, Mrs Lewis, aged 73, and with very little English, suddenly said, 'Would you like a snow-ball?' What could I say but 'Yes'. So I stood patiently waiting for the break. Her first effort failed, so I told her to 'press the snow harder'. While she groped and grovelled I noticed that the shadows of snow were like the casts of the moon. She came nearer this time, grew nervous as she approached, giggled, and again the snow showered as soon as it left her hand. Old Mr Jones passed me wearing his flam-boyant red and green striped holly scarf.

January 4th   *Snow Story, Mr Jones*

Again I met Mr Jones wearing his red and green striped holly scarf. There was still snow on the ground at the time. And it always made me wonder how the older people of the village managed to keep warm by never wearing an overcoat. He told me that a few years back he remembered 'it was especially bad on the Chapel road. Even the day was black and the snow had reached the full height of the Chapel walls, so that there was no division between the main road and the tombstones. Like death everything was levelled up to the one level. By the slopes of the field the walking was not bad, but along the Chapel road where this girl had to go, the snow was more than over her head. This girl, she was very stubborn, knew she would be buried if she slipped off the Chapel wall, so she mounted one tombstone after another, knowing that there she was sure of higher ground. Eventually she found her way across the fields. The going was quite simple after that.'

March 6th   *Empty Cottage*

A staunch Welshwoman living alone – they always seem to survive their men. At last she dies. With her goes the Welsh tradition, good and bad, yet much of it worthy of being retained. Her stone cottage, whitewashed, surrounded by a garden sheltered with lilac bushes and rented out at £5 a year, is now offered at 10/- a week. No one wants it. Within three wet and frosty months, the roof has caved in, the small 'taxed' window is cracked, the walls split in two as though an earthquake has passed under them, the boulders of stone slackened by frost have rolled out of place. The old lady who lived in it, Miss Trehearne, was in her ninety-ninth year, and until last October lay or sat in her four-poster bed like a pickled Elizabethan. She was loved by some, cherished by others, and occasionally honoured by a celebrated visitor. One of these was the well known writer and founder of Everyman's Library, Ernest Rhys, who conversed with her in Welsh. He told me sometime later that to console her he told her that he was a hundred years old, and she was delighted. To Miss Trehearne most of the villagers were 'strangers – not of my generation'. 'They don't know what work is.' 'They would not do their hair tidy.' And sitting in the shade of her room, she would complain to me 'I can't be be up and about to tidy the garden'; 'I don't like the dark nights and I long for the moon.' 'It keeps me company at nights', she said. And true enough, beside the faded photographs of Tomb inscriptions, Graveyards and Chapels connected with her dead relatives plastering the whole wall, she had little else. Now all this has gone. Within the year perhaps many other buildings of the village culture would go as well.

'Paulinus' suffered a similar fate, dusty and neglected in the Carmarthen Museum.

This Saint whose cromlech remains
Whose burial height grieves in straightened stone
Stands, in a dingy corner of a museum's frayed side,
Neglected by man, as the bald-brained councillors
Neglect man, who flit through its impersonal ruins.[30]

April 23rd   *Notice to Quit Tygwyn*
                                               20 Lime Grove Av.
                                                      Carmarthen.

Dear Mrs Rhys,
I hereby give you six months' notice to quit residence known as 'Tygwyn' Llanybri as from April 24th 1942.

                                               Yours truly,
                                               (Mrs) W.T. James.

May 18th   *Bird Notes, Woodpecker*

Chaffinches, blue-tits. Three jays flitting from stream bush to open tree, there and back, there and back. This was the first jay I had ever seen. This was in the Cwmcelyn Valley. What impressed me most was their wonderful colour of cinnamon. From the distance from where I saw them, they appeared a warm cinnamon colour all over, which of course I knew them not to be.

Returning home along the Coomb road, where there is a small neglected quarry, tall overreaching trees, and hot medicinal air rising from the stone face of these pink Sienese rocks, I noticed a large splash of brilliant scarlet, a secretive flight from tree to tree until whatever it was hid deeper and thicker among the leaves. This sudden sensation of flight in colour disturbed me considerably. I was such an amateur where birds were concerned, I had no idea what this could have been. It was so large. The Scarlet Cardinals in Buenos Aires, yes I had seen many of those, and flights of wild emerald-green paraquets, but this vivid flash ...

Further on, skirting the hedges of 'Plasnewydd', a flock of yellow buntings kept rising in scallops above the hedge. Sunning occasionally to keep their yellow tan. A great titmouse was also seen, with its long black bib, and young fledgling thrush with its wide open orange mouth; the beak doesn't seem to have formed and the general impression is of a rather loose and shapeless mouth. Wagtail in flight towards a stream. Marsh titmouse. A goldcrest on the ground in Mrs Lewis's garden and another bird which I could not identify at sight: roughly the size of a small thrush or large bullfinch, long yellow band lying horizontally along the wings, yellow on the upper tail coverts, yellow on lower abdomen, and the rest a dull green-brown, perhaps a greenfinch in winter feathers.

When I got home, I looked up *The Handbook of British Birds* (edited by Witherby, Vol II, p. 283) and found that my scarlet adventure was no myth but none other than the Great Spotted Woodpecker.

June 3rd   *Flower List*

Wall Pennywort
Mallow Musk
Tansy
Field Scabious
Coen Feverfew
Yellow Toadflax
Meadow Vetchling
Tufted Vetch
Bush Vetch
Sea Purslane
Germander Speedwell
Bog Pimpernel
Sea Thrift

Hedge Woundwort
Wood Sage
Common Comfrey
Forget-me-not
Wild Thyme
Spurge
Self Heal
Ramping Fumitory
Cranesbill
Jagged-leaved Cranesbill
Greater Bird's Foot Trefoil
Meadow Sweet
Strawberry-leaved Cinquefoil
Creeping Cinquefoil
Common Agrimony
Hairy Willowherb
Lady's Bedstraw
Giant Goosegrass
Common Bugle

June 5th   *Wine Making, Pub Drink*

'My mother gave me a pure white book with thick leaves and in it I
pressed wild flowers. I got a prize for this at school, as they'd never
seen such a collection.' Rosie told me this when she found me
surrounded by elderflowers while I was preparing to make some
wine. The subject naturally turned to all the bouquets of homemade
wine including the praise of Gorse, which was considered one of the
most fragrant and potent. As we drew towards the subject of Pub
drinking and the general tendency for women to drink, Rosie said,
quite beside the point – 'God can read my heart. In the old days
they wore anything – nothing in particular – we came naked and
will go back naked to God, so what's the use ... Oh, what? "You
make your own homemade wine", they say. They wouldn't dream
of going to the Pub for a drink, or having one in public, *but* they'll
do it locked behind doors. But God can see them, so what's the
good.'

June 12th   *Air Crash*

At unexpected moments, when I was working in the cottage,
washing, or out in the garden, I would remember odd experiences
of a closer war that I had encountered. There was that long London

raid which lasted from nightfall 6 p.m. until 6 a.m. the next day ...
the longest raid London had ever had. In it I had lost my memory.
The shelling in Dover while standing on the promenade in the
middle of the raid. A near death on the East Coast when a Jerry
plane merged in through the moist sea mist, striking a bomb onto
the pier, and as it approached below the cliff level it had suddenly to
swerve to avoid a crash. Keidrych, used to the bombs, dropped to
cover behind a concrete block. I saw a soldier standing alone, and
preferred to stand still as well. There was no room for three. A few
seconds later the plane exploded, brought down by a battery a few
hundred yards away. The soldier, unknown to us both, came over
and asked Keidrych if he might shake the lady by the hand. I
suppose he thought I had been brave. But I was not brave, as I told
him, for I could not dive down and leave him standing alone.
Anyway, in that split second, I was too surprised to consider danger.
To see a plane so near and unexpectedly, as I shall never see a plane
again in my life, was strange, and this held my attention. High above
the cliff, the soldier and I leaned against the railings overlooking the
misty beach. No sea could be seen. It came in straight for the cliff ...
unknown of course to the German pilot as the mist had obscured
the view. It was a miracle, as they all said later, that it didn't crash on
the highly fortified beach.

  Then there was my visit to the bombed East End. And my stay at
the Inner Temple when I turned up while the library buildings were
still smouldering and continued to burn for another five days. The
Round Church wet and empty like a grotesque seashell. Out of this
experience I wrote my poem 'Crossed and Uncrossed'.[31]

  But the tragic event which made the most impression on me was
a young pilot's death. For several nights I had had a nightmare that a
plane had crashed in the field behind my cottage. And that by
running and reaching the plane first I managed to save the pilot's life
... the pilot being German. As I was in charge of the First Aid for
the village, I took this responsibility very seriously, far too seriously.
Now truly a plane could be heard to choke and splutter, it came
down the sky quickly. I ran. I knew where to run as I saw a huge
pall of smoke like a vaporous hearse hovering in the air where the
plane was falling. I flung my First Aid satchel over my arm, and no
doubt because of these previous nightmarish dreams I became
highly susceptible to every incident. I saw a human body drop and
bounce sideways as I entered the field. The bullets were flying out
of the fallen plane at a terrific speed, my knees shook under me and
I took the quickest cut through those bullets thinking that I might
save the pilot's life. I was the first at this side and another man, a

stranger, middle-aged, and the stranger disappeared. The pilot was
dead. An evacuee friend of mine took off her apron, said a prayer
and covered his body. His eyes were also closed for him. And I went
away. As I was in charge, I had the pilot's papers handed over to the
RAF personnel when they arrived. I did this not as interference, but
because I noticed that one or two of the many people that had gathered other than the villagers were touching his personal belongings.
His name, and I write months after the incident (roughly early June,
1941) was Petwick Lawrence; he was stationed at Pembrey and
carrying at the time TNT. He had been previously stationed at
Prestwick and had a lovely photo of a girl and, I believe, an address
of High Street, Plymouth. Anyway my natural inclination was to
contact this pilot's mother and wife or girl and to let her know that
his death was instantaneous, and that it was my belief that he tried to
avoid the village in coming down. I wanted the mother to also
know how the villagers felt, and how his death was respected by all
who visited the field. I mean, for instance, when the Polish doctor
arrived with a lorry and took the body away on a stretcher.

The air crash is mentioned in one of my poems in which I have
also related an air crash nearby, though not at Llanybri. The poem is
called 'Lamentation'.[32] The very bad Swansea raid which we could
see distantly from Llanybri is mentioned in the long heroic poem
(Feb 19, 20, 21) 'Gods with Stainless Ears'.

August 4th   *Simple Living*

I spend my days quite simply. As simply as any person could, and
'the Shadow Remains' is a good poem of my v. simple life. I bake
my own bread, fetch water from the well. A tedious job to say
nothing of the journey, as the arm and thumb get very tired pressing
the brass button which will only run when it is pressed. It is bad
enough on railway trains, but it is very difficult if you are filling two
3-gallon cans. The fire is made of coaldust and clay, and I frequently
bank it up at night and aerate it with holes made with a poker to
keep it in.

I feel wretchedly lonely. The village, most of them have turned
and treat me as a spy. The malicious talk seeping in so far that it
infilters the minds of the children and they throw stones at me.
Worse, outside the village PO a young boy kicked my dog in the
stomach ... just to get at me.

So my energy becomes consumed by my own creative waiting or
by the energy used in rebelling against these villagers.

I will not pretend that my suffering in this matter is light, but grave and penetrating. The then Minister of Education for Carmarthen, Mr Mason, went as far as to advise certain educative authorities from London not to come and see me. This person happened to be editing a Poetry Anthology at the time but came just the same. As usual, during this victimisation, I immediately warned the stranger of what was said about me. He then told me he was very gratified to hear what I had to say as he had already been warned not to have anything to do with me. For this sympathy and understanding – for it was, then, a courageous visit – I shall always be grateful. So I wrote about the gossip and suffering in 'Raw Salt on Eye': 'Was accused of spycraft to full innate minds with loam. Was felled innocent'.[33]

May 7th   *Welsh Composers*

A Brandenburg concerto is playing and behind it a few hours ago Dr Mansel Thomas gave us a lecture on the future of Welsh music.[34] But can there ever be any with the present barrier which is set up to protect and prolong the traditional music of yesterday? We were offered during this session three young composers and vocal examples of two. Then there was Grace Williams's developed style out of the 'Rough Rocks' of early Welsh folklore, full of vitality, strength ... Arwel Hughes gave us a shouting Lullaby with a swaying movement, containing a second development in the theme of the 'Erl King'. Of the composer, Daniel Jones, we heard nothing, though we were told that he had music of his accepted by Sir Henry Wood and the BBC on several occasions. I should like to have heard something of his, even though it were only one score. The BBC was praised for its encouragement of music ... CEMA,[35] the BBC. No, if we are to be truthful to the future ... let us say it has done more harm than good, and no doubt will continue unless a stern disapproval is shown.

What have we in Wales today ... good ears and voices ... and how do they use them ... as an outlet for suppression ... go and see *The Silent Village* and you will see what their puritan and stony religion has given them. Today, this afternoon, the final rendering of the National Anthem was no different ... and it is a sad solemn rendering ... blown out with a huge emotional outlet which dragged, slurred and poured one note into another.

This is what will have to change ... the negative approach. Until we get the fundamental correction to the purity of music we cannot progress. The pallor ... sentimental Eisteddfod singing MUST GO, and we must have instead a positive and active inflection in the voice ... then yes, we can speak of progress ... overthrow those teachers who would encourage middle class taste; and overthrow all authority, no matter how high or where they stand, who in any way oppose the young creative musicians' own instinctive individuality. And I say this because today I feel there are such young persons among the community who have been overlooked ... just in the same way as they have been ... squashed ... side-tracked ... and mocked in the literary field. We are Sir Chairman, of the twentieth century, and everything should be done to counteract any person who would wish us to escape and represent every other. We are already, if we are willing to accept it, at the birth of another great Era.

I believe the Welsh records of folklore to be adulterated. I have heard folklore songs in Spain and elsewhere: but I find the Welsh representation suspiciously complicated, both of harmony and melody ... the rhythm is acceptable.

Dr Mansel Thomas, who stresses education of music rather than the creative side, mentioned that because music was a universal language it should be taught well. This is of great importance for the future of basic English ... but music, if I may interrupt Dr Thomas? is not universally understood for the barrier of taste is already misunderstood between nations. When he started saying, 'We want a Welsh Schubert, a Welsh Beethoven', ... I began to feel bored. Why can't the wretched composer, if ever he can manage to get through all this Welsh red tape ... why can't he just be himself?

Worse ... Dr Thomas went on to say, 'The Youth of today has better opportunities to make known his work.' I know this cannot be so.

So we are offered three young composers as examples of the future promise for Welsh music. Grace Williams, Arwel Hughes, and Daniel Jones.[36]

Grace, we are told, has a musical brain of the first order and the ability to produce symphonic works. We are to expect Arwel Hughes to be slightly influenced by his master, Vaughan Williams, with regard to incidental music. and his attractive settings to Poetry. Daniel Jones – who has written many overtures – has much thought and fertility of melodic invention. We then heard songs by two of these three composers.

A lullaby by Arwel Hughes. But it was too much a shouting lullaby ... and too influenced by so many of the lullabies we have heard in the last two centuries. A Welsh Elizabethan would have been a better model. The second song was also by Arwel Hughes. Here the accompaniment was more defined, fresh to the ear, but the voice somehow seemed of secondary importance. The second theme was poor and made a muddled attempt to revive the 'Erl King' mythology ... I still remember those three small chords which were absurdly commonplace.

Grace Williams. Her collection of Oxen songs are well known. A native of Glamorganshire. 'English folklore à la BBC', I see I have jotted down as my immediate impression at the time. But she has a clear and definite vitality: and her accompaniment to St Athan was cheerful in a time like today.

The settings of Vaughan Thomas to 'Cangannyedd Ar nos ar brief' [sic][37] had all the plaintive desolation of the Russian composers; and rendered for me the desolation which now exists in Wales ... I believe that the piano for this medium was a little thin and think the music could be improved with a fuller accompaniment of instruments.

R. Parry Williams's poem to the wind, set by Dr Mansel Thomas, was then played and sung. Here the accompaniment was clear and strange, as it should have been, but not sufficiently so to acquire the uncanny atmosphere, echo wailing of the wind. I should have liked an occasional single line of cadences.

Far too much stress for chamber music (l.p.).

Even advocated that every county should have a Directorship of Music as had the counties of Denbigh and Merionshire. Also exchange of students from abroad ...

Folklore *Dance of Four Clogs* ... good ... the beginning of the record was pure, the rest adulterated ... refrain like the final movement of

The Holly reminded me of Grace Williams's work but better. Full of sparks and wet spines.

He recommended in particular a National Orchestra.

June 28th   *Chicken Mash*

The mash reduced to so small a ration that the farmer is compelled to use his own initiative. This morning, after sixteen sleepless nights rebelling at the mechanical and impersonal death which these robot planes cause, I arrived here in Llanybri and gathered young burdock leaves. 'Cut them into thin strips and stirred them among stale bits of bread warmed and softened with hot water.' This food was then thrown on to the floor boards of the chicken coops. 'This instead of the green that they cannot get themselves as we cannot let them go out,' said Rosie, 'the rats and carrion-crows are dreadful' she continued. The pigs now £7 apiece at the age of six weeks, and at the outbreak of war you could get them for thirty bob each. And food is hard to find for them as well. It's so hard to find anything at all ... just a bit of wheat grain and flour in warm water. The percentage of pig production falling by half since the beginning of the war. 'That accounts,' I said, 'for pork, pork, and more pork being offered to us week after week by the London butchers.'

This drastic search for food has led us to respect the smallholders; and they in the struggle to retain their livelihood, have had to fall back on new ways of feeding, find resources of their own. Some have turned to burdock, and revived their knowledge of herbs, which until recently had been replaced by synthetic foods, linseed cake, and dried milk, etc. etc. This fight for existence – so obvious among themselves – must be extended and exposed by the pen of the writer. It must be made known and publicised in all columns wherever space arise. And in no way confined to just the agricultural magazines. Whether in *Lilliput*, *Tribune*, *Vogue*, *Statesman and Nation*, *Time and Tide*, *Sphere*, *Horizon*, *Life* AND *Letters Today*, *Our Time*, *John Bull*, etc. etc. It does not matter so long as these rural hardships are realised and understood. It is, and I say this with a stiff face, mind, and heart, it is of a deeper and graver consequence than any of the horrors of blasted bodies and homes. These to some extent are fatalistic ... it may be you or I. But as repelling as this fate is to me ... is it not worse, to have whole sections of the people sink, forced to face pestilence aggravated through malnutrition, and as a result of a callous survey and lack of foresight directed towards this rural day? A result – depending on how we face it – which will affect not one generation but generations to come.

We have, as a life on this land, an offering of peace and security for the soul. A pastoral root which is wholesome and cannot but stimulate anything but the mind's conditioning: and this is of a more vital significance than anything else since the pulse of humanity has been obliterated by the machines of monstrous war. Yes, *was* I say, and now ask, where are we, those who repudiate this icicle of death? Where, and how, are we to break through this paralysed crust of earth and mind? There are two conditions open to us.

We can go backwards. Back to the primitive and rural crafts of the land. This school of propaganda is much in evidence just now. Led by Professors, who seem to live backwards anyway, Philanthropists, Hypocritical Vicars, who think farmers are idyllic illiterates provided they keep out of the pubs. And our Civil Servants or State Officials dabbling in the Arts? Thanks to them we cannot have a large-sized kitchen in which we can all eat together in Wales – farmers, labourers, children, cats, sheep, dogs, wife, boys and girls.

We need such a room big enough to hold these and give sufficient space as well to boil the pig food, boil a bucket of water to wash the clothes. Instead, are reluctantly given the one room cut up to fit the floor-space of two. We are given, and have been given, a *large* parlour and small *narrow* kitchen. And as a result of this, since, in Wales at any rate, good customs do not die out; the families squeeze into this one small kitchen, at discomfort to themselves, in order to eat, or sit and talk, on the chair, boxes, or settles, whatever is provided in order to share each others company of sadness or joy. The parlour they *never* use. Not even on Sundays. Not even during the Harvest Feasts.

A person like John Betjeman, who can pretend he cares for Wales, and can edit a book containing Welsh Landscapes and allow reproductions by John Piper, of Grongar Hill, when it is not Grongar Hill, and no attempt is made to make it as such, is sufficient to prove that he not only disparages Wales but the whole meaning of art as well.

And why not have the courage? Where is the faith we should have today in our own generation? Can we not put up as good a village or building as our early ancestors? Can we not use ... shall we not put all our modern research and scientific knowledge to the good purpose of humanity? And when a new gadget is invented, check it, use it, rather than let it be bought up and the patent destroyed by some monster fearing industrialist. And when the gadget proves false, chuck it skyhigh, blast it with all the power and objectivity of a robot plane. Tradition can be evil when the root of its repetition is associated, as it is so much today, with FEAR. Tradition is apt to exterminate the young and frustrate the fresh spirit of our generation. The word, *tradition*, is really a substitute for fear when it is used by the Tories, Industrial magnates etc.; when it is revived by a group of State Artists; flattered into position by popular Art Critics. Today let us retain only what is good of the past ... and not copy ... copy ... a ... cat. Rather let us have the courage to be adventurous, face up to our own generation. Above all to grow. And to grow means peace, plenty of light and air. Good roots and a home in which to extend those branches so that they may be fed.

August 2nd   *Birds Not Recognised*

Two birds I cannot recognise. Through the kitchen window I can see them separating the seeds of the sow thistle from the plume. Somewhat alike and no doubt of the Hawfinch family. The forehead, neck, back and lesser wing coverts are beaver brown and somewhat furry in texture. A rather broader band than most finches have covered the greater wing coverts and formed a light stripe of cream across their backs. The primary and secondary wing and tail coverts are a blue coal-grey. The tail feathers longer than the wing feathers. The beak broad and cured. And a small patch of white under their tail coverts. As the stem bends under their weight they lift a claw and cling at right angles to the stem like a tight-rope walker trying to find his balance on a slackened wire.

Passing the manure yard, and rich clumps of pasture leading down to a small stream, I could see a large flickering of birds flitting from branch to branch and disturbing the leaves. They flew here and there, and seemed to favour a variety of small-leaved willow whose name I do not know. They were long-tailed tits, fledglings and mature birds, covered with a predominance of grey feathers; a black stripe running over the crown of their heads like a middle parting on the head. They varied in number from 20 to 30, and every now and then a short-tailed tit with a full black crown could be seen feeding amongst them. Similar flocks had been seen by the farmer, Mr Williams Ivor Davies, from time to time, whose field this is. They had not nested there but would visit the meadow; on another occasion feeding on a young oak tree.

The willow, with its small, pallid and dry leaf, greyer and tougher than most willows, reminded me of Corot's Ville D'Avray where I had spent many an evening, sitting at this same hour around the lake. Today these blurred mists and mellow tones in life and nature are put aside. All is sharp, hard, and must be clear and factual. Bright colours, crude and violent for all purposes, are rushing through the press. Life and thought spin along on immediate and tangible values; while the recesses of our mind and feeling remain neither accepted nor described.

These mists have been expressed by some on the past; and nearly always to the advantage of humanity, including the blur and haze hovering over the Celtic legends; Whistler's Thames; Picasso's blue period; T.S. Eliot's fog 'that rubs its back upon the window-panes';[38] the mysticism, damp and unexpressed haze which penetrated Russian characters by writers of the early revolutionary period; gauze and atmosphere created in films; in photography, manners and clothes. The peace and mist rising from this stream here in this meadow in the middle of war, during the most successful month of the robot machine. Near a tree, quiet and grey as those growing in Southern France, filled with the joyous notes and movements of birds. A peace permeating sky, grass, and leaf. Even the caddis and larva appear hazy, so that when a wood-pigeon flies heavily from a thick-leaved tree, we are surprised that she does not carry a branch of olive in her beak.

August 5th   *Birds from Plasnewydd*

Coming back from Plasnewydd, I find it hard to know what bird is singing against the sun. The song is varied, some of the notes not unlike the early churrs and first phrases of a nightingale. Both Rosie and Mr Carr who passed us on the road they were sure it was a goldfinch. 'A young one' they said to cover up their indecision. But I remained stubborn and unconvinced. The field glasses were of little use. The bird seemed to be mostly a fawn yellow in colour, but when we caught a glimpse of the narrow and sharp strip of lemon running along the outer edge of its wings we all shouted, 'It's a green linnet' and walked away.

On the way home, Rosie spoke of the Hound's Tongue and of its value as a cure for burns. She reassured me that it was good as she had tried it out herself. 'It's all right if you peel off the skin of the fern along the rib of the under side ... just wrap that peeled side next to the burn ... like a bandage ... so that the juice from the fern can get through to the wound ... it's that which cures it.' I had heard of another cure, and that was the inner bark of an elm. To wrap this green and moist stripping around the burn. I do not know if it is effective for open burns; but when Phil Davies who had been called up for his medical suddenly found himself with a huge 3-inch blister on his arm, he had this cure recommended to him. He was very keen to join the RAF and anxious that it should disappear within 24 hours, he tried the experiment. Within 12 hours all the moisture in the blister had been absorbed without either puncturing or piercing the skin. He was accepted, but I regret to say has since been killed in action.

As Rosie and I wandered on in silence, for I had also told her how this boy had used the bark ... I broke the strain when I saw a butterfly resting on some agrimony. I spoke of my difficulty in trying to buy a butterfly net. How I had already tried the Angler's Shop in Carmarthen ... and made suggestions from there until we arrived at the Tygwyn farm, of what I might use if I attempted to make one myself.

Flowers – Found on the field while turning oats and barley
Corn Marigold
Heartsease
Viola tricolor (6 to 8 inches tall, foliage a light tender green, flower

white miniature pansy face with deep yellow pencil streaks radiating
to the centre with sepia-brown and white furred nectary.)
Cornmint
Snapdragon
Sneezewort (*Achillea ptarmica*) Note: disc-ray white; pounded leaves
used as snuff.

August 6th   *Crows and Potatoes*

I helped turn the edges of three fields of mixed barley and oats in
order to make room for the machine to come along to reap and
bind. Here I found quite a lot of flowers which had escaped my
notice; and as many were not entirely native to cornfields I was
quite surprised. Corn Marigold, Heartease, the tall and short varieties (*Viola tricolor*) white flowers with deep yellow centres.
Cornmint, which had a most unpleasant smell and attracted more
than one butterfly. Wild Snapdragon, and Sneezewort with its white
central disc florets and outer ray.

As we shook and turned over the corn, for it was very heavy and
damp, we kept coming across a small size of potato lying among the
rows. These had been stolen by crows from nearby plots. They had
flown away with them in their beaks, and through accident, or with
deliberate policy to hide, they had dropped these potatoes in the
cornfield. In the immediate distance, on a hard green meadow
running up the opposite side of the valley, eight or nine sleek crows
can be seen pecking at something grasped between their claws. Plas
Isa's field had been harvested the previous day. They brought in a
splendid crop of large and healthy potatoes. Much too large in my
opinion if the potatoes were to be well-flavoured and sweet. The
smaller ones had been left on the field to be picked up for feeding
the hens and pigs, for they were useless as seed. So it was that these
black Carrion-crows had swept down overnight and flown away
with more than they could eat. There was one farmer, the late Bill
Howells, Rosie's brother, who when sowing corn used to add seven
extra bushels of corn for every seven acres for the crows. Casting the
grain fairly thick, for before he had finished they had arrived in
flocks from the Coomb woods and covered the whole field with
their black and shining feathers.

Now that we had the Saw Mills working, and so many trees had
been felled in the last two years, the Carrion-crows, Rooks and
Jackdaws had all fearlessly penetrated the village, arriving even as far
inland as the slated roofs and air-raid shelters of Carmarthen. Here
they would prowl like cats, scavenging in the early hours of the

morning among the dust bins. I cannot say I like these species, or their Gestapo walk. But their pure black outline, shape and tone, seem to intensify the view in much the same way as the Japanese use black to clarify their woodcuts or heighten a design. These birds are a new change for Carmarthen: but I am not sure that the sea-faring call and elegant flight of the gulls flying white over the River Towy are not sweeter to her streams, appearing like white flocks on the ploughed fields. And that today these Carrion-crows and Rooks are just the final setting and last resistance to her Puritan background.

August 7th   *Pimpernel*

'Do you remember when Jack Vaughan was alive, and he was helping to turn in one of the fields, his wife passed, bringing in the cows and shouted "You'd better hurry, Jack Vaughan, it's coming to rain." "How do you know?" he replied. "I can tell by the little red flowers," she answered him. "Oh you, and your flowers," he roared back, red as a pimpernel in the face himself. Now these scarlet flowers are known to close at noon. And they also close when it's coming to rain.' So far I had not bothered to observe their reactions, either towards the sun or the rain. But I shall, as these are a particularly interesting family in Carmarthenshire. Besides the common yellow varieties, a blue and purple have also been seen.

August 10th   *Flowers*

I found what I believe to be a Woody Cranesbill (*Geranium sylvaticum*). I met Mr Percy Jones, F.L.S., in Llanstephan and handed this and two other specimens over to him. The next day I heard that he was seen wandering about the lanes trying to find a better spec- imen of the *Geranium* variety which I had given him. On my way home, I noticed that the Dusky Cranesbill had ceased to flower. And that the plant had been cut down with a bill-hook when someone had trashed the hedge. Over the Fynnonolbri Bridge I found a freak specimen of the less hairy Rose Bay. The petals of one flower were white while those of the second flower rising from the same main stalk but on its own slower-stem, were a deep pink. These are beside me now in a milk jug. There is also another flower which I believe to be a pink Bladder Campion. The leaves and stem are hairy and somewhat fragrant. And a cutting from the Great Hairy Willow-herb from the stream. This plant was about 4 foot 6 inches in height.

August 11th   *Woodpecker*

That wretched green woodpecker came right up to the vegetable garden today. It yaffled among the elm leaves, but I could not see it, then disappeared.

August 13th   *Flower List*

Berries, Woody Nightshade
Greater Celandine
Malva moschata
Stork's-bill
Knapweed
Tuberous Bitter Vetch
Lathyrus macrorrhisus
Enchanter's Nightshade (stream variety with scarlet sepals above calyx)
Burdock
Blue Sheep's Scabious
Common Eyebright
Cudweed

August 14th   *Butterflies*

Caught with homemade net:
Hedge Brown
Meadow Brown
Small Tortoiseshell
Common Blue
Small Copper
Wall
Green-veined White
Large White

Not bad going for a first attempt. All the butterflies belonging to the brown range had appeared so much the same to me before this; likewise the white varieties. The net had been made from some sky-blue net which I decided was a good camouflage. It was fastened on to an elder stick and bound to a frame made from floral wire.

August 15th   *Butterflies*

Two tortoiseshell butterflies starting to hibernate on the bedroom rafters.

Gooseberry moth (*Abraxas grossularicta*) seen in lower field, lying with open wings on a white Flowering Nettle. The white surface of its wings was striped with orange bands and small black patches. The body as it drew up and closed its wings was also orange shading to a paler hue and somewhat softened with dark silky hairs.

August 16th   *Library and Bookshop*

Went to the County Library where they told me they had no books on butterflies or moths. I went out, and crossed over to D. Williams's Bookshop on the opposite side of the street. There they had no technical books on the subject. I asked if I might order one, they implied that I might be disappointed as no book on this subject was being reprinted just now. I then remembered the shelves of secondhand books at the back of the shop. There was a large dark and dirty enclosure as secondhand books should have. I must have remained there an hour. In all the shelves which had been filed under various headings, there was only one other person interested. And he, of course a minister, had to be delving in the same shelf as I. I say of course a minister because, today, they seem to be the only people left who are interested in Natural History.

Most of the books on *Lepidoptera* were Victorian. Out of date but fascinating, both in description and with the frigid colourings which no butterfly ever carried. I bought E. Meyrick's *Handbook of British Lepidoptera* for the beauty and precision of its prose. If a writer can describe clearly and concisely the individual shapes of each vein cell and the fragile powder as it rests in colour on the surface of the wings, and write it so well that the reader is fascinated, he has in my opinion gone a very long way towards mastering his own language.

Rev. J. Seymour St. John's *Larva Collecting and Breeding* – I bought this so that I could get to know the natural haunts and feeding grounds. And *British Butterflies* by Edward Newman, F.L.S., F.Z.S. father of present Newman who is authority on lepidopterae and has his own farm and collection in [illegible] not far from here, where I have been to see the rare living butterflies. Many are released each year and have been seen as far as S. Wales, he told me. When I returned to Llanybri, I found that a previous signature, 'Parker', had been signed in pencil at the top of the page. Was this, I wondered, T. Parker, author of *The Natural History of Carmarthen-*

shire, published in 1905? I turned over a few more pages, and here and there read the margin notes, still written in pencil. The dates fitted in with my belief. And though when I showed this volume to others I was rebuked, I was finally rewarded when at the end of the book I found two full lists of every butterfly found at 'Oaklands' with separate date and descriptions similar to that contained in his *Natural History of Carmarthenshire*.

August 17th   *Colour Charts*

Perhaps the best description for all flowers, birds, and butterflies, is the first impression. Take, for instance, the frail shaded Meadow wing. Impersonal, yet as striking and subtle in its change of tone as a Siamese cat. The second rule of order, is that colour should only be defined from one regulated chart. It is not sufficient to call a flower pink when another reliable botanist may refer to the same flower and shade as orange or blue. A check on this, to confirm what I write, needs only a quick reference to the description of the Meadow Cranesbill in various botanical books. The chart should cost a penny, or at the most threepence, when perhaps a waterproof surface is provided. This would enable field collectors to take the chart out with them in all kinds of weather. Would a chart taken from Oswald Siren's thesis on colour be a good foundation to work from? The plate and choice would have to be standardised; possibly printed through the responsibility of one firm, so that no discrepancies of tone or shade could arise. And this could only come into effect after all the naturalists, entomologists, ornithologists had consented to the basic and authoritative colours on the chart. In every book on any of these subjects a leaflet of the colour chart could be included and in this way scientific research of the various changes which take place, either in flowers living in different soils, or in birds which shed and renew their colours could be made. The demand for greater accuracy would also enable amateurs to know whether a reference to 'pink' fell into the blue or orange range; whether it was as fierce and arresting as the clear shock pink of a Campion, or mellowed with mauve and grey washes like the Common Mallow.

August 18th   *Llanstephan Estuary*

What I cannot understand is why some notice is not set up to the effect that certain stretches of the Towy Estuary are dangerous. Today the sea went out further than usual owing to the harvest tides, the sand could be seen rising in banks, lightening under the sun, dry except for a narrow channel which carried fishing boats out towards Pembrey. Here, at this brackish edge, almost 500 yards from the mark of high-tide, round, hollow, spiral holes have been left in the sand. These were dry; but it was obvious that as soon as the tide came in, the water would seep under the holes and filter high up through the sand, filling these holes with water like sinister pools, treacherously and imperceptibly. In attempting to test these pools, a foot could be trapped. The suction of the out-going tide would draw it further down, deeper into its shifting base. From the scale pattern left on the sand of the conflicting currents, it was obvious that these were whirlpools. They were not large in size, only pools varying from 1½ feet to 3 feet across. Though they were small and known to the local bathers, it was not fair to the children or visitors to the village who paddled near them that they had not been warned.

After scraping up enough cockles for supper, I followed up the tide, out as far as I could. Fishermen stood around the curve of the Bay facing the West Marshes of Laugharne and Pendine. Their lines drifting out to sea for bass. The crabs too were plentiful, so that all the lug-worms which had been dug up with so much care and patience, had practically diminished. As far out as it would seem almost impossible to walk. Over to Pembrey where there stretched a pale and virgin sand like the beginning of a new world. Here, captured in long slender pools, lay shells, Whelks (*Fusus norvegious*) accounted to live in forty and fifty fathoms of water. A scollop, in rich tawny colouring, fluted and spiked (*Pecten maximus*), edible mussels (*Mytilus edulis*), and numerous Tellin and Razor shells. And one other (*Littorina rudis*), a shell which solved a whole problem for me. When I had walked towards Cwmcelyn Bay, I had often noticed transparent pale pink snail shells lying among the hedges. As they were similar but smaller in shape to the average varieties of 'garden' snail, I had concluded that perhaps these might be one of the same family but extinct now, and characteristic of this particular part of South Wales. I now find they are no more than striking varieties of the periwinkle, some having black or white circular stripes on pink and apricot backgrounds. The frequency with which these pink shells can be found among the Spring violets and primroses can mean but one thing; that at one time the sea must have covered this particular part of the valley and had since withdrawn.

August 18th   *Making Straw Rope*

A dreary wet day with N.E. wind blowing. No butterfly day. The corn had been cut and bound and Rosie had to decide whether they would put it up in stooks or leave it over the weekend. By the afternoon the clouds had lightened and we all went out. Rosie, Mr Davies, their daughter and myself. We all worked hard, very hard. The wretched machine had bound some sheaves ineffectively, so that whole rows of corn had to be bound by hand. This was easy for the others, tedious for myself, as I had never attempted to bind by hand. I found the knot hard to manipulate; the wiry stacks of the barley cutting into my hands, crawling up my sleeves, down my neck, raising weals of red which inflamed my skin. Had it been wheat, the whole operation would have been easier: then I need only have twisted the wheat stalks and bound them tight around the sheaf. I had it explained to me, since I did not know, that wheat could not have a knot when it was bound into a sheaf as it germinated too quickly. And that if rain rested for some time in the cracks of this knot, and grain caught in it might grow, then, when threshing took place, the wheat would have a mixture of green and golden-ripe grain, and that would be bad for the flour. It would make it bitter.

I learnt other things which interested me. I was told that it was not so long ago that rope was practically impossible to obtain, so that some of the binding which had to be done for thatching had to be pegged down with hand-made twine. This was twisted a little differently to the straw-rope that [was] used for binding wheat. A stick plucked from a hedge would be attached to the first strand of straw. This stick was twisted, and the layers of straw regulated and fed from a loose stack lying on the field in much the same way as wool is fed and twisted from flock into a long strand. When working, out in the haggard, where the big trusses of hay had to be carried, the same straw twists were made; but as they developed into rope they were curved into scrolls. Like the beginning of a straw beehive or enlarged raffia mat. These ropes were usually made to the length of five or six feet. They were made and piled up in coils until the day of carting. Then, on that day of carting, they were opened and thrown forward to catch the huge trusses of hay. Bound securely around these heavy loads, the hay was easily carried and easily held in the hand by the straw rope ends.

August 23rd   *Potato Harvest*

We heard that the potatoes harvested from John Davies's Plas Isa field, had gone over to our troops in Normandy: as a shipload from Swansea. This was a relief, for only a year ago, from the very same port a ship-load of potatoes had been sent out of the harbour to be dumped. They had found no market: and instead of distributing them to the farmers as feeding stock, the controllers remained indecisive, until the answer was given too late. Eventually they rotted and were good for nothing. The potatoes I mean. And how many thousands of lbs of hake had been condemned recently by the M. of H. at Milford Haven?

August 26th   *Butterflies*

A Silver-washed Fritillary flew over the bramble hedge. Just missed a Red Admiral on three occasions. Twice the butterfly lay open-winged on a fragrant mauve thistle (*Cnicus arvensis.*) And on another occasion it rested on a spray of green bramble berries. A large dragon-fly passed swiftly across the marshes, having no apparent colour when in flight. The wings were transparent and about 3 to 4 inches across. Several Wall butterflies flew fast flying low to the grass. They all appeared unsettled, unable to rest or feed. The 'Whites' have the largest flight just now, covering the ground tirelessly from marsh to garden green: while the Red Admiral returns to his favoured haunts and is exceptionally swift in moving, especially when I was attempting to catch him. I would say that he does not zig-zag for protection as so many of the other butterflies do, but rather disconcertingly rises in one dignified glide, curving in an arch like a swift, warm and close in flight but well out of reach.

I found, since I am an amateur in these matters, what I thought to be a young field rat lying in the kitchen. It was dead, and I thought it strange that the cat had not eaten it. I had often seen her eat sparrows, feather and bone. And knew her habit of bringing her catch into the kitchen so that the sheep dogs would leave her undisturbed. What was it then? Could it be a vole or shrew? I took it out and placed it on the stone wall, calling the cat at the same time. She took no notice, so I knew by her refusal that it was a vole. Poisonous to her nature, and a mammal not frequently seen.

It is often by studying the relations of other animals between themselves and their choice of food, that we learn so much. The entomologists may learn the names of hundreds of insects entirely through their study of larva breeding and imago feeding. The ornithologist may notice the shape and leaf of trees: and when studying water birds in particular, the names of shells cast on the shores, the small fish rippling on the water-scales of the tide. And so, whether we are conscious of it or not, the intense and penetrating study of one or any of these branches in the field of a naturalist will in the end grow, until it covers an area of the whole field. Sky, plant, tree, animal and soil strata included. And in this way a natural conclusion and unity is reached, which politics, industrial problems and scientific research cannot achieve. These are essential qualities for today: but his gap which they have created in most of us today, together with the crooked outlook of religion, is such that we are left in ourselves disunited, yet as one apart from the disintegration of the world.

August 27th   *Stacking Sheaves with William Ivor Davies*

Again I went out to the fields. Towards a two acre stretch sloping down over the Laugharne Estuary. This time William Ivor Davies and I worked single-handed. The work required much patience for no sooner had we got the first two sheaves to stand and walked away to fetch the next pair, when the wind spiralled, curved over the hedge, gave a sharp blow, and blew down the whole lot. This happened quite often. Now, to put up a good stook is not to consider what it looks like today, nor whether it will resist the immediate sharp wind. But rather will it stand after many days of drenching rain or hard-hitting hail? For this is Wales, not the sunny south of England nor the dry east plains of Anglia. Will these stooks retain their vigour and the gaps left under the bundles continue to aerate the sheaves so that the stooks do not collapse individually, and rather that the upper stalks of grain are free and not matted so that the fresh air and sun may dry and ripen the grain. Besides the difficulty of overcoming the wind, the sheep dogs kept burrowing under the stook, sending a rippling movement right up to the tips of the grain so that they collapsed or slipped wavering to one side. We tried to draw the dogs off towards the hedge where they had already caught a rabbit, but the fun for them lay in catching moles under the stooks and from this gaiety they refused to be distracted.

After a pretty good spell of work, Mr Davies offered me a Woodbine. But he should have remembered that I do not smoke. He then suggested that we should sit down and handed me an apple and penknife from his pocket. He had picked up the apple from Amelia Phillips's tree which she had grown from seed forty years ago. He had managed to pick up about two dozen apples without any of us realising it! They were all stored in bulging pockets. Like a magician he kept putting his hand in and drawing out three or four apples at a time.

We were standing at the back of the cottage waiting for the Sunday papers. William Ivor Davies had gone into the next vegetable garden but one to see if he could find his broody hen. She lay somewhere in the hedge between this garden and his field. Taking the pole from the washing-line, he bent and struck at the dark roots of the hedge. It was when he was in one of those striking attitudes that he had managed to fill his pockets with eating apples. They had originally been picked fresh, for the tree spread its leaves and branches low over the wall. Of course, later he told Amelia Phillips about this, but for a moment, for an hour or so, we were all amused.

This small and trivial incident is like so many in the village that brighten a day's work. In the rush of town work this same incident would remain mocked at. In town our sensibility and choice of pleasure becomes hard and more definite. A lack is felt of the 'play' of things arising out of the people themselves: lack of magic, of simple delight. The French have retained it ... in Paris, for instance, the rural qualities of a peasant are not so far away from the soil; the *modistes* have it, *femme de menage, boulanger* etc. ... but we have not.

I will write of two other events which delighted us this same afternoon. About the sheep dogs. Rosie arrived with freshly baked tarts and a milkcan full of sweet tea. She spoke proudly of the way these two sheep dogs, Fan and Tips, never took anything from the kitchen table. No matter whether they were in the house or not. And to these words of praise Mr Davies added 'Have you noticed the way Tips runs, different from all the other dogs and the way she hangs her tail?' I said I had not. And they called up the resting dogs from the other end of the cornfield. Iris, who had joined us for tea, also stood up calling them backwards and forwards, encouraging them to run up and down the field long enough for us to observe their differences and Tips' superior pace. The strange thing was that she never ran like most four-footed animals but used her two forefeet first, springing and bounding up high in the air and then lifting her hind feet. In this way 'Tips' set up a see-saw rhythm which Mr Davies aptly described as 'gambolling'. This was her only method of racing on the field, and though abrupt and joyful, it was no less swift than Fan's.

The second incident which we enjoyed was when Tips was caught taking out the last of the five remaining tarts from the wicker basket. An act which rather deflated Rosie's pride in her.

Earlier this afternoon when Mr Davies and I were talking, he spoke of oat-bread made on the grid and said how good it was. 'That is good when the oats were homegrown, threshed and milled on the farm and eaten newly baked from the grid. Sweeter than barley. You can taste the barley in the National bread when we get it sometimes.' I peeled away the husk and tasted the grain of both oat and barley. The oat grain was soft and exceptionally sweet and nutty in flavour. And the barley grains were mealy. 'The grain will take some time to harden,' Mr Davies said. 'It will probably have to remain in stooks another seven days or more.'

1945

February 10th   *Dialect and Husbandry*

The basis of a dialect depends on four main issues: occupation of the community; whether they have been conquered over a long period and how suppressed; weather; and mythology, that is customs, healing cures, superstitions, religion. In all rural communities there is a similarity of basic rhythm, ritual, and sad melodic flavour, contrasted by the festive joyousness of the gatherers of the harvest. And in particular, a similarity of exact syntax can be traced between the idioms of the Irish, Bretons, Provençals, French, Spanish, North Italians, Friesian islanders, Swiss, Flemings through ancient laws of husbandry.

May 3rd   *Fisherman*

It was unfortunate that often when John Roberts walked across the Taf Estuary with his flat fish alive and skipping in his basket, for he had caught some on the way as he felt for them with his feet, that at the same time Mrs Jones from Llangain would also arrive with her load. This meant a congestion of fish; but rather than discourage such a wholesome effort I would always buy from both. John Roberts always arrived while I was in bed and his shouting 'Fish alive O'. It meant putting on anything and racing down to catch him before he sold out. Mrs Jones of Llangain came later on the Western Welsh bus which arrived at Llanybri, its terminus, at 9.30 a.m. Her fish were also exceptionally fresh, firm and clear. But they had all been cleaned and weighed beforehand and each portion, roughly two fish at 1/- per lb, wrapped in grease-proof paper. Whereas John Roberts had his flat fish hanging so many on a willow strip or lying in his basket and just guessed approximate weight. Those he had felt with his feet under the sand as he walked across the sea bed were still loose and flapping in the spacious basket.

When I bought from Mrs Jones I thought I would ask her how she kept her fish so fresh – she ought to know. 'Now let me see, to keep the fish fresh, slit only one side and draw out the insides, then wipe with a clean damp cloth and fill with salt, leave the head on.' Did I know how to test if it's fresh? I did know but told her I didn't. She said, 'Look to see if the gill is red, if it isn't it's not fit to eat. Do not give it to your children if the gill isn't red for that's where trouble starts.' I judged by the sunken eye of the fish.

June 6th   *Coracle Men*

The Hunting men are trying to eliminate the fox. If they succeed it will become a sacred animal. But they won't succeed because 'on its natural run' their whole pleasure depends. It's much the same as these poor coracle men, who with the tremendous force and push from the linesmen, have had the Law turned against them, so that they will not be allowed to use their coracles any more.

'They catch all the salmon', is the continual protest of the fishermen in the press. And with the same breath of protest, they will do their best to procure a coracle at a degrading price in order to sit in it and fish with their rod and line in the pools they could not otherwise reach. The Teifi coracle men have had a raw deal; and I am sick of debating with well known linesmen on the subject of their defence. I am proud of my article on 'The Coracle' in *The Field*, but it is not enough; and another is required to reveal the injustice and the harm that is done. But I haven't the time. The material would have to be carefully collected.

With regard to the cost of coracles, a secondhand one costs £2.10 and a new one, which takes about three weeks to make at the right time of year, when the wood is just right, costs about £5. Of course, the calico has to be supplied by giving up clothes coupons.

It was inside a Carmarthen pub, built facing the River Towy, on a settle shining with a yellow varnish and scrumbled to resemble oak, that I learnt the result of a case concerning one of the local coracle men. About one whom I neither knew nor had visited. He had been found guilty of absenting himself from three Home Guard parades. He had a staunch defendant in Mr W.H. Rogers: but even he could not undo nor penetrate the military knot. The accused pleaded that he was both a plumber and a coracle fisherman by trade, both reserved occupations, and that this left little time over for other duties. He said that he had not been accepted for military duty when he volunteered at the outbreak of war; and on the three occasions when he absented himself from the Home Guard parades he was physically unfit.

He was fined £1 on each of the three charges.

Since then I heard of another incident. On a moonless night a coracle was found on the same River Towy with a tidy load of fresh butter. This had apparently been stolen from the Cow and Gate factory close by. And as for their instincts in finding the new shifts of

sand in the river bed, treacherous quicksands, small whirlpools large
enough to upset the coracle, strong tidal currents. No nautical or
scientific training could teach them this. I had this put to me by a
young sailor I met on the Cardigan coast, shortly after he had
returned from the Normandy invasion: 'The lads they send out now
from the Naval Colleges are no good ... mathematics, use of instruments, technical training, they've done all that. But once on our
ships, they're useless. Take for instance, the intricate coast on which
we had to land. Every few yards the depth varied. There was the
echo-sounding instrument needing sums on paper before an answer
could be given. But the Breton and Cornish fishermen, at the job
for years, they use a new sense they have acquired.' And the coracle
men working on the rivers, the play of magic, ritual, superstition,
prophets of the sky and foretellers of the ocean bed, these attributes
remained a force in their trade, both for their gain and their protection.

   J.G. Frazer in *The Golden Bough* has analysed this. They can tell
the depth of river or sea bed by the smell. By the smell of the sea bed
on the lead; or by a strip of seaweed caught on the hemp. They will
tell you whether the water is shallow or deep. And what they tell
you is reliable. It is their life.

June 8th   *Lyrics and Weather*

The weather extends in rural communities into the very life of the
people. The rain and interminable mist of Wales. The sadness recurring, and enveloping them. And nearly always that mist is green,
sea-green, drifting in from the coast. Then as suddenly a crisp clear
sky and leaf, sharp and decisive; and their vision and premonitions as
clear. Their summer carols, Daffyd ap Gwilym's crystallised lyrics all
belong to this group of magnification. And in their voices of today,
as in the past, the contrasts of light and shade can be observed. The
language doric ... minor ... with the clarity of island-weather ... so
frequently to be found among the islands of Greece so hard and
pure. Alun Lewis wrote his poem 'Peace' to me though we had only
corresponded by letter. I sent him an invitation which was titled
'Poem from Llanybri'.[39]

   The continual subjugation of the Welsh by conquerors has made
them distrustful of strangers. They have grown accustomed to using
their wits. It is also possible that the strong mixture of Goedelic and
Brythonic blood may have produced a strong conflict in their
natures, for I find them, on the whole, ambivalent. The Irish also
possess this dual quality. They say one thing one moment and at

another moment something else, yet they mean both. Then which do they mean? It's just that they have two visions instead of one.

August 15   *VJ Day*

A most disturbing and magnificent victory anthem by Vaughan Williams, which I hope everyone has heard broadcast this very same day. To me in such despair concerning the hypocrisy of the various Churches, I feel here in this old Welsh composer we have something deeply stirring, and more important still, he has given us a vast musical score of great dignity in our own time. In an age of disintegration and destruction, of our selves; of our nations; and of our allies; we become the greatest hypocrites because of our material outlook and twisted righteousness: for who are we, that create atomic bombs to sneer and condemn the flying rockets? Who are we, who allow our men ten days after the surrender of Germany to turn our enemies into the future mothers of our race. Today statistics show that 4000 German girls are pregnant by our soldiers and many of them to become their wives. Where then was the enemy ... the true enemy ...?

I cannot go to pray in the solitude of the Church as I would have liked, for the door is locked. Neither can I go to the Chapel for to me it is in a foreign language; one in which I cannot take part. So I have heard the Service of Thanksgiving on the wireless ... here alone in my home, with my baby daughter asleep in her pram. Meanwhile, I console myself that others are also listening to this programme, or can hear the Victory Anthem again sometime.

Keidrych is away for the day; he left this morning to go to Aberystwyth. He may not be back until tomorrow.

War will continue in this human world. War will exist until women become freed from slavery ... it will exist until they become no longer the slaves of men but their leaders towards a preservation of life. There IS faith in our people, thank God ... more hope from them than from the Church. People live, suffer and *surprise* us with their wisdom.[40]

September 28th   *Butter Print*
                                                                     Llandeilo

Dear Mrs Rhys,
Received your cheque and order safely many thanks for same. We shall send them by rail as soon as possible but next week we shall be busy with the potatoes.

Regarding the butter print that you ordered, do you want it in a pound box? Or print only.

I don't think I can get the bread board the size you want, but shall send the largest we can get.

Yours faithfully,
Joshua Thomas.

	£ s d
2 Stools at 10/–	1. 0. 0
Butter Print and Mould	7. 0
2 Bowls 3/–	6. 0
1 "	2. 0
1 Plate	2. 6
1 Rolling Pin	2. 0
1 Potato Masher	2. 0
2 Ladles 2/6, 1/6	4. 0
6 Small Prints 1/3	7. 6
1 Spoon	9
	£2. 13. 9
Carriage	1. 2
	£2. 14. 11
Cash by cheque	£3. 0. 0

With thanks
Joshua Thomas.

1946

March 21st   *Who Owns Tygwyn?*

To: Keidrych Rees Esq., of Tygwyn House, Llanybri.
We the undersigned as solicitors and agents for and on behalf of
David Emlyn Jones of Brynderi Llanybri in the County of
Carmarthen your landlord HEREBY GIVE YOU NOTICE TO
QUIT and DELIVER UP to him or to whom he may appoint
possession of the cottage garden and premises known as Tygwyn
House situate at Llanybri in the County of Carmarthen which you
hold as tenant thereof in the 29th day of September 1946.

Dated this 21st day of March 1946.
(signed) Walters and Williams.
31 Quay Street Carmarthen.

Note my letter to Mrs James: sent March 22nd 1946.
There is a rumour in the village that you are no longer the owner of
Tygwyn or my landlord. I understood that there was to be a six
months' notice on either side; I am therefore at a loss to know to
whom do I pay my rent?

May 6th   *Fisherman (Whiff)*

When John Roberts next called, I showed him an engraving, from
Pennant's *Tours in North Wales*, of rather a rare fish called the Whiff.
I thought I had had one delivered to me on one of his willow sticks
as an edible flat fish, which looked quite distinct in its markings from
the rest. I remembered this especially, as I didn't care for the creature's face, and disliked it more when I tried to fillet it and all the
hooks stuck in my hands and cloth. 'Yes, I believe I sold you one of
those … I've seen them.'

I had a tubular steel cot resting against one side of the kitchen
wall. The two sides consisted of strong string netting. The fisherman
noticed this and in his own idiom said 'That's good knitting.' When
I apologised that I hadn't a cup of tea ready, as we had had maté[41]
instead, he said he didn't mind and wouldn't wait until I had made
some as he wanted to go back on the bus. I gave him a sandwich:
'I'm very fond of cheese, mm.'

As he started to turn down his trousers over his bare legs and feet

– he had very nice legs – he asked if I'd remember him when I had one of the 'boss's' coats to throw away. 'Yes, there are salmon at the estuary, and the sandworm is as good as any bait.'

August 17th   *TB Windows*

With windows too frequently closed: and others, where they are wanted, will not open. In the two cottages I have lived in, the measurement of each of the opening windows in both the kitchen and the living room were at the most 8 by 16 inches. The window frame giving light was of course larger, but the air space, especially in summer, was far too inadequate. In the older thatched cottage made of stone and culm, such as Miss Trehearne lived in, the window measurement was not more than one foot square to each of the two rooms. And I do not believe they opened. This was an example of the tax window, and the two small windows, under the curved eyebrows of the sodden thatch, looked just like two black eyes. My suggestion is that we should fight against the legend that a window should be broken after a death to let out the spirit. We must break all such windows and replace them with something more worthy.

What have we? A disastrous prevalence of TB contaminating the whole community, cattle and people alike. A correction for this is upheld by the State. They urge more Sanatoriums and more Hospitals to be built. The hospital beds are there but the nurses are missing. Yet the *damp* houses continue to be built like open graves.

But this is no solution. The solution lies far deeper. It is in the prevention of the cure itself. And this means a complete survey and corrective design for all rural buildings. These in themselves would then become natural sanatoriums without all that awareness of the close walls of death.

1947

January 12th   *Snowbound*

This is certainly New Year. Snow is supposed to have the property of cleansing the soil and air. And after such an ugly interval of war with evils crashing together from both sides perhaps this is just as well.

We are one of the snowbound villages; and hope to get some bread tonight, after a lapse of three days, if a group of men can manage to get a tractor down as far as Pilglas. We do our best in the meantime to fetch water and go out as little as possible. When it is possible. I mean by this, after someone has dug us out.

Each morning Keidrych has to get a shovel and dig out a trench, in some places five or six feet high, as far as the road. Once the road was reached it was just a means of wading up on top of the snow-drifts that lay horizontally like shifting sandbanks. These were not hard to overcome. It was the wind, the strongest I have ever known. I went out once and returned with my hands bleeding and torn. There was no post going out so I had to send a telegram. But I couldn't get into the kiosk. Each time I tried I was either blown down the ice-bound road or landed on all fours; eventually Bertie Howells of Plasnewydd edged along, and holding on to the sill-edge of the PO with one hand, shoved me in with the other.

I noticed on my return that 'The Shop' couldn't shut its doors as a snowdrift had landed in the passage and wedged the door open.

Water was a headache. Everyone waited for someone else to thaw the pump. Winding straw around the pipe was pretty useless and the only effective method was to collect all the straw and light a bonfire under the spout. The result, of course, meant depending on one pump which went continually dry. The thing to do then was to rush out as soon as the sound of pumping could be heard. Fortu-nately, as always in winter, and with the added quietness of the snow, all sounds were considerably amplified. The tractor starting up and chugging off as slowly as a steamroller could easily be heard in all parts of the village, and when the chains wound slowly near, we saw it pass, from the bedroom window, strengthened by men shouldering spades, and hooked on behind it in an attempt to carry churns of milk on a market trailer.

January 25th   *Land Grabbing*

Sometime ago John Ormond Thomas[42] again came to see us. This was his second visit. When we first met him he was studying at the University. He was now working for *Picture Post*. He had come to Carmarthen to write up a stern protest that was being sponsored in Wales by all parties against the land-grabbing habit of the War Office. This was published today as a first article in *Picture Post*. I wish they'd write more about Wales.

Keidrych is fed up at not being able to go to the office, and the farmers at the Black Horse or Farmer's Arms make it no easier, for they, too, are unable to do anything. Their milk is ruined. There have been no buses for weeks. The food stock is diminishing far too quickly. Then quite unexpectedly Keidrych decided to ring up the CC and ask if he might organise a party to dig a way out. This idea was supported by others in the village, and the plan was accepted. So

Lynette Roberts, Keidrych Rhys and their daughter Angharad, Llanybri.

within a few hours, men and women, about fifteen of them, joined up and ploughed a way through the snow drifts. They chose the Chapel road as this would free the road and relieve the milk congestion, but it would not enable the Western Welsh to come up to the village. It was tremendous work. It was to be paid, of course. And many sly jokes were made about 'working for the CC'. This continued for some days. The drifts were solid and in places ten feet high. When the Llanstephan road was attempted a few days later, each spadeful had to be first hacked out with an axe before the blocks of ice could be removed. They became ice-colliers in fact.

During all this winter we did our best to feed the birds, which dropped dead as they fed. Others, mostly starlings with frozen legs, were unable to move. I remember in particular feeding robins and blackbirds but can claim at seeing no rare or unusual garden bird on the feeding ground. Blue tits, more than most, seemed to be the sturdiest birds more able to survive. Perhaps their nests were more secluded.

February 6th *Winter Birds*

Now only one blackbird remains. And that bird I shall keep alive. The robins have all disappeared, presumably dead. In the village no robin has been seen. I am particularly attached to this national bird. And it is my intention one day to write a poem on this masterful young creature.[43] Not a 'garden spade' poem: but something which holds the whole measure of this bird. Of its migration, communal interest, clear personality and sweet voice which somehow seems to follow the rain so that its song contains the mingled freshness of the rain and clearness of the sun.

After reading David Lack's *Life of the Robin*, I wanted to find out how many robins had completely disappeared in villages all over Great Britain. I made an attempt and sent a letter in to *The News Chronicle*, but I regret they did not use it. A survey will have to be made sooner or later. It would have been easier before the leaves covered the branches.

April 16th *Gardening*

There can be no defined way of gardening any more than laying down rules for animal-rearing. Each country has its own methods, and I think when living with each of these it is best to adopt those. So we set the garden at the time of John Brown's Fair. The soil then has the right temper and should be free from frost.

Lynette Roberts in the garden of Tygwyn, Llanybri.

In most of the gardens here two-thirds are taken up with potato seed, with a row shovelled up for broad beans, cabbage and parsley, and a small finer bed about 3ft by 4ft containing lettuce, carrot, leeks, shallots, beetroot and perhaps a little cress and radish. This makes a cottager independent as he seldom requires any other choice of vegetable. One or two plants have almost died out which were once prevalent in most gardens, and that is wormwood, grown for medicinal purposes, and savorifach.[44] I still grow these last two plants. Before she died, Mrs Phillips, a friend and neighbour, gave me a splint of wormwood as a gift. 'It is good for you,' she said. It is a laxative. This was before we lost her. She was the best gardener in the village, as far as culture goes. At 89 she was still digging her own garden and would work, as she always did, slowly and thoroughly, the old bucket or perforated enamel basin filling with roots as she dug steadily and bent and cleaned up the soil. I had seen her year after year working at the garden, the first garden but one away from my own. She used the method we all adopted. On the newly dug soil and working in clogs we would mark out the lines by following-up the twine with a small clog-print on either side of the string. So the string was then lifted and a shovel used with a long Celtic handle similar to those I had seen used in Brittany and the Channel Islands. It is pressed forward like a hand-plough, throwing up the aerated soil on either side so that a furrow is said to be 'opened'. This open row or furrow is filled with manure and then closed with soil, either before or after the bulbs or seeds are set or sown according to their culture.

The final effect of this work in all village gardens in Wales is one of neat precise rows rising at intervals to 1½ feet. The smooth top of each of these rows is about 2 ft across, sloping down gradually on either side to the original level of the soil that is 1½ ft down. The rows are kept in continual circulation as the crops grow by shovel-

'Photo to illustrate gardening the Celtic way with a long handled shovel. A spade is never used. A fork occasionally to break up the whole allotment. The aerated and crumbled soil is then lifted and smoothed into set ridges. This makes the soil warm and keeps it from getting water-logged. The continual movement of the soil with the shovel also prevents any weeds from getting a good hold.' Note on back of photograph: 'Keidrych in garden of Tygwyn, Llanybri using Celtic shovel with long handle as used by peasants also in Ireland, Normandy and South Wales. About Nov. 1939 or Feb. 1940.'

ling up the soil between each row as the roots deepen. This method is particularly successful for dry summers: or for any region where water is not to be had on tap. The continual movement of the soil also disturbs any appearance of weeds.

For ourselves I again put in sets of strawberry plants, one old root with a few young runners to each set. They are not popular here as they are said to spread all over the garden. They don't, of course, if the runners are cut, but this is not considered. I also tried again sweet corn. I have only succeeded really well with this vegetable about three years ago, when everyone kept asking what they were, but they look so beautiful in all their various stages of growth and have never failed to produce a few cobs of irregular quality so that I don't mind taking the risk.

Why so many potatoes are grown I can't imagine, unless it's for the pigs and chickens due to the shortage of mash or it may be habit. Today they can be bought by the cwt fresh from the fields.

The perennial border onion has lifted and become slippery. Therefore useless – this is a pity. I had some buds given to me by Mr Davies Dyffryolcwm but they must have been lifted at the wrong time as they never thrived. Chives, sage, mint, parsley I had from last year's sowing; also spinach, which I consider one of the most healthy vegetables that we have, and more than useful since it grows all the year round and seldom cowers under the bite of frost unless it is exceptionally bad, such as it was this last winter: but even with the Spring these roots remained vigorous and gave a quick yield of fresh green leaves when there was nothing to be bought elsewhere. I use horse manure for the whole garden, one of the few. I have a fad about this as I believe cow manure draws bacteria and is infested with dormant insects, chrysalis, fly maggot etc. The blacksmith will supply anyone who cares to fetch the manure themselves, and is only too glad to get rid of it. For this I remember I owe him a couple of pints.

May 2nd   *Woollen Factories*

The trouble with the Welsh is the old trouble, that of jealousy. It infects all the young shoots of its generation and is steadily getting worse. Universities, Libraries, Professors, Religious Centres; even the Welsh Regional Centre suffers under this malignant complaint. I have wasted precious time, in trying to collect authentic facts about various sources, before I could proceed with the material I had gathered for my own writing. I am used to delay ... delay to the extent that you come to the conclusion that either your letter has been lost, or that 'they' are high-handed and will not reply. If and when it does come, then too often it is (for me) worthless since the information is either out-of-bounds, or some out-of-date material that has been sent hoping it will keep me quiet. Well, it doesn't succeed with me so I write off again. The result is again useless but at least I have the satisfaction of feeling that I have done my best.

Before writing an article on the sacred 'British White' cattle[45] I wanted to consult the Rev. John Storer's nineteenth-century book as this was the only written source on this particular breed. I have failed so far to get it. The National Library at Aberystwyth have their hands tied as it is in the Robert Owen Collection, for in that Bequest no book is allowed to be posted out. I cannot receive it at the County Library even if it were transferred there as I cannot leave my two babies, one under 2 years of age and a son of 4½ months. So, humiliated, I had to write and beg from a stranger. A major living miles away in Norfolk.

When I wrote my article on the Coracle for The Field I was quite prepared to find out first hand and watch the crafts of today being made. I visited the Coracle men, wives and children on several occasions in their homes and on the river, and still do. They are my friends. But when I asked for an up-to-date statistic on the subject from the Fishery Board all I received was a pamphlet of their Annual Report dated 1933. I was amazed as this was material which only the Fishery Board held and could give.

Again for the Welsh Blacks: the secretary is courteous and charming: I receive all the obvious pamphlets, the choice of well known out of date photographs from the pamphlets if I require them. But I want NEW and fresh photographs. You feel, after going to see various herds and writing them up because they are of good quality, that new photographs should be available. Then again, only the out-of-date statistics are given. Those of 1944. But this is 1947 and I want to know the exact number of Welsh Black breed today, i.e. May 2nd 1947.

With the Woollen factories it is equally depressing. They enjoy the idea if you tell them that you have written 200 or 300 words about their Mills; but they cannot and will not take the initiative and have photographs taken. In fact, some of them have never had photographs taken of their factory.

There is then this deplorable reticence to retain knowledge among themselves, and withhold facts which are really public property. Such material should be available to the whole world today. And I refer here, as well, to the extraordinary muddle in the literary field where no research worker can get at the fundamental and original documents of his own Country. Yet the professors have the audacity to sit on high perches and flay you in reviews because you have not studied particular papers. They are far too much like antique dealers who want to sell their hidden treasure but are at the same time reluctant to do so, with the result that they soon turn into junk shops and crumble in their own parasitic fervour.

July 8th   *Bulls*

For the last few weeks I seem to be inundated with bulls and the subject of bulls. By this morning's post I received a photograph of Dr Vivian Jones's Stock bull, Penback Victor, taken when he was a year old. A week back I received two other photos of Welsh Blacks. One was the famous bull, Egryn Buddugol, reared by Mr Moses Griffiths, and another was a group of the Egryn Herd again reared by Moses Griffiths. And the matter didn't end there, for besides the photos of Welsh Blacks which are dotted along the mantelpiece, another two came in, sent by the secretary of the British White Cattle Society. All these were required to illustrate articles which I had recently written on the subject. And how good they looked on the mantelpiece.

Now, I am used to these quiet pedigree bulls for I was born in the Argentine. The Argentines fatten them up, sometimes giving them as many as three dozen eggs a day in preparation for the Agricultural Shows. But what I cannot welcome is a bull walking or grazing in a field. I always feel it is pretending to do this, whereas really it is planning some incredible act of evil. What is more, I believe bulls are not allowed out in the open; and to suddenly come across one is terrifying.

It so happens that this recently occurred here, and because of this one incident I immediately remembered others. Then I had even more horrible stories related to me.

Angharad, my daughter aged two, loves what she terms 'bull-cows'. So when we went down to the spring well about 400 yards down the hill to get our water supply, Angharad was naturally drawn towards a large black and white creature staring at us high over the hedge. Intuitively I didn't like it, so rather sharply I pulled her away. Later I heard that this same bull got loose and that it had joined another herd in the field next to our cottage. Here, two children, also aged two, were stopped from entering the field. The bull then came rushing out and went up into the centre of the village and terrified a small boy whose impediment of speech had already been caused as a result of a cow tossing him when he was a baby.

His fear again intensified when he became too paralysed to move, even though he saw the bull coming towards him and had a chance to run – he couldn't. Instead, he howled, and remained sitting on his small toy truck. Fortunately, Lyn Thomas, the son of a farmer, diverted the bull just in time. Later it entered Plas Isa's farmyard, and in attempting to get out again, leapt the stone wall, and not clearing it was left for a while balancing backwards and forwards like a see-saw on the top of the concrete ridge. This was just one bull.

There was another last summer that was always left free to graze in the field but this bull was chained. The chain was padlocked between his front and back leg so that he could only walk. But the wretched thing had a habit of getting loose and appearing at unexpected hours like Bacchus with trails of convolvulus and streamers of greenery flowing from his horns. He would crash through a hedge anywhere and take everything with him. He was a white bull, and might have been a sacred bull but for the dreaded clanking, which sent everyone, on hearing this sound, scurrying into the nearest house or shed for protection. One day the white bull seemed to almost run up the hill. I pushed in Angharad and a young boy standing beside her and slammed the iron gate. In a matter of seconds the bull passed, he had broken his chains and was off on his rounds! Again he had broken through a hedge and branches and flowers trailed from his horns like a pre-Raphaelite train. He snorted and entered Mrs Dyer Brynderi's yard. I heard a young child crying and knew her to be alone. No one could reach her without touching the bull which stood across the stone drive digging into the wallbank and tossing his horns into the clods and stones which flew over to the next farm. He did eventually move ... and was not allowed out again.

But the trouble with these small, but what might have been serious, accidents is that the owner is seldom near to pacify or fetch the bull in. This is what happened on both these occasions. The farmer was either in Carmarthen or out some acres away tending to the fields.

A third bull recently chased some girls who were trying to cross the ferry to get over to Laugharne. And that is quite enough.

1948

When there is any big event in the village there is a sense of charged energy. On the road Mrs James and her neighbour talked fast and excitedly, and though I could not hear what they were saying – neither was it different from any other day that they should be talking together, both were relatives each washing out their hall and polishing the doorstep – but I just felt that there was something. But what.

Further up by the post office, another group was chatting with some lively expressions on their faces. As though the news had given them a new spurt or incentive to think. That the event was changing the normal working order of their minds.

The steam roller was on the road, a large tar cylinder mounted on a lorry, and many strange men. This looked as though the CC were going to do more than fill in our pot-holes this year, and I wondered if by having our own District Councillor, he had asked for these repairs.

One child was crying as I passed, and when I asked her why, she replied 'It's hot.'

The steam roller always appears to have the same antiquity of design as that of a sewing machine. And I like the design of both.

I was on my way to get my fortnight's rations. This grocer's shop is traditional of most other village shops in that it is exceptionally crowded, littered with paper, crates, packets, weights still hanging from the ceiling, weights which used to be used for weighing dead pigs, more sacks, pop, and casks of vinegar etc. In fact, how Mrs Davies ever managed to keep the shelves tidy and the numerous tin cans in groups of any kind I don't know, for she was always serving someone or other. And talking quietly. She was like a kitten. And far too many of them walked in slowly or quickly, depending on their age, visiting the shop each day for companionship or for a chat. They often didn't want to buy but had to think of something as an excuse. It was quite early, about ten-ish, and the vicar of Llanstephan was there getting his rations. Some tomatoes, butter. These tomatoes were the first of the season and came from Guernsey. I was looking up and down the shelves to see if there wasn't something new and different from the familiar tins which we had seen over and over again throughout the war years, when Mrs Davies said, 'I'm afraid I have something rather unpleasant to tell you and I don't like to tell you.'

She told me that she had decided to sell the Shop ... give it up ... and that she would require that part of the house in which we were living for herself. I replied that I quite understood her point of view and that I would do my best, but as she had brought up the housing question I could now tell her how very seriously we had tried to get another house. She had always known that I wanted a more hygienic home with proper sanitation. Keidrych had put our name down for a Town Council house in Carmarthen. And in addition he had written from his office asking if they might not consider him as a Carmarthen citizen as he was born in Carmarthenshire and had his permanent office in Carmarthen which he attended each day. To my amazement, though I don't think I showed it, Mrs Davies

'Photo of me outside Ivy Cottage, Llanybri, where we had notice to leave, as the owner did not want to have a grocer shop any more. Here in the photo is myself with my young son, and my Siamese cat. I used to breed these and lost the mother and eight kittens which I fed all myself, due to the terrible cat-plague which came into the village from Plasnewydd. Cat after cat died and each kitten was known to me by name and each one of their personalities. "Spitfire" was my favourite. The wheelbarrow was an exact copy of a Llanybri wheelbarrow made by the carpenter Mr Howells. It was holly green outside and bright orange inside. How much better than all these silly toys, It would take my son for rides, it would take the cat for rides, it could be used to carry stones, sand, and even weeds.'

suggested we might go into a hut – that they were much better inside than they looked. i.e. the huts which the prisoners of war had recently evacuated.

The following day I again went round to the shop as the cheese and bacon allocation had not arrived. Her daughter, Lilian, then asked me how I felt about the whole matter. I told her that I wasn't going to let this worry me this time as it did a year ago when under similar circumstances we had a solicitor's letter of acquittal, as the owners had, unknown to us, sold the property and the new owner wanted us to go. This was when we left Tygwyn.

But I had to admit that I had not slept that night, and she said her mother hadn't either, and that she wished it was all over.

I asked her if she knew what the prisoner of war huts were like, and she replied that she had not been inside but she could arrange it as she had an Austrian friend living in one of them. Now what interested me was this: Who had suggested a hut to them? That anyone should be forced out of a house and condemned to a P. of W. hut still surrounded by barbed wire. Only a year ago, or less, the German Prisoners of War were living in these huts and were barricaded in, and some barbed wire still remained as a boundary fence. I am not frightened of life under any condition; and can easily face up to the situation of living in one of these huts if we had to to. I COULD DO IT. But as there are families sleeping six in one bedroom thirty yards from this cottage and two doors away from that, another house where the tenant has had notice to leave as the owner wished to sell, and neither of these had ever thought of going into an ex-prisoner of war camp: and furthermore, that next door to Rosie Davies where Marie James is very ill and not expected to live, people have already applied for her house before she has even been buried, it is strange that the Hut situation should arise.

Anyway, I tried straight away to get one, or rather make enquiries from the sanitation inspector about their structure but his telephone was out of order.

I rang up again today, June 5th, and spoke to Mr Williams. He said that there were no huts and that all the huts at the Ystrad Camp which I referred to were already filled and that there was a waiting list of 300; in addition to that we cannot be turned out anyway because we are protected by the new Rent Restrictions Order. I knew this. But alas, in a village the situation is somewhat different. All are friendly, communicative, and to fail to move for a friend when you were living on their property, they too needing a home, is very difficult.

In the evening Keidrych went up to the Black Horse for a drink.

He said they discussed this new move of Mrs Syd Davies's of the Shop, and the move, which I have not mentioned before of the Post Office saying 'Llanybri was failing', for on these two shops depended the whole structure of the village. Not the church. Keidrych said that James 'Black Anchor' had told him that the vicar was behind Mrs Syd, advising her.

After he had told me this, and turning in late to bed, I could not sleep, and my mind dwelt on all the silly things that might not happen until all the thoughts ran ahead and tumbled into a dreadful cloud swept along by the beating fury of the wind, and so the night outside my window was dramatised. Over Pembrey the lightning struck along the flat surface of the water. Other charges lit up the sky at various points, with the occasional clouds frustrated and set – they looked like the vicar whose mind I knew to be sharpened against us. The black cloud changed into a rat and dissolved. I then went downstairs and disconnected the wireless set.

June 22nd   *Grave Lettering*[46]

This was a road we frequently took out of the village, because it was smooth, and continued for some time without a hill until after reaching the Chapel. Chapel Newydd was a pompous landmark whose foundation stone, much to our disgust, was laid by one of the squire's family, a Mrs Morris. Related to the Kylsants and in no way

Lynette Roberts and Keidrych Rhys with their children Angharad and Prydein.

a chapel-goer. Why they should have been so silly as to choose her
I cannot think. But it does go to show up the weakness in the
Chapel to this very day. Too much compromise and willingness to
please both sides. 'All friends, we attend both Chapel and Church,'
they say in a big manner, and appear smaller as a result of saying it.

The weeds on the top of this graveyard are more varied and plentiful than those found on the Church, or on the Hen Chapel wall.
They consist largely of the rockery families and were ablaze when
we passed with yellow stone-crop, flax, and seed which had escaped
from a nearside grave, the mauve-pink dianthus. There was a
constant tapping coming from the graves and I knew this to be
someone at work. I am curious to know who. So I decided to call in
on my way back. I knew the graves had been cleaned and that some
friends of mine in the village had been annoyed because the cutter
had not come this twelve month to do the headstone. I hoped it was
he at work.

The grave I had in mind was no other than that of Rosie's
brother Bill, whom I had admired and enjoyed talking to, long
before I knew that they were related. I walked over the tiled
entrance, the tiles were exceptionally well kept, and then turned
round to the left from where the tapping came.

It was an old man who just half sat and half knelt on his knees
working away at some letters at the bottom of the headstone. His
eyes were grey and dim, his hair white or rather silver blending in
with the dirty-white marble on which he was working. A case of
chisels lay open at his feet, red powder dye, and a strong hammer.
The whole base of the headstone had already been covered with the
red dye, a terracotta I would call it but to all rural people in Wales
whose farms and outhouses and cattle were coloured with this
shade, it is always known as red. Over this red could be seen the
rough and casual marks of the letters sketched in and not yet
finished. They were suggested with a soft pencil. Lines had been
drawn across horizontally, but only a rough estimate for the width
required between each letter.

'What I'm trying to get is something like the top man, I don't
know at all who did it. I keep looking up to compare and get a just
likeness.' He went on working as we all talked.

The word DEATH was just finished and stood out crisp and
clean. A new death. Fortunately the lettering was good as far as
typography goes. A classical one no doubt. Anyway, he stabbed at
the rest of the phrasing as quickly as possible as it was starting to rain.
It was not Bill's tombstone that I had thought he was working on.
But I gathered from one or two of his remarks, that he had no

intention of coming again to finish them for a very long time. 'I'm stabbing them so that the rain does not wash them away. Then they can be left as long as I like without coming to any harm before I return. If I don't, then the children may come and start scribbling on the dye or rubbing my letters out. Now, in all graveyards I've been to, and I've been to many in my time, I have never seen one as good for lettering as this. Or not many as good. I don't care what they say about the country. These townsmen who think they know everything. But it is the country folk who have the best headstones by far.' He then turned and spoke Welsh with Keidrych, who afterwards told me he was upset by the way the community destroyed themselves. Those nearest to him were the quickest to throw a man down ... those of his own birth-place.

When Keidrych told me this I asked him if he had noticed his exaggerated mannerism ... how excited he appeared in the middle of conversation, got up, threw himself sharply around a tombstone, then returned as quickly, on the side that you least expected him, shouting something about Lloyd George or other. He said there was little appreciation for the trade, and unless his name was on the stone nobody would know about him or any of them. He walked rapidly over to another new and ugly structure which to me looked like coarse granite with very shakey and bad lettering finished in what appeared to be a grate-polish glaze laid on repellently thick and bought in a tin from Woolworth's for a few pence ... Creosote it looked like. Well, this, the worst in the graveyard was his work, and the name on it as large as the corpse, read G. Phillips Gorslas.

Some of the Tombs, the new ones, were in polished granite with electric flower designs engraved in short panels down the sides and handcarved lettering filled in with gold leaf down the centre. One tombstone looked like black Victorian glass, but really it was highly polished grey slate. Some graves were particularly repellent that lay along the earth because the body formation of the baby or child was shaped in concrete. I very much disliked this.

The old man, after touching on many subjects which we vaguely listened to, for he was far too excitable to talk with, swivelled round the Headstone and crouched snapping up the tin box, closed his case, throwing in the odd tools and rulers, in order, he said, to go and get a cup of tea. I told him that if he had nowhere to go he could have a cup at my cottage. He asked me where I lived and I told him the first house as you enter the village. He reminded me of the strange people I had seen who on occasions go in and out of the Mental Homes. A poor wretch, who seemed to be suffering from some persecution or other. One who suffered all the time the sharp contrast between his lonely job of crouching over a dead man's corpse and hammering in his identity, without receiving any praise or acknowledgement for his efforts, this should, I imagine, make anyone unbalanced. He lacked human contact. And here in front of me was the result.

June 26th   *Mr Rowlands's Grave-making*

Walking again along this same road, I thought I would look at some of the earlier tombstones and compare them with the craftsmanship of those I had seen at Llandeilo Abercwyn. Within only a few days the honeysuckle had sprung out of the hedge, and foxgloves grew up from the centre of the banks so that they broke the quiet outline which had controlled the Spring.

When I reached the Chapel gates I realised to my great disappointment that I could not get in. The iron gates were padlocked and I did not care for the look of the spiked railings. This gate was, of course, *as both the Church and Chapel always are ... locked ... locked against humanity.* It is through this very misconception of religion that they will, and are beginning to, destroy the very essence of faith and natural prayer. The consoler and aspiration of mankind with all its mystical sources which thank Heaven no scientist has yet been able to penetrate.

So I read, as I could, over the stone wall, finding it hard sometimes to see between the various weeds and flowering grass which fringed the whole of this wall. As I leant, the whitewash came off, as it had recently been limed for the Singing Festival. The best gravestones were those of natural slate, when their stabbing was exceptionally deep, so that the letters stood quietly out in spite of the handicap of years and their dullness of colour. Far better, in fact, than any other of the more recent cuttings on stone. The best date were those cut in 1846 and round about that time. The shoulders or steles were simply sloped with a slight decorative interest, and a small elegant scroll of the two letters E.R. crested the top of the memorial. It was about this time that I wrote my poem 'Chapel Wrath'[47] about the cult of the tombstones.

But it so happened, as it does in villages, that the very person I wanted to see was coming down the road. It was just an idea at first, something about the slow-drooping walk; the way the flannel cap was pushed far back over the forehead; the pale and slender face of this old man – Mr Rowlands. He worked mostly on farms. Consistently on one, until recently, when he gave this up owing to his age. As he came nearer I knew it was he and shouted down the road

Lynette Roberts with her children, on the road to Cwmcelyn.

'You're the very person I want.' After what seemed to be a very long interval, he reached the Chapel padlock and let me in. I had forgotten that death meant a grave, and suddenly realised that he had come as a gravedigger to open one up for young Mrs Thomas. He had already thrown up a lot of rock so that it fell on canvas upon someone else's grave that lay alongside. The mound of broken rock-stone was rising halfway up the headstone. It was red sandstone rock and the grave stone alongside it was made of white marble. I couldn't see Mr Rowlands for he had already dug a good way down. This was the first grave and it therefore had to be below seven feet. He had just covered his own height which was about five feet six inches. There was no soil … no earth anywhere … the saying 'into dust you shall return' or whatever the quotation was … failed, for this grave was not other than that of hard red rock.

So Mr Rowlands after helping all day to cart in the hay had now arrived here, far too fatigued, I thought, to try and finish off this relentless job. The work was strenuous, and because it could only be done in the evenings after the labour of the fields, there was little else he could do but to start digging as soon as the body died other-wise he could never get the work finished on time. This was his official job. He was the Chapel Gravedigger, and got £2.10 for opening up a new grave. He was also the Church gravedigger. He told me they paid £3. Both were terrible. Both solid rock, but the Church had this one defect, they struck water every time a grave was dug. There was the time when Mr… was buried. It was so bad that the digger had to go on baling out the water right through the service so that the coffin could go in as dry as possible ... and even then it was filling pretty quickly, 'floating' in no time before the service around the grave was finished.

Mr Rowlands was keeping the shape pretty tight, I thought. And the opening had the same outline as the waisted coffins which Mr Howells, the local carpenter, made. These were very smart affairs. I remember visiting Mr Howells's workshop shortly after the outbreak of war, when he had a galvanised shed leaning against Croft Cottage. At one end of the shed the galvanised ribbings were completely stacked up with manufactured coffin panels which he had bought wholesale and which only required the necessary dovetailing when an order was made. I remember asking Mr Howells if he got used to putting people in coffins and measuring them out. And he said there was scarcely a death which did not affect him, as they were nearly all known to him, and those mostly for life. So with the same feeling I realised that Mr Rowlands was not digging this grave without a certain amount of emotion. This young wife died of cancer. Her illness became obvious during the snowbound winter months of 1948. She was leaving a daughter aged fourteen. And had a foreknowledge of her death a few days before she died, even though she had not been told of the cause of her illness. Among her wishes were, that her daughter should wear black and white at the funeral and that she should be told beforehand that her mother was going to die. I do not know what happened. The funeral is tomorrow. 'But it is a sad one, for they have many relatives around here. Then too, the husband has been a loyal and tender husband, nursing and massaging her far better than any district nurse, they say.'

July 10th   *Parc-yr-Hendy Painting*

Mr John Griffiths called with some poems. He was a native of this village and though he is a retired Headmaster and over 81 years of age, he thought nothing of springing on the Western Welsh bus as it started to leave the village. He was born at Parc-yr-Hendy and remembers the old Chapel quite well when it stood without a roof surrounded by jackdaws that flew wildly in and out of the trailing ivy. And across the road from the Old Chapel was our former cottage, Tygwyn. When I pointed this out to him, he said it was 'there' when he attended the Infants' School. It was like one large barn with a gallery at one end and he was continually punished for drawing. One day when he was caught, he was made to stay in late, and the punishment consisted of having to make another drawing. His brother, he told me, really enjoyed painting, and may have been the artist who made a water colour wash of Parc-yr-Hendy. I remembered seeing this at Mrs Phillips'. As it was a local picture I asked Mrs Phillips if she knew who had painted it, but she couldn't remember and just said she liked it very much.

In the 60 years he had visited Llanybri he said he did not remember one new house being built up or one lost.

November 18th   *Angharad's and Prydein's Bird Lists.*

Bird list known by Angharad Rhys, aged 3½ years.
1   Crow
2   Finch (meaning hawfinch)
3   Greenfinch
4   Goldfinch
5   Chaffinch
6   Bullfinch
7   Yellow Bunting
8   Starling
9   Long tail (meaning wagtail)
10 Great Blue-tit
11 Blue-tit
12 Rash (meaning thrush)

Prydein Rhys with birds.

13 Blackbird
14 Robin
15 Gull
16 Green Woodpecker
17 Woodpecker (To Great and Lesser Spotted)
18 Cuckoo
19 Owl
20 Corrant (meaning cormorant)
21 Swan
22 Goose
23 Duck
24 Long-tail Duck (omitting word 'tail')
25 Corrant (for Red-breasted Merganser)
26 Starling Duck (for Great Northern Diver)
27 Pigeon
28 Chicken and Cockerell (for cock pheasant and hen)

She also knows well (meaning repeatedly) penguin, sparrow, gold-crest, swallow, nightjar, heron, curlew, but either forgot or misplaced them altogether when tested. These examples were all taken from bird plates, Ludwig Koch's Bird records. She only knows by sight the few that feed outside the window from day to day.

Bird list known by Prydein Rhys, aged 2 years.
1   Crow
2   Greenfinch
3   Robin (meaning chaffinch)
4   Yellow Bunting
5   Long-tail (meaning wagtail)
6   Blue-tit (meaning great titmouse)
7   Blue-tit
8   Chaffinch (meaning Robin)
9   Woodpecker
10   Owl
11   Rabbit-owl (meaning long-eared owl)
12   Honk (meaning goose)
13   Corrant (meaning Red-breasted Merganser)
14   Pigeon
15   Chickens (meaning pheasant)

How does this compare with the bird observation of other children of the same age?

than usual owing to the harvest tides, the sand could be seen
rising in banks, lightening under the sun, dry except for a
narrow channel which carried fishing boats out towards Pembrey.
Here, at this brackish edge, almost 500 yards from the mark of
high-tide, round, hollow, spiral pools have been left in the sand.
These were dry; but it was obvious that as soon as the tide came
in, the water would seep under the holes and filter through the
sand, filling these holes treacherously and
imperceptibly.   In attempting to test these pools, a foot could be
side. The suction of the out-going tide drawing it further down,
deeper into its shifting sand. From the scale pattern left on
the sand by the conflicting currents, it was obvious that these
were whirlpools. They were not large in size, varying from 1½ feet
to 3' across. Though they were small and known to the local
bathers, it was not fair to the children of the village who paddled
near them had they not been warned.

After scraping up enough cockles for supper, I followed up the tide, out as far as I could. Fishermen stood around
the curve of the Bay facing the West Marshes of Laugharne and
Pendine. Their lines drifting out to sea for bass. The crabs too
were plentiful, so that all the lug-worms which had been dug up with
so much care and patience, had practically diminished. As far
out as it would seem almost impossible to walk. Over to Pembrey

102

Page from the typescript of Lynette Roberts's diary for 18 August 1944.

Village Dialect: Seven Stories

Fox

The sky is green and transparent. It holds that sudden flash which announces the sun but has no tie with the living green of the soil. It is a green impaled by age, that knew the pagans stretched before their gods. Now the trees twice as tall, appear blacker than usual under this astringent light. Out towards the Mill Bridge, the valleys are ringing with water. Streams have filled overnight, and steep lanes that have turned into waterfalls flow close to the hedge. The sun rising, threads through every crevice of the Prescelly Mountains, flares up and over towards St Clears, Pembroke Bay, cutting out the outline of each wave and leaf as they sparkle with a million separate lights. The ploughed fields are sweating, drawing out a blue blaze the colour of a new ploughshare.

From this surrounding mirror of pristine clearness, this valley is hidden, is engulfed by the rising vapour of streams warming into monster dinosaurs drifting up funnels of smoke blown and angered by the wind, then to fall like transparent snow, iridescent on the brows of cattle waiting patiently to be milked.

Walking another half-mile through this opaque and sifting air, I suddenly reached the outer walls of a farm.

'Not much timber.'

'Not much milk after that raid.'

Rosie walked beside me, and wiped her hands on the canvas apron as we turned into the yard. She pulled up the latch and the chickens ran with open wings into the field. A sitting hen shook its eyes and furious tongue as she bent to lift the stiff feathers and count the yellow heads of ducks.

'That's one, two – we've lost three.'

'Fox?'

'Sure to be – but they're such smart fellows you can't be cross. I remember years ago, there were little ones in the middle of the cornfield. Five of them. And they had made a little playground *right around* their home. After milking we would watch them close – on the brow of the hill – close to the farm. Quiet as the sun was going

An Introduction to Village Dialect, with Seven Stories (Druid Press, 1944).

down. We saw the mother with them. The father was there, too. O their colour was lovely, a rich dark red. You may not believe it, as the two parents left to go out hunting and the little ones followed, at the first sign of danger the mother just sat down and went swish with her tail – bang like that on the earth, and immediately the little ones ran to *cwtch*.[1] Another day just after milking, my mother shouted out: 'Run after the fox, it's taken a duck!'

'Of course I couldn't. It was one we had fattened for Christmas, 5½ lbs. A while after my mother said: 'Whist, I expect the young ones could do with it!'

'They weren't far away – just in the cornfield, and took the bird from under our nose. They were left by us, and we loved to watch them. We were living on the Kylsant Estate then. One day a man came and took two of the young ones away to put them in the wood for the hunting people. Silly, really, they would have gone on their own had he left them to themselves.'

Tiles

'I just can't pass without asking how you are. Never mind, I'm disturbing you; I'll come some other time.'

So Rosie went when really I wanted to tell her how ill I felt. I was doubled up with pain, and the pig screeching louder and louder as it was drawn towards the yard. After a short interval she passed the back door, so I called her in.

'It's killed but it won't lie down … O, I can see you're ill. Don't you get up now; I'll have a fire in no time.'

She lit my fire with five sticks, plastering the grate right up to the top with *pele*,[2] making a hole or two with the poker for the flames to draw through. In a Castle at Laugharne, not far from here, I had seen a whitewashed hearth with an orange woodfire glowing from the centre.

'What do you think of that?'

'Well, it's like this: I'll tell you right. For myself I would not like that at all. Imagine if I was ill, that whitewash would worry me somehow; you can't just sit and gaze into a white hearth; myself, I prefer the black.'

So I realised how foolish my thoughts had been. Yet I still wanted the bricks limed under the grate. Rosie was now on her knees in an attempt to scrub the floor.

'It's a pity they're not tiles; almost every cottage has them but mine.'

The knots in the boards were sticking up like elbows. And Rosie sat back on her clogs to rest and talk awhile.

'I'm telling you right, there was an old lady living just below our farm in Plasnewydd and mother used to send me down with a piece of bacon or some milk. She was very old and doubled up, and you could see the pleats and bows on her back as she bent over her stick. She wore a cap with white frills and loops, and a flannel apron. She'd go to a box and offer me an apple. "Here *merchan fach*,[3] this is for you." Once a week she would do her floor over with a burdock – no, dock-leaf, I mean – with the point. She'd go like this.' And Rosie stood to make the circle and placed a dot in the centre. 'She'd do like this, and make another, and another, all around it, and over the whole lot, until when you came to look at it from the door, it looked like linoleum. Sometimes she did other designs such as triangles, or small circles like trefoil, or squares. Round the hearth she would do stoning in another design. Under the grate was also white.

She's dead now, I know; and I remember these things when I was 14, now I'm 46. It must be on cement and it comes off a dark green.'

The room was clear. And the fire slowly rising to a blue flame. I lay back in peace, and rested for the whole of that day.

Steer

'Don't you put your hands in the earth; I'll fetch these for you. She doesn't look very well – the broccoli, I mean. Where do you want them put, on the other side of the gooseberry hedge?'

When we entered the cottage, Rosie saw that I had not tidied the grate. 'You sit quiet a minute and I'll rise the ashes.' I had found setting the garden too much, and was glad to rest. Friends had come, some daily. And their gifts: two-thirds of an apple pie and a packet of biscuits from Mrs Lewis; toffees, a chicken, eggs and chips, a pudding to myself, whole meals, a white kitten from Plasnewydd, and always the cup of tea.

I could hear Rosie riddling outside. She flew in through the window and filled the room. The bowl of *pele* rested on her hip, while the bucket and sticks hung from her sunburnt arm and goose-feathered wings. The milking was finished, label tied to the churn and lid knocked down, so I begged her to stay ten minutes or so before her son returned from the Timber Mills.

'I'm not fit to come in with my canvas apron and all.' As we spoke we watched the kitten sitting with turned out paws in front of the warm glow of the hearth. Rosie thought it might run back to Plasnewydd, two miles out of the village, and to stress her point she continued to tell me a story, which I shall now repeat:

'Once my mother sold a steer, two years old. It was for 12 or 14 pounds, I can't remember which. She couldn't be bothered to fatten it herself, so the farmer to whom she sold it took it away. Down to St Clears, along the clear high road to Laugharne, six miles away. A few days later a white steer was seen by farmers swimming across the River Taf. The tide is very quick and the currents strong as you know. He, the steer, I mean, swam and swam, for he drifted and was carried out of his way, and the men watching thought he would never arrive. Soon, the steer found his feet on the ground, and rushed across the marshes, sprung over the Mill Bridge, straight back by the shortest route, a way he had never travelled before. Of course, my mother was pleased in a way, pleased to have him back, sorry to have parted with him. The next day the farmer fetched him back. Back again from the Plasnewydd farm.'

Graveyard

'We won't sit here, but press against the bank further up. In the grave since Saturday – and there's poor Joseph up there under that headstone and white chipped bed – the earth has a good heart to care for.'

This was a modern grave, dug six feet down to the red sandstone rock. In the distance the thick headstones of slate were sinking to the level of their neglected trades. The engraved symbols of carpenter, mason, blacksmith, farmer, were beginning to dissolve. They should be lifted and preserved I thought, and grieved. The heavy granite and deeply polished face of the red and black 'chessmen' should be abolished. The loving hand of the *teulu*[4] had gone; commerce even stood at the head of the grave. I wondered how much deeper this evil had penetrated and inquired from Mrs Lewis, who looked 70 at my side.

'... Ay, they go out like a candle. The undertaker brings the cover to put over them, just on the top. Underneath they have on their shirt, the men their pants, stockings, no boots. The women have their nightgown on. I don't like women much about a funeral. Lots of men is what I like to see. When Joseph was alive he was always telling me about the long processions who had to walk nearly two miles with the body and how they broke out into song most of the way. If I'm sad sitting alone, waiting to join Joseph, or in want, I just say to myself ... the ... Lord ... is ... my ... shepherd ... I ... shall ... not ... want ... the 26th Psalm, I think it is – and the pain goes like a flash, and I'm alright ... he maketh ... me ... to ... lie down ... in ... green ... pastures ... he leadeth ... me beside ... the ... still waters ... through ... I walk ... through ... the valley ... of death ... I will fear no evil ... There, the rain is coming on; I don't know what you'll do for you're more simple than me.'

I had forgotten my coat. I looked up; the heavy brows of the yew straightened my thoughts. We took shelter under its slender branches while the rain continued to splash down on us. The clouds freshened by the rain, were moving fast. They sailed overhead and fell apart like a jay's wing over the bay.

'I often wonder how far I could go in the sky to reach the blue, O, I wish I could see proper, get about. There's Amelia now, 84, out cleaning every day. Up at 7 every morning at Miss Trahearne's, rising the ashes – cleaning the grate and making her a cup of tea. And then look at me.'

She was half-blind and a huge growth covered part of her face.

The chapel emerged clear and hard, the mathematical precision of the slates a brilliant peacock blue. The yew we had left illuminated into a fountain of dark green jet, each metallic branch tipped by the sharp edge of the sun. Tombstone, bell-glass of china flowers, grass blade and riverstone, all stood magnified and isolated by the wet face of the sky. The epitaphs shone with a new rejoicing.

We strolled out and down the muddy lane. The cart ruts standing high in their ridges; past the cattle standing in the pool. Over the bare rock which was exposed at the top of the hill. Nearer now to the hedgerows, where the flowers breathed out the warm scent of the grave.

We were going to pay a visit to Mrs Jones, Parc-yr-Hendy,[5] to find out how she was progressing.

'She won't be long now. She thought she was going to be sent from here – to the workhouse – and started to get very common – not bothering about herself – dirty and untidy – and not going to bed at nights. She'll probably go in her sleep,' Mrs Lewis added and started to tell me a tale of which I have no copy but the facts were roughly this:

There were two women who slept together in a bed which drew out of a cupboard. (I don't know why she described the bed, for it has nothing to do with the story, and I had already seen a similar one in a village outside Carmarthen.) In the next room her son lay sleeping. The mother was not expecting death, neither were her son nor the woman with whom she shared her bed. Yet on a certain night, for some mysterious reason, as inexplicable as death itself, this son arose and lay beside his mother. Remained with her, until she died; then returned to his own ironstead in the next room. Through all this tension and tragic loss, the woman sleeping beside the corpse neither woke nor was conscious in her dream of any strange event.

Pub

'Alright then.'

'There you are.'

'Didn't I say it?'

'Are you sure you're not robbing him? Mind you, the flames get cooler as they rise. The best place in hell fire would be on the white coals themselves.'

They were as heated as the subject of their debate. And the fate of Hitler was still left undecided. Someone knocked, for it was after hours. Two farmers and a policeman in civvies came in.

'One of them's the third Devil entering.'

'Here comes the man of the mind.'

And not knowing to whom they referred, they all three sat together on the settle, Williams wearing his most evasive smile. He had become attached to a land girl evacuated to a neighbouring village who spent most of her time going places in corduroy trousers. She lived in the wing of a farm, which had been converted from a stable, and it was this particular incident that symbolised their meaning.

'Well, Williams, how's the new pony? Have you put her in the stall?'

'Now look, Williams bach, it's a pity to use good straw, all you need is a white sheet to lay her on.'

'Cover her with,' said another.

'Shove her against a rick, mun.'

'Now stop. I've just come back from the mart and I'm tired. I bought a pig tidy before the war for 30 bob apiece, now they're asking three to four ponds. The Farmers' Union is no good; we've all retired from it. Its only use is to enforce tax on the poor bugga of a farmer, that's the only point they have taken up. What's happening now: the uniform standard of meat is one shilling to the lb – one-and-six to the customer. Is this an encouragement for good quality farmers – to only breed quantity – by weight rather than quality? And anyway the officials can't even guess the weight proper just by lifting the beast. Can you let me have five woodbines?'

'Yes, if you fill my pipe.'

'It's too big, mun.'

The blacksmith with a smile like set iron said:

'Anyone who can drink a pint and smoke a woodbine should pay a farmer's tax. Anyway they're rich.'

Williams turned on his rival who also owned a farm:

'Who's rich and owns a farm?'

The blacksmith bent the poker with his two hands.

'Well, it's like this. I'm the part now.' And Williams stood up. 'If there's a farmer who doesn't drink or smoke he should be in the grade one and pay first tax, for he's sure to be tight and have plenty of money. And the others belong to category two. I'm taking a calf up myself on Wednesday, but have a good mind to sell it locally – kill it myself. I'd get three pound notes for it instead of one.

'I'll have the head, Williams bach.'

'I'll have half the liver.'

'Trouble with Tweed, he is only one of them. They're six of them at the top. They'll be trouble with Brooke when he comes out of jail. I like the man myself. He's a nice fellow. Funny how he headed the poll ... the Prisoners' War Fund with 10 pounds (sterling) in the *Carmarthen Journal*.'

'And that Councillor friend of his. I met him in the Boar's Head and said, "Fancy sending evacuees to a village like ours where we have no water supply: all the wells drying up each summer and us bickering as to who should get the water, the cattle or the people." There's the county well down at the bottom of the hill, 400 yards out of the village with nothing but a push button to release the flow. I've been down there myself waiting two hours for a bucket to fill, drip, drop. And they're thinking of sending us 40 more.'

'Old Vaughan said he would break the damn pusher. They could easily have a hydraulic ram to pump it up into the village.'

'And the same Councillors bring us the ARP pumps. But where's the water? Where's the water mun?'

'We had that fire the other day when the hen roost caught on fire. Where were we? They all got roasted by the time we had the thing under control – and that plane! I'd sooner use my pop-gun. And the planning, planning for parlours when we don't use them and only want our Ty-bach[6] buckets taken away ... TB dried out of our homes.'

'What we want is some scent about the place. Look at Jack Vaughan. I was up there the other night and he was smiling all over himself because he had got this job at Pendine. Four pound ten for cleaning out the barrel of a gun. Breakfast sixpence, and bacon as much as you like. He was just stretching over for a scarlet box when his wife shouted "Now then, Jack Vaughan, that's Muriel's."'

'Aye, he's a terror for scent.'

'Going to Muriel's box, shaking it over himself before he takes out the cows – Lavender is what he likes best.'

'Lavender, I'm told, or Carnation.'

Swansea Raid[7]

I, that is Xebo7011, pass out into the chill-blue air and join Xebn559162,[8] her sack apron greening by the light of the moon. I read around her hips: 'BEST CWT: CLARK'S COW CAKES, H.T.5.' I do not laugh because I love my peasant friend. The night is clear, spacious, a himmel blue, and the stars minute pinpricks. The elbow drone of Jerries burden the sky and our sailing planes tack in and out with their fine metallic hum.

Oh! look how lovely she is caught in those lights Oh!

From our high village overlooking the Towy we can see straight down the South Wales Coast. Every searchlight goes up. A glade of magnesium waning to a distant hill which we know to be Swansea.

Swansea's sure to be bad. Look at those flares like a swarm of orange bees.

They fade and others return. A collyrium sky, chemically washed $Cu.DH_2$. A blasting flash impels Swansea to riot! Higher, absurdly higher, the sulphuric clouds roll with their stench of ore, we breathe naphthalene air, the pillars of smoke writhe, and the astringent sky lies pale at her sides. A Jerry overhead drops two flares; the cows returning to their sheds wear hides of cyanite blue, their eyes GLINTING OPALS! We, alarmed, stand puce beneath another flare, our blood distilled, cylindricals of glass. The raiders scatter, then return and form a piratic ring within our shores. High explosives splash up blue, white, and green. We know all copper compounds are poisonous, we know also where they are.

Bleached, Rosie turns to fetch in the cows. I lonely, return to my hearth, there is a quiet clayfire with blue flames rising that would bring solace to any heart.

Fisherman

An irritating iron blue sky, that lifts the green from out of the leaves so that they are reduced in hue to a yellow fragility. As though winter, a cupboard of darkness, had extended too long, and the etiolated branches give out a curious light of their own. The wind under pressure and lowered by the sky, clatters down milk cans, whips straw from off the ricks. And such a speed and shout to hold them down, that birds stretched out of their timidity, dip and snatch at the new box of milk strainers. These no longer made of cloth, but tissues discs, which blow up foreshortening their muled winds as they drift helplessly in the steel of the gale. At such a time as this – round lamentations of grief – Giotto halos – damp angels from the Chapel walls of Padua.

The fire grey and low, sparked as a stick was pushed through the *pele* crust; through each hole made overnight in order to preserve a breathing space and permanent life in the hearth. The wind banged and whined through the keyhole, lifted the sacking and animals from beside the door, brought with it a call, known for years, as familiar as the cuckoo disturbing all early routine.

Fetch a plate he's on the way.

The call came nearer.

Fish-alive, Fish alive, Alive-o.

We picked up shawl, coat or sacking and ran. Marie shouted, 'would I or she fetch for us?' and the spittle flew out of her mouth like pointed glass.

Fish-alive, Fish alive, Alive-o.

The wind and our speech wound in and out through the boisterous trees, distorting the voice, and throwing it back in our faces with a cold salt sting.

'There should be a fine catch with the spring tides.' And I imagined him sitting in the middle of the estuary, a cormorant with fierce emerald eyes, hunched in a navy blue silence. We waited. The breeze unravelling our aprons and hair. He might go round the other way. This was an anxiety we often suffered in the village, as it had been planned in a circle.

FISH ALIVE. FISH ALIVE. ALIVE-O.

One stick of fish, I smiled, How much?

A goose turned out of the lane. A brilliant white bird against the blue sediment of the sky; her feathers and pride pushed well out of place by the scurrying scrolls of air. The breast petals fluttering in all directions, light as strawberry flowers; than as quickly dimmed, grazed with a frozen grey light. We turned to watch the orange webbed stride, and laughed as the blue eye and bill were lifted higher and higher, her iron claws gripping the road to steady her gait.

The last of the aristocrats. A proud people who checked their horse's head.

I felt sad. How much? I said again.

A tanner. Six pence.

The fish, drab flat fish with scarlet spots, bounced about in a freshly woven basket of reeds; others hanging from his hand had been threaded on to slim strips of willow.

John Roberts[9] known for years to the village, and as much attached to them, as they were to him, stood in front of us now in his rough Breton suiting; his burnished flesh glowing like coals of fire; trousers rolled up above his bare feet and knees. I wanted to ask if it were true that he had dropped two of his relatives into the river by the full curve of the moon. But I was scared: scared of his answer. For I depended on him, as did many others to be ferried entirely at his mercy over that particular estuary. And like them, had been thrown across his back, lifted over sand and rock, dropped in the boat and quietly rowed over a mirrored water of birds. This morning we all knew, that at the lowest ebb of the tide, he had walked three miles from Laugharne, crossing the River Tâf, like St Cadoc, through all its shifting sands and quagmires, without once entering his boat. An attempt few could achieve. Then over another hundred yards of slippery seaweed, up to the Bell House, and along the fringe of the Pentowyn pastures.

O it's nothing. But I can't get back awhile the sea's right up to the pokes.

The galleon engraved on the cliff – the one by your cottage?

Funny only you and one other have noticed that.

And Emlyn has he been called up yet?

O he can play his pack of cards better than any of them.

Swallows screamed to within an inch of our ears, flew high above the washing wires, then dipped under the eaves of the Chapel. An old Chapel with many of the slates ripped off by the impeding gale. The skeleton rafters peering through the gaps – the inner ribs of his boat; the roof of his mouth as he threw back his head to watch the astringent flight of the swallows – a white ridge of herring bones.

Will you be coming again?

The soldiers camped near us will be taking more than I can find.

Restless as the wind, he shifted ready to move on to the next group of women waiting outside the farms: leaving me with two fish bouncing as vigorously to free themselves from the willow, as a young calf tied and pulling to free himself from the mart.

An Introduction to Village Dialect[1]

Note. For technical reasons I have made a distinction between Cymric and Welsh writers in the same way that Histories on Scottish Literature refer to Gaelic or Scottish poets, etc. The term Anglo-Welsh having no origin but a superficial one, had to be dismissed.

Before I can discuss the subject of contemporary Welsh dialect, and endeavour to prove that it has both a tradition and root, I have first to point out that there has been practically no acknowledgment of Welsh Literature in the past. This lack of recognition in the History of English Literature has yet to be adjusted, and it will take several minds of astute and singular purpose to achieve it. In the meantime because of the tragic deformity, I am compelled to raise certain manuscripts out of the dust; and I will examine these in as clear and sound a manner as possible.

George Saintsbury in his surveys of English Literature (e.g., Macmillan 1929, pp. 16, 42, 63, etc.) has somewhat neglected the Welsh contribution: but in no way is this as serious as Professor G.L. Craik's. In his *Manual of English Literature*, there are isolated chapters on 'Scottish Chaucerian Poets', 'Scottish Poets', 'Scottish Prose', which include a prose passage on the translators of Gaelic and Latin MSS, from the middle of the sixteenth century to the end of the nineteenth century. In this chapter he writes:

> Before the middle of the sixteenth century a few prose writers had also appeared in the Scottish dialect – (and later) – it is worthy to remark, that ... we have unquestionably the Scottish dialect – *Scottis langage* as the author calls it.

All this is courteous to Scotland; but to balance the History of English Literature, a chapter or two devoted to the Welsh and Irish writers would preserve a more mature survey; and this applies to all historians compiling an 'English Literature', not only to Professor Craik.

Gildas, we are told, is British. Yet his habit was twisted by the Saints of Demetia with whom he conversed, by St Cadoc, in particular! That Gildas was a bard in his native tongue, studied in Ireland, had Welsh and Breton biographers, and attacked his countrymen as they do today with avid ferocity, still prevented a claim that he was Welsh. There is Nennius, a monk from Bangor. Bishop Asser (*Asserius Menevensis*) born in Wales and brought up a monk at St Davids, who became King Alfred's translator and biographer. Attended the Wessex court because in Alfred's own Kingdom 'he could find no distinguished man of learning'. The translators of the *Lives of the Saints* from the Latin and Cymric tongue. Layamon, a priest who lived and wrote on the Severn bank and Welsh borders; who adapted the surrounding Welsh folklore and legends into his 'Brut' which at its source, as was Wace's before him, was derived from a Cymraeg MS, found in Breton by a Walter Mape (a native of the Welsh Marshes), and put into the Cymric tongue by him. There are other grave omissions and lack of recognition, but I shall deal with these only when they contact my subject.

Saintsbury opens his *History of English Literature* with *Widsith*. Here I think an identity with Taliesin should be made. I will quote so that this statement may be considered:

Priv vardd cyssevin	Primary chief bard
Wyv vi i Elfin ...	Am I to Elfin ...
Bum mi ben ciwdod	I have been the chief director
Ar waith twr Nimrod;	Of the work of the tower of Nimrod;
Mi wyv ryveddod,	I am a wonder
Ni wyddis vy hanvod.	Whose origin is not known.
Bum mi yn arca,	I have been in the ark,
Gan Noah ac Alpha;	With Noah and Alpha;
Mi gwelais ddiva	I have seen the destruction of
Sodom a Gomorra;	Sodom and Gomorra;
Bum yn Africa	I was in Africa
Cyn seiliad Roma;	Before the foundation of Rome;
Mi ddaethym yma	I am no come here
At weddillion Troia.	To the remains of Troy.
Bum gyda vy Rhen	I have been with my Lord
Yn mhreseb asen;	In the manger of the ass;
Mi nerthais Moesen	I strengthened Moses
Drwy ddwvr Iorddonen ...	Through the waters of Jordon ...

This dramatic recitation of events, genealogy, travelogue, is still demanded by the quieter villagers when a boy, returning from the Forces, enters the pub – that diminishing Bardic Hall – and is encouraged to relate his adventures. I have been ... I was over ... I have seen ... I was with the Huns (*quoted from Widsith*) and repeated by an ex-sailor one evening at the *Black Horse* ... until a dark farmer hidden in the corner, relates with sharp crescendo a story not so diverse in idiom to that used in the Cymric MS of St Beuno, a saint of the sixth century (*translated, from a MS in the Library of Earl of Macclesfield, and collated with another MS in the Library of Jesus College, Oxford, by Rev. W. J. Rees, MA, FSA*):

'Ha, woman, stop a little while until this is done'; but the child was crying, so that it was not easy to endure it. 'Ha, woman,' said Beuno, 'What causes the child to cry?' 'Ha, good saint,' said the woman, 'there is a cause for it.' 'Ha, good woman,' said Beuno, 'what is the cause?' 'Truly,' said the woman, 'the land which you possess, and are building a church thereon, is a township of the father of the child.'

These mounting phrases and the withholding of wit until the end of the story are to be found in most dialogues of Welsh dramatic speech. From the book I have just quoted, *Cambro-British Saints*, I can only find other examples from the translations of the Cymric MSS. And this goes to prove I think that there is a genuine Welsh dialect which reaches the surface, however tampered or late the translation. (Among the Bretons, Pierre Loti's *Iceland Fishermen* is another example). So as not to appear dogmatic I will quote from the translation of the Latin and Cymric MS on the Life of St David, and in this way, leave the suggestion open for discussion; I shall quote from the passage where St Patrick is ordered by the Angel to go to Ireland and leave Demetia in the hands of St David:

'Thou must leave,' said he, 'this place to one who is not yet born.' And he became angry, and said, 'Why has the Lord treated his servant with contempt, who has been serving him with fear and love, and hath chosen before him one who is not yet born, and will not be born for thirty years.' And Patrick prepared in himself to leave that place of the Lord Christ; and the Lord loved Patrick much and sent his angel to pacify him ... And then the mind of Patrick was set at rest.'

'God,' said he, 'has not appointed this place for thee, but for a child who is not yet born, nor will be born until thirty years are past.' And Saint Patrick hearing this, was surprised, and sorrowful; and being angry said, 'Why has the Lord despised his servant, who from his infancy has been serving him in fear and love, and has chosen another, who has not seen the light, and not to be born for thirty years?' And he prepared to flee and forsake his Lord Jesus Christ, saying, 'Since my labour in sight of the Lord is considered in vain, and one who is not yet born is preferred before me, I will go away, and not submit to such usage.' But the Lord greatly loved Patrick, and sent to him his angel to appease him with friendly expressions ... Then the mind of Patrick being pacified, he willingly gave up the holy place to Saint David.

The first quotation is from the Cymric MS, the second from the Latin (*Cott. MSS, British Museum, Vespasian, A., XIV, collated with Nero, E.I.*). Other curious idioms from this same book which are consistent with today, are:

'And he was a brother in the faith to David.' 'I know not indeed, said Aidan.' 'Scuthyn arose and said "thou shalt not serve said he ..." 'today; I will, said Scuthyn, be the servant of this day.' 'Then he went, and having set down, was beheld with surprise.' '*There is no one of us*, who can preach to so many; and we have all of us tried in our turn, and we have seen *that no one of us* has ability to preach this multitude, look, and consider, and inquire *whether there is any one* who is worthy, and is able to preach to the large number here assembled.' 'I shall not go there ... *but go you.*' 'And which is yet a high hill visible to everybody, *and it is flat everywhere about it.*' 'And the like to him they never heard before, and after him they never will hear.'

Apart from this distinctive dialogue, there are also customs which prevail to this day. When St David says to his disciples Deiniol and Dubricus: 'Go to the sea to catch fish, and bring here clear water from the fountain,' would the demand from a rural mother be so different: 'Go off and spike the fish, fetch clean water from the well.'

The hand plough is used down at Cwmcelyn, and on the hills sowing of corn by hand, the toilers work side by side with modern agricultural machines. The reverence for bees by the Saints, and the many legends about them, 'For the honey comb proclaims his (*St David's*) wisdom, for as the honey is in the wax, so he will hold a spiritual sense in an historical instrument.' The superstitions arising out of the swarms in the village today: of the swarm that sailed to Ireland on the prow of a ship ... on the making of mead, *Medd*. I was told only a few months ago how to brew mead in the village: with all the asides as to how the wax was melted down and poured into wooden moulds and sold to the Chemist for extra money. The veneration for the fox by the Saints and how they allowed a watchful eye to close as the ravenous beasts ran off with a calf, whelp, or young pig. Such tolerance for the wild beast has not left our pastures, and in the story 'Fox' at the end of this introduction, that appreciation for their pagan beauty and hunger is understood. The pig is another devoted idol of the Saints. And where they found it often became the site for a new church or monastery. This was due to the continual submerging of the land, and the earthquakes which occurred around Demetia at that time; the Frisians arriving with their own legends of submerged and eroded coasts, forced the monks to take special precaution, and not having faith in themselves, they turned to the pig which was not only idolised by the Druids for their defence, but was also wise in his choice of a firm burrowing ground. The pig has its own feast day on the bleak plains of Hungary and is brought nearer to us today by Auden's translation from one of the Icelandic songs:

Sleep you black eyed pig,
Fall into a deep pit full of ghosts ...

to the stanzas attributed to Myrddin, in which the pig becomes a symbol of the Christian peoples of Wales:

Hear O little pig! sleep not too long,
There comes to us a lamentable report
Of little chieftains full of perjury,
And husbandmen that are close-fisted of the penny,
When there shall come across the sea, men encased in armour,
With horses under them having two heads,
And two points to their spears of unsparing havoc.
Fields will be lying unreaped in the country of war,
And the grave will be better than the life of him who sighs,
When the horns call men to the squads of conflict.

This prophecy says Thomas Stephens, was no doubt written by a bard at a later period than Myrddin and suggests the eleventh century. He goes on to give us two very apt proverbs. One from Kymry (note the Greek K. and not the Norman K. as the Nationalists wrongly conclude): '*Y mae yn gwrandaw fel mochyn mewn soff*' ... he listens like a pig in the stubble. And the Carmarthenshire proverb: '*Y mae mor sifil a hwch mewn soff*' ... she is as civil as a sow in stubble. About two years ago a pig ran straight through my cottage; I was told that this was a good omen. In the same way I have heard villagers console each other when a cow wanders into the garden leaving huge craters in the softly shovelled soil.

Before I leave the twelfth century, I must again refer to Wacc and

Layamon. Their value towards the study of *Welsh dialect and folklore* has been neglected and research and comaparison in all MSS, deviating from Walter Mape, Caradog of Llancarvan, Dr David Powel of the sixteenth century, Geoffrey of Monmouthshire, Geoffrey Gaimar, Robert of Gloucester, and the former two which I have already mentioned, might result in some interesting examples of Welsh dialogue and custom. Wace in translation retains all the purity and directness of a true Celt:

> Vortigern looked closely upon the brethren. Shapely were they of body, bright of visage, taller and more comely than any youth he knew. From what land have you come? Tell me now the place of your birth? (And the King Hengist spoke of his land and birth.) When King Vortigern heard the name of Mercury as the god of their governance, he inquired what manner of man these were, and of the god in whom they believed. (After Hengist had related the many gods, Vortigern replies.) 'Ill is your faith, and in an evil god you put your trust.'

The same sectional speech composed by Layamon in the English is a striking comparison:

> Vortigern sent to them, and asked how they were disposed, their business; if they sought peace, and recked of his friendship?' (Lack of space prevents a full quotation.)

But I suggest that a similar comparison should be made with the dialogue outside the Carmarthen Gates between the child Merlin and the swaggering knights. For it is in sections such as these that an example of Welsh dialect might be found.

Owing to the abridgement of Layamon's 'Brut' we get an over-burden of facts which to some extent, have already been sifted by distinguished men of letters; it is as though too many MSS were put in the *cawl*, so that in the end no particular broth could be distinguished; but of his language my people would say, 'his speech is rough about him', and I believe if I had the time I should be able to quote some very strong examples in favour of the Welsh dialect. With Wace the situation is somewhat reversed. The framework of his poem bears a truth of subject and understanding with his Celtic neighbours, the dialogue shines, but only occasionally are there similarities of rural expression such as we get today. The proportion being less than that spoken by the Bretons in Loti's *Iceland Fisherman*.

Recognition in Wales has always been given a first place in the laws of her sociology. But it is this, above everything else, which she has never been granted outside her own country. Giraldus Cambrensis (*Itinerarium Kambriae*) gives us a terse illustration. The Cymry, christianised before any other part of England or Scotland chose, among other differences, their own date for Easter and an individual cut for the tonsure. When Augustine sailed over to promote unity and remain himself top-dog, he called together the seven Bishops of Cambria. And they journeyed to the confines of the Saxons – the Bishops of Hereford, Worcester, Llandaff, Bangor, St Asaph, Llanbadarn, and Glamorgan – this remember, somewhere about 604 AD, roughly 400 years after the Cymry had accepted Christianity.

> When the seven Bishops appeared, Augustine, sitting in his chair, with Roman pride, did not rise up at their entrance. Observing his haughtiness, they immediately returned, and treated him and his statutes with contempt ... (And today we have the Welsh MPs!!)

In the village the foundations of the *teulu* remain somewhat unchanged. A certain distance is kept, and with exceptions, recognition and grace among themselves is strictly adhered to. The word friend ... life friend ... pal ... is not understood in its English sense – they are a community. To those they like they speak to: to those they dislike, they remain silent.

A few chapters ahead Giraldus includes Chester in his itinerary through Wales, and remains there over the Easter recess (*circa* 1188). 'The Archdeacon Rogers, saw the Chester Plays in 1594, when they had been going on for something like three centuries in all', and it was then the Water-Leaders and Drawers from the River Dee took chief part.

> From comely Conway unto Clyde
> Under tyldes them to hide:
> A better shepherd on no side
> No earthly man may have.
>
> (*The Three Shepherds.*)

In some of the maps made during the Medieval period the River Clud is marked for the Dee. F.J. North, D.Sc., FGS (*The Maps of Wales before 1600 AD*, Cardiff, 1935, p. 32) suggests:

> that *Fl Clud* is the river Dee and that its mouth has been confused

with the Vale of Clwyd, but there are symbols representing the
Roman Walls, of which the more southerly (or Hadrian's Wall)
almost reaches the river, while the other (obviously misplaced) is
drawn to the south of another river Clud, beyond which is
Galeweia (Galloway) ... it would seem that the whole of the
coast between North Wales and South of Scotland has been
omitted ... *Fl Clud* may well have been intended for the Clyde.

I do not wish to imply that these Plays are in any way Welsh.
They are not. But I should like to point out that there may be more
Welsh influence in them than has so far been admitted. 'The Welsh
had Miracle Plays acted long before this period in their own Cymric
dialect in extensive amphitheatres constructed for the purpose ...
one of which, at St Just near Penzance, has been restored.' In Wake-
field's *Second Shepherd Play*, Mak the Scottish gillie calls on two
Saints, St Stephen and St James. The three shepherds appeal to St
Thomas of Kent, and St Nicholas. St Thomas canonised 1172, was
the Protector of Wales and a shield to all her Christian peoples and
principles; at his death one of the scribes from Llanbadarn Fawr
Ceredigion wrote in Medieval Cymric:

> Y vlwydyn rac uyneb y llas Thomas archescob (keint) gwr mawr
> y grefyd ae santeidrwyd ae gyfyawnder, ae gyghor, ac (o) annoc
> Henri urenhin Lloegyr y pumhet dyd gwedy duw Nadolic ger
> bronn allawr y Drindawt yny gapel ehun yg Gheint ae escobawl
> wisc ymdanaw, a delw y groc yn y law y llas (achledyfeu) ar
> diwed yr afferen ...

St Nicholas (Greek saint of sixth and seventh century) was introduced to Wales by the Flemish, whom they had adopted, and where
there still exists the coastal town of St Nicholas, named after him,
not far from the precincts of St David's. So both saints were acceptable to the Welsh Border audience. Again, the mock of the pipes:
'Who is that pipes so poor?' is a reminder of the Bard Glyn Cothi's
ironical satire when the bagpipes were introduced at an early
Eisteddfod. And the sly reversal of Taffy was a Welshman, when
Mak is represented as the sheep-stealer and is tossed in canvas by the
three shepherds. The Play, written as far as I can judge, for I have
not seen the orginal spelling, in middle English with a dig at the
Southern dialect of Wessex:

> M. I shall make complaint, and make you all to thwang (find
> mirth)

At a word,
And tell even how ye *doth*. (My italics.)
S.   'But Mak, is that *sooth*?
Now take out that southern *tooth*,
And set in a tord.

This I believe to be a jest on the termination of the southern *th*. The termination of the Northern *es* is used by Mak, and only on one occasion by the three shepherds when they return Mak's dialect as a refrain for his baby:

M.   Nay, go' way: he *sleepys*.
S.   Methink he *peepys*.
S.   When he wakens he *weepys*. (The italics are mine.)

Again when Mak is asked who are the wicked gossips over the child's birth. The culprits are not given Welsh or Scottish names, but English:

Parkin and Gibbon Waller, I say,
And gentle John Horne ...

The alliteration, assonance, especially the *internal rhyme*, should be observed, also the titles attributed to Myrddin, *Bardic President about the waters of the Clyde*.
A refrain in the Lullaby *A dylly-downe, perdie*, brings us to the Ballads. In a modern Book of British Ballads, an editor writes:

A similar group of Welsh Ballads was projected, but after a careful investigation of the principal periodicals and collections, and some correspondence with *students* (the italics are mine) of Welsh Literature, I have concluded that for English Readers, there exist but few Welsh Ballads of any merit.

This may be so, but I doubt it. What of the translations of Welsh Ballads, Telyn, Rondo, Trioled, Penillion, by Ernest Rhys, Alfred Perceval Graves, and others whose names I do not know. Yet in this same Book of Ballads I find 'Three Ravens', 'The Bonny Lass of Anglesey', 'Kemp Owyne'; the note to this poem runs:

This has been associated with Owain up Urien the King of Rheged of North Wales who is celebrated by the bards Taliesin and Llywarch Hen.

'Clerk Saunders', which should read 'Clerk William Saunders' since
the ballad is often printed with 'Sweet William's Ghost'. And
'Thyme and Rue' taken down from the recitation of S. Baring
Gould at Mawgan on Pyder. If I quote to claim an association with
Welsh customs and traditions I hope I may be forgiven. From *A
dylly-down perdie* ... to:

> There were three ravens sat on a tree,
> *Downe, a downe, hay downe, hay downe ...*
> *With a downe, derrie, derrie, derrie, downe, downe.*

'The three Ravens,' we are told in the Mabinogion, 'belong to the
armorial bearings of Urien Rheged, a King of North Wales, and are
still retained by the House of Dynevor ... At one time they represented the 300 Ravens which descended on their master Owain to
help him in battle.' It is possible that the three ravens represent the
community of Owain's cantref, and is of symbolic origin, in much
the same way as the pig symbolised the Christian peoples of Wales
in Myrddin's stanzas. Of the origin of the refrain, which extended all
over Britain and is even found south in William Cornishe's poems
'*Dyry, come dawn, dyry dyry come dawn*' (I quote from memory), the
source is traced to Wales. *Hob y deri dando* is a refrain belonging to
the stanzas of Myrddin, one of which I have already quoted.

> An inquiry into the meaning of this refrain by Sir Hubert Parry
> led to an analysis which traced an origin back to the Druidic Era
> and translated means 'pig (go or come) to the oaks under cover: it
> may later have been associated with the calling of herds at night'.
> The word *Hob* now only survives as a flitch of bacon; formerly
> pigs were called *Hobau*: but now they are called *moch*. (Thomas
> Stephens, *Literature of the Kymry*, Llandovery, p. 258.)

Another custom, prevalent in the village and found in the folklore of Wales and among other nations, is the persistence of death:
seen not as a ghost, but as another identity tracking down its victim.
I have so far only found two examples. One is the already well-
known poem 'Angau' (Anon.), where the second stanza is:

Galw am gawg a dŵr i ymolchi,	I got me up and called for water,
Gan ddisgwyl hynny i'm sirioli;	That I might wash, and so feel better;

| Ond cyn rhoi deigryn ar fy ngruddiau, | But before I wet my eyes so dim, |
| Ar fin y cawg mi welwn Angau. | There was Death on the bowl's rim. |

(Welsh Folk Verses, trans. Aneirin ap Talfan)

and so the poem continues with Death beside it, following the man to chapel to sit straight up in his pew – back home and through the door which is locked, to rise in front of the victim from under the floor boards. In a Tuscan folksong there is a similar theme:

I hear Death's step, I see him at my side,
I feel his bony fingers clasp me round;
I see the church's door is open wide,
And for the dead I hear the knell resound –
I see the cross and the black pall outspread ...

(Translated by Martinengo-Cesaresco)

Mrs Lewis, who is my neighbour and lives alone in a two-roomed cottage similar to mine, told me once that 'death kept on sitting beside her and that she could not get rid of the bugga' (the word bugga, frequently used in the village, conveys no meaning to the rural people other than old nuisance, old wretch). Another saying conveyed to me by Mrs Davies when I was accused of being a spy, was, 'if you sweep before your house everything will be clear'; these were not the exact words, as at the time she could not remember the proverb. Her explanation was, if I kept myself good, clean, I need not worry – and on top of this she added another interpretation: if I kept the dirt or harm they were creating, out – swept it outside the doorstep – I should not be troubled. Anyhow the saying exists; and is well-known to authorities on research as a representation of the Middle Ages. It may have arrived in Wales via the Bretons, a language communicable to them today: or through Auguste Brizeaux's poem 'La Poussière Sainte', which, if the rendering is based on the genuine superstitions of his people, lengthens the age of this charm by several hundreds of years. Here in this poem, the conflict between pagan and Christian rites are very noticeable:

... Sweep, sweep my broom until my charm uprears
A force more strong than sighs, more strong than tears;
Charm loved of heaven, which forces wind and wave,
Though fierce and mad, our children's lives to save.

My angel knows a Christian true am I;
Not Pagan, nor in league with sorcery.
Here I dispense to the four winds of God,
To quell their rage, dust from the holy sod –
Sweep, sweep my broom, sweep on ...

Letters I have received from Carmarthenshire and North Wales
have often returned for me the period of the Elizabethans. For
instance, Puttenham will substitute the word 'he' for verse (line in
its correct sense); he writes:

If ye ask me further why I make what first long and after short in
one verse, to that I satisfied you before, that is by reason of *his*
accent sharpe in one place and flat in another, being a common
monosillable, that is apt to receiue either accent, and so in the first
place receiuing aptly the sharpe accent he is made long ...

Now there have been times, when a peasant, sometimes illiterate,
has attempted to express herself directly out of the Cymric tongue,
and the attempt has left me as delighted and vague as Puttenham.

'She is not very well, the broccoli I mean' (Llanybri).

And when I asked this same person, Amelia Phillips, to give me the
date of her eightieth birthday, she said 'Indeed, I do not know.' And
when I asked her if she knew the date of her daughter's, she said
slowly and with difficulty:

'On the ... First ... Day ... of the ... Last ... Month ... of the
                                                           Year.'

Other quotations from Elizabethan prose in which the syntax or
idioms are similar with that of today, are:

'There is not forgotten.' 'That is he misseth nothing.' 'They busied
themselues.' 'Nowe I think most meete to speake somewhat
concerning.' 'This opinion shall you find confirmed throughout
the whole workes.' 'It is to be wondered at of all, and is lamented
of manie.'

All these quotations were found in the rather awkward phrasing
of William Webbe.
    The narrow-minded schoolmaster – England for the English only
– Roger Ascham, whose

doing thereof would be more pleasant than painfull, and would bring also much proffet to all that should read it, *and great praise to him* (that) would take it in hand, with just desert of thankes,

compared to a letter received from South Wales last year:

When I got back she had the place tidy and had made the Welsh cakes, *it is great praise to her* that she did this ... now stick to do it and try to please the Head that you may come on as it is very important because people after this war half of them will be without work. Do not make up with common people: keep away from them as they only make mischief and draw you the same way.

But as regards rhythm, Gabriel Harvey is the exception among the group of Elizabethan critics. His pastoral ear carries a cadence of words so that they fall out naturally, and are governed by that pasture rhythm. With James Joyce, and most people working on the soil it is the same.

'Now canst thou tell me nowe, or doist thou ...' to '... Well, you know or don't you kennet or haven't I ...'

From Gabriel Harvey to James Joyce (*Finnegans Wake*) who, among other great attributes, linked up the close mythology and dialect between the peoples of Eire and Wales – the Liffey – 'Towy I too.'

Now that I have arrived at the essence of all languages of the soil, and by which phrases are governed, rhythm: and though unconscious to the speaker at the time, there is invariably a set pattern, to which accented words are added to balance a phrase. Later I hope to prove this with quotations from my own collection of idioms and representations from other rural communities. But to show its growth and tradition I must first consider the carol, rondels, their shape, time, and repeat of one word or set of words, before I can hope to be understood. 'Carol has a dancing origin, and once meant to dance in a ring: it may go back, through the old French *caroler*, the latin *choraula*, to the Greek *Choraules*.' W.P. Ker in his chapter on *Danish Ballads*, refers to the Carols in churchyards as mentioned by Giraldus Cambrensis in *Gemma Ecclesiastica*:

When a priest was so haunted by a refrain that he heard all night long, 'that in the morning at the Mass instead of *Dominus vobiscum* he said "Swete lemman thin are ..." "Sweet heart, take pity".

There is another reference by Giraldus to the circular dance of the Welsh and this is from his *Itinerium Kambriae*, 1188 AD:

You may see men or girls, now in the church, now in the churchyard, now in the dance, which is led round the churchyard with a song, on a sudden falling on the ground as in a trance, then jumping up in a frenzy, and representing with their hands and feet, whatever work they have unlawfully done on feast days; you may see one man put his hand to the plough, and another, as it were, goad on the oxen, mitigating their sense of labour, by the usual rude song.' A footnote to this by the editor, W. Llewelyn Williams, reads: 'This same habit is still used by the Welsh ploughboys; they have a sort of chaunt, consisting of half or even quarter notes, which is sung to the oxen at plough ...

Of the few translations of the Cymric carol which I have seen, there are two very noticeable characteristics: a tragic and dark note which is usually contrasted in the same carol by a joy and brilliance of light: and the recurring persuasion to the people not to be afraid – to come out of their hiding places:

'All poor men and humble,
All lame men who stumble,
Come haste ye, nor feel ye afraid;
For Jesus our treasure,
With love past all measure,
In lowly poor manger is laid.'
(*O Deued Pob Criston*).

'*Lift your hidden faces*
Ye who wept and prayed;
Leave your covert places
Ye who were afraid.
Here's a golden story,
Here be gifts of glory
For all men to choose.'

Here I shall not hurry as the subject is too serious; neither will I allow lack of space to restrict my thought. Of the rondel which grew out of the carol. The most perfect example of time, with its counter pattern of 6-4, is one which I found through my own analysis in Chaucer's 'Balade of Bon Counseill'.

4	6	*a*
6	4	*b*
4	6	*a*
4	6	*b*
4	6	*b*
4	6	*c*
6	4	*c*

and the first stanza fully quoted:

> Flee fro the prees, and dwelle with sothfastnesse,
> Suffyce unto they good, though hit be smal;
> For hord hath hate, and climbing tikelnesse,
> Prees hath envye, and wele blent overal;
> Savour no more than thee bihove shal;
> Werk wel thy-self, that other folk canst rede;
> And trouble shal delivere, hit is no drede.

This is an exact copy of the original Chaucer poem, including punctuation, and it was taken from the print of Louis Untermeyer's *Albatross Anthology*. The 5th line having a diaeresis after the 4th syllable which completed the pattern. Here are others of a similar pattern and tempo (from Venetian rondels translated by Martinengo Cesaresco):

> 'He is at sea, and he has sails to spread.
> I am at home, and I have beads to thread.'
> 'Wouldst thou my love? For love I have no heart;
> I had it once, and gave it once away;
> To my first love I gave it on a day
> Wouldst thou my love? for love I have no heart.'

Philip Sidney's rondel, 'My true love hath my heart, and I have his' and the strict pattern of caesura or diaeresis emphasising the rhythm in most of the rondels and ballads is so deliberate that I venture to say that there is the possibility that they were based on certain steps used in the original circular dance; but to find this out would take many years of research.

6	4	*a*	6	4	*c*
10		*b*	10		*d*
4	6	*a*	4	6	*c*
10		*b*	10		*d*
6	4	*a*	6	4	*a*

The persistence with which these tunes haunt and remain in the mind, resemble pagan chants; neither the dance nor song can be said to have an ending. When stories were told to me out of the past, and repeated five or six times I have always been most careful to go over the first draft to see if I had left out a pause or added an extra word. In practically each case I can say that there was little alteration to be made. This proved for me how a story could be remembered by a peasant – simply by the stress of a repeated phrase, or one word accented and repeated in a pattern. In everyday speech there is naturally less precision, less tension: but it is the pattern and rhythm which holds the story together and prevents it from getting lost. Milton, who has been flicked off the page too easily, realised the importance of this and in *Paradise Lost*, Eve is given a voice which runs parallel with the rondel. Phrases are set up in 6 and 4-syllable intervals, and the repetition of a set group of words carry the refrain:

In me is no delay; with thee to goe
Is to say here; without thee here to stay
Is to go hence unwillingly; *thou to mee*,
Art all things under Heav'n, all places thou,
Who for all my wilful crime *art banisht hence*.
This further consolation yet secure
I carry hence; though all *by mee is lost*,
Such favour I unworthie am voutsaft,
By mee the Promised Seed shall all restore.
                         (The italics are mine.)

This might be termed counterpoint of phrase; but it is not full counterpoint as it is understood in prosody, which includes contrasting metre and accent.

The succeeding quotations are taken partly from letters, printed page, or the voice. The first three are from letters and belong to the Carmarthenshire dialect:

'The weather is *wet*. I dressed and went to meet the van but it was so *wet* and though you would also see it too *wet* to meet me there.'

'Awful weather for the *corn*, lots of *corn* out this way and fields of *corn* have gone with the flood to the river some from Llwynfach and the island Llanwrda.'

'If I could *come* to Carmarthen, *would you COME to meet me there*, most likely I would *come* by van the 10.30 from here … and *come* to the depot the office if *you could meet me there*.'

'It was a hard *calling*, and yet the *calling* is not so bad after all.'

'Outside it was *light*, eternally *light*, but it was a pale, pale *light*.'

'Is that all *grannie Moan*? Is that all *grannie Yvonne*?'

'On the last day *in vain* had she tried. *In vain* had she sought in her head.'

(These last four quotations are from Pierre Loti, *Iceland Fisherman*).
Another example from a Breton is Wace. The opening paragraph to his *Life of St Nicholas*:

'Nobody can know *everything*, or hear *everything*, or see *everything*.'

Gerard Manley Hopkins who used Welsh metres: wrote his finest lyrics at St Beuno's near the Vale of Clwyd; attempted to learn the Cymric language, used, as I have said the Chester players may have before him, the rural dialect.

'What work? What *harm's done*? There is no *harm done*, none yet.' 'And I do not *repent*; I do not and I will not *repent*, not *repent*.' 'Here he feasts: lovely all is!' 'What is it Gwen my girl? Why do you hover and haunt me?' 'You came by Caerwys? I came by Caerwys.' 'There needs but little doing.' (*St Gwenvrewi's Well*)

'He puts all his *gold* into a bag. Then he went over to the other farm, and threw in the *gold* in front of him.' 'Is that all *gold*?' said the father. 'All *gold*,' said O'Connor (Synge: *The Aran Islands*)

'*Did you hear the* thunder, it was very cold last night. The *thunder* it was terrible. Did you hear the *thunder*, Mrs Davies?' (*Llanybri*)

'*Worms*: if ever you have the *worms* I've heard of a very good cure. You take three or four *worms* alive from the earth. Place these in a small bag and tie them round the neck. Right next to your skin. When the *worms* die in the bag they say you won't have any more.' (*Llanybri*)

Even in certain idioms there can be found relationships between peoples of the soil elsewhere; in Spain, Ireland, Italy, France, Iceland, Brittany.

'There's no sense in it.' (*Llanybri*)

'What sense is this? it has none.' (Hopkins' Poem *St Gwenvrewi's Well*)

'Is there any sense in it? (Loti – *Iceland Fisherman*)

'In our village we go *after* the cows, or we sometimes say *fetch* them in … and when one dies we are sorrowful *after* her.' (*Llanybri*)

'My thoughts are *after* you all day' (Llanybri), also 'going *after* you all day'.

'My thoughts are going *after* her.' (*Petrarch trans.* by Synge)

'I'm lifting up all my thoughts.' (*Petrarch in trans.* by Synge)

'I'm thinking like this or I'm thinking to myself.' (*Llanybri*)

'I'm thinking looking downward.' (*Petrarch trans.* by Synge)

'I have been not at all well. I have not been very well myself with cold. I had the bronchitis very bad.' (*Llanybri*)

I now hope that by proving in as short a way as possible that there is both a tradition and root to the Welsh dialect, I shall be able to discuss, at a later interval, the history, mythology, weather, craft, custom, literal syntax and idiom of the Cymric language, in relation to the contemporary dialect in this village. I hope further, that this introduction will help dispel the false misinterpretations used both by radio and amateur writers to represent the Welsh-speaking peoples; that it will promote in its place a stimulant and conscience towards the light of research and genuine speech.

And to end as I began, but from the words of a distinguished critic, W.P. Ker (*Collected Essays*, Vol. II, *Iceland and the Humanities*, c. 27, p. 117) when attacking the intolerance of some of the professors:

If the liberal way of thinking were more generally known and appreciated it might lead to some interesting discoveries, even in places not far from our doors. The Island of Britain has never yet been thoroughly explained to its inhabitants. Few people know anything of the poetical traditions of Wales, of the ancient and elaborate art of verse as it is still practised there, where a postman is quoted as an artist in metre, and a policeman writes the history of literature. Does not even a casual glimpse into this unfamiliar order of studies add something to one's knowledge, add something to the character of Britain?

WELSH ESSAYS

Llanybri interior, painting by Lynette Roberts. 'Mrs Phillips putting the "pele" on the fire. She saw this painting of herself and giggled and loved it. Showing the metallic strip on the mantelpiece, the way the washing was aired. The way the small amount of crockery and cutlery was kept together in one basket. We all did this. The way so many still had photos up of Queen Victoria or King Edward the old king. The paraffin lamps, exact copy. The black oilcloth table cover, and quarry tiles. This was (apart from the harmonium) my kitchen in Tygwyn.'

Simplicity of the Welsh Village

We are told by many distinguished architects that there is no Welsh architecture. English visitors often find the outlook foreign, cold and bleak, and they sense, many of them, that they are no longer in their own country. Now it is just this change, whether of atmosphere, land formation or a particular architectural feature, that must be analysed if we are to find out what makes the distinction between these two countries.

The first, to my mind, is colour: the blue slates and greener pastures, the two predominant colours of the Celt, the sharp outline of the whitewashed farms and houses as they stand against the skyline; the way in which the walls project geometrical planes of light that resemble still-life models of squares and cubes. This cold austerity is so suddenly upon us, and contrasts so vividly with the rich, mellow tones of English farmhouses, that we are estranged and left singularly apart. I, who have lived almost consistently for six years in the village of Llanybri, find the adjustment between England and Wales most difficult to accept. And, though I prepare myself for the change, it is always a more acute and vivid perception than that which I imagine.

There is that intense wildness of growth, quick greening growth that springs so freshly from the low boundary walls which surround every rural dwelling; that clear shining grass that fringes the edge of the tarmac road; and against these blades of grass the hard stone white wall; the black iron gates, split and turned by the village blacksmith to keep out the cattle wandering to and fro to the fields; the bleak chapel and unsheltered tombs. Here, on a sunny day, it is possible to penetrate each slate, stone and blade of grass. There are no nooks, screens, rockeries, or pergolas. The gardens are easily seen, set out in shallow ridges with slight or no division between each property.

The houses can be understood by a child, for they are the first statement of simplicity; and it is this plainness, I believe characteristic of most buildings made by the peasantry, which outlasts any of the adulterated and passing fashions of a century. There is a radiant

The Field, July 7, 1945.

and illusive mystery about their presence, largely due to three causes: to the people who have never failed to exercise the flexibility of their wit to conceal their thoughts; to a piercing light, which I shall discuss later; and, thirdly, to the sea and valley mists which tend to fold and thread through the whitewashed dwellings as though to conjure up the older legends and fuse them with the newer ones now being created in our homes. In England I would suggest that the situation is reversed. The English villager is straightforward; unlike the Welsh, we know fairly accurately what he thinks and what his home life is like. But architecturally, his house and garden tend to obscure our insight.

An English village is often termed *picturesque* or, more sarcastically, *a prettiness prevails*. We are uncertain of what we may find around the next privet hedge, around the protruding gable, sunny bay window extending to the lawn. In a Welsh village a certain symmetry is maintained throughout. The simple structure of the house is a pattern, as I have said before, that even a child can accept. A rectangular stone dwelling with one window, then a door, than another window built level with the grass. A further one window, two windows, three windows, built above this same structure, would make a house or mansion. In fact, the plan for a cottage, farmhouse or mansion has varied so little over the many centuries that all Dr Iorwerth C. Peate describes in *The Welsh House* can be found today, not only in my own village, but over the whole of Wales.

What we need, then, is not so much to preserve the rural architecture of Wales in a museum behind glass, nor to build an exact model of a Welsh village retaining all its craft and folklore, such as Hazelius founded in Sweden, and was later developed in Denmark and Norway, etc. This is good if it is kept to Dr Iorwerth Peate's original purpose and not misinterpreted to mean a pseudo Hollywood village, part modernised with concrete bathing-pool and cinema, together with a mill such as the novelist Michael Gareth Llewelyn suggested in the Welsh Press. But what is far more urgent, is to have the support of valuable persons like Dr Peate to help preserve and repair the numerous farms and cottages, no different from those which he wishes to represent in his Open Air Museum. Here, in whole villages, or on isolated farms, exist the very buildings of the peasantry, together with the natural mode of life and craft which goes with it. And what are we doing to encourage and adapt these buildings to the living conditions of today? What are we doing with the severe frost and rain, with the younger generation gradually being transferred to England or conscripted to war. The villages are deteriorating. It is happening now in my own village.

The question arises, then, in agricultural Wales, [of] how are we going to approach our building problem. Are we going to build on traditional lines, or allow the county councillors to bring in their callous suburban villas, totally unsuited to our culture? Or are we, when building a new village or isolated farm, provided it harmonises with the surrounding rural architecture, going to be courageous, and allow our generation to experiment and build with the most up-to-date materials. I believe the only method of approach is to meet the need of the workers in the simplest way possible. By that I mean the most sound and mature: to repair where needed the standing buildings and keep as near as possible to their classic style of architecture.

It is universally recognised that there is similarity between most peasant architectures throughout the world. I have seen this similarity among the white-washed farms and dwellings growing out of the soil in the village of Mezokovesd, in Hungary, in houses designed by Van der Vlugt and J.J.P. Oud in Holland, in Northern Italy, in Bavarian and Austrian villages, on the island of Tresco in the Scillies, and on the pampas of South America. If modern rural architecture is to be at all wholesome, it must spring directly, or be inspired in the process of its creation, by the local dwellings of the peasant. This is exactly what has happened with the most successful modern rural building in the past, and, because of this and the severity or truth of outline which Wales has retained in her own native style, she has with other Celtic countries more chance and opportunity to lead and go ahead. Her place and sphere of influence in these matters might well be that of Sweden after the last war. A good modern building does not look out of keeping in Celtic surroundings, as I have seen so many appear against an English rural landscape. Readers can see for themselves what I mean in the village of Talog not far from here, and again in Laugharne – or, more clearly, if they look up the Modernised Dairy Farm in France, illustrated in *The Field* (January 27th, 1945), planned by Le Corbusier. Here the white geometrical planes of the walls and their polished strips of window sheeting are all plain, and blend with the austere whitewashed farms in the distance. The tall tapering yews; stunted grotesque attempts at topiary, whether the evergreen bushes are found in the graveyard growing behind the boundary walls or standing at the back of a vegetable garden to dry dishcloths on, they all tone in with the architecture and help to intensify rather than diminish the quieter green fields that curve gently over the hills.

We have then, in Wales, the perfect background, and extensive peasant democratic tradition which will harmonise with modern architecture, the added advantage of atmosphere conveyed by the sea and valley mists and the penetrating power of the white sunlight. This last condition of magnesium light alters the whole panorama of Wales so much that I think more should be said about it. It is a light which glazes every building, stone and tree, and I hope I may be forgiven if I say a few words about it, before I come to the actual requirements needed for our rural reconstruction. It is the clear condition of light, I believe, that has helped more to effect that change which exists between England and Wales than any other defect or attribute. The fresh and burnished illumination of colour is partly due to this light.

The rain, the continual downpour of rain, may also compensate us indirectly, by giving us that pure day which precedes it, which everyone in Wales must know. During those intervals the rain water is reflected back to us through a magnetic prism of light. The sea, which surrounds two-thirds of Wales, throws up another plane of light. And a third shaft of light reaches us at a fuller angle through the sun. Here, then, in Wales, we frequently get three concentrations of light, where normally most countries only have two. This third eye, or shaft of light, gives us the same privilege as many of our scattered islands hold, which are devoted to the Saints. The light magnifies, radiates truth and cleanses our dusty spirits.

With every home a separate unit and centre of the nation's culture, we should endeavour to preserve its value, and break down every barrier of hypocrisy and adulteration which certain architects are grovelling to put across. To quote from *The Carmarthen Journal*, Mr Alwyn Lloyd, F.R.I.B.A., when referring to post-war rural housing, said: 'An interesting point was the placing of the range, whether in the living-room or scullery.' Mr Lloyd advised the living-room, for 'if placed in the scullery, people would use the room as a living-room. If people thought it was unsightly, there were companion ranges, which had a cover that hid the range when not in use.' But we do not want small kitchens in an agricultural area, far less the kitchen range in the living-room. Neither do we necessarily need a parlour. What are the county architects putting up for us now? And what is being addressed to the public in lectures by the authoritative town planners? Last year, in the whole of Carmarthenshire we managed to build ten agricultural cottages! My own, the one in which I am writing these notes on the kitchen table, is a two-roomed cottage which was condemned before the war as unfit for human habitation. There are other buildings in the village in a similar condition.

What are our most urgent problems then? Boldly, they are *lack of water*: often the County Council well, 400 yards at the bottom of a hill and outside the village, goes dry, and then rain water caught from the roofs is our only supply. We are worse off than our Welsh Colony in Patagonia. Yet springs are arising out of the lanes every year, water underground abounds everywhere; the water dowser has told us that much. *Lack of space*: neither the women attending to the cooking for man and beasts, nor the men and children grouped around her, have sufficient space to sit around their hearth, eat or sleep. In the 34 dwellings around our chapel I cannot think of any well-spaced exception. The width of many a kitchen is often the length of the hob, fire and oven, and, by the time the bucket of swill covers the hearth and the sheepdog and cats have placed themselves gently in front of the fire, there is little room for anyone else in the room; unless, of course, he or she happens to be an older member of the family sitting in his or her *cwtsh* all day, like a still portrait over the settle.

Dampness in all homes: this serious defect upon our health must be overcome. *Lack of fresh air*: many of the windows are remarkably small for they were built to avoid the window tax, some roughly 18in x 12in. in size. Other glass panes are what we call 'deadones', a term used for a skylight when it does not open. Other windows, that should, do not open because they have swollen with the rain or have rotted away, allowing grass to grow on the indoor sill. All these defects are prevalent in most of the agricultural areas of Wales, and can be overcome with little or no alteration to the outside structure.

But the first and most profound adjustment, in my opinion, is to prevent the increase of TB in Wales. If, instead of having to await attendance, and grieving because no room in a sanatorium is available, we got down to avoiding this tragedy by planning our own home as a health centre, this would do much to alleviate the impending disaster. There is no reason why we should not benefit by every bit of sun that graces this soil. And we could not do better than study the Health Centres at Peckham and Finsbury, where research on light, and experiments carried out by the architect, Sir E. Owen Williams, and that collective group of architects, Tector, have so successfully helped towards the social progress of our nation. I do not mean that the outline of the buildings must be interpreted into our housing scheme, but that their experiments towards capturing sunlight and maintaining dry conditions in the home would be well applied to our own sphere of domestic architecture.

A house such as the one partly built off the ground and standing on concrete pillars, by F.R.S. Yorke and Marcel Brem at

Angmering-on-Sea – an architectural feature, I believe, started by Le Corbusier – is one method of overcoming dampness, and obtaining drier conditions in the rural home. Long strips of glass extending over the whole length of the upper floors can today be drawn back to form upstairs balconies or downstairs terraces such as Chermayeff planned at Halland, Sussex. In every home open air sun-traps should be a compulsory feature, together with a wholesome water supply and damp-proofed walls. A new preparation of cement which dries similar to whitewash might improve those dwellings which are already built.

This, then, is merely an outline of the main rural problems as approached by a cottage dweller. In conclusion, I should like to stress that, besides upholding the best of our traditions in the main structure of peasant architecture, there are many sympathisers already interested in this subject; and I feel more strongly that the more vigorous and courageous drive should be devoted towards the younger architects. For the sake of our country in years to come, let us give our generation a chance to go forward, and experiment with the new building processes now being manufactured. Many of us can accept nylon for fishing lines and textiles, glass bricks, plastics and steel sheeting for aviation, cars and household use; but, somehow, when we hear that these materials are to be used for building in large quantities, we flinch.

And it is this lack of courage, great fear of change, that has resulted in our falling back architecturally since the pioneer work of such invincible architects as Frank Lloyd Wright, Peter Behren, Walter Gropius, Le Corbusier and Van der Vlugt, prior to and preceding the last war. It needed a war to jog us towards the progress and research which we have made in aviation; it would be grave if only another war – this time a civil war – were needed before we found the courage to experiment and go ahead with a style of architecture which was absolutely adaptable, and a fearless expression of our own century.

Coracles of the Towy

Perhaps the first recording of this craft was in ancient Jewish history, when Jochebed took 'an ark of bulrushes, and daubed it with slime and with pitch ... and laid it in the flags by the river's brink'. At a later date, it is known that the coracle was used by the early Egyptians and Britons, and was mentioned in despatches by one of Julius Caesar's generals; and a context from one of Taliesin's *Pillars of Song*, that he was cast into the sea in a bag of hide and left to drift until he reached the River Dyfi, seems reasonable enough, when we read that 'three missionaries, in 878, sailed from Ireland to Cornwall in a coracle made of only two skins and a half'.

Five hundred years after Taliesin, Giraldus Cambrensis describes these boats in such a way as to make us believe that the rough part of the hide was used on the outer side of the craft; so that, when men carried the coracle, they looked like a group of wild horses rearing and pawing the air. This incident is quoted by Giraldus from a famous fabler of his time: "There is amongst us people who, when they go out in search of their prey, carry their horses on their backs to the place of plunder; and, in order to catch their prey, they leap upon their horses, and when it is taken, carry their horses home again upon their shoulders.'

When carding and spinning factories arose along the river banks, the coracle men found flannel, treated with tar and pitch, a lighter material for their craft, the weight varying from 80lb when ox, cow, and horse hide were in use, and falling as low as 30lb with the new cloth. This waterproofed flannel may have been used in the sixteenth century, gaining favour as hide became rare; but it infrequently covered the wickerwork in the eighteenth and early nineteenth centuries, when most of the wool was sent over to England and the Welsh were reluctant to go forward with the loom weaving machines. In a bad fishing year the cost was often too much for these coracle men. If a benefactor could be found, such as we read in the *Book of Llanegwad*, 1798, when 'John Harry overseer do purchase flannel and other things necessary to make a coracle for John Lot', well then, good; but too often they had, against their

The Field, 5 January, 1945.

better instincts, to use a substitute. This was canvas, a heavier cloth and not so durable, as it was liable to crack.

In 1870, a courageous coracle man (it needs so little to tipple or send a staff through the boat) started to experiment with calico. This Henry Evans finally succeeded in his efforts. He lightened the craft by 10 to 15lb; and, with the help of others, he boiled together pitch, linseed oil and other ingredients, so that the cotton remained pliable and was less inclined to chip. Towards the end of the July floods, 1944, I was standing in a coracle yard overlooking the river Towy, talking with three generations of this distinguished craftsman; with his grandson David Evans, aged 62; with William Evans his great-grandson, aged 37, the winner of last year's coracle race; and with his great-great-grandson, young Evans, a 12-year-old. Each is still in the trade.

The small and black coracle of the child rested against the glistening white walls, and beside it lay six other black coracles, drying on their sides. Each, in outline, formed a primitive circle, varying individually, just as the circles drawn by Neolithic men varied in the caves; slightly blunted to face the coracle man and somewhat pointed at his back, with slats of wood adjusting and strengthening the shape. One net hung, folded in a figure of eight, inside the open cottage door, and another was stretched across the whole courtyard. The sand and white mesh was as delicate as that of the fly-nets thrown over race-horses on French and Argentine tracks, while it was shaped and spun like a tent of lace, as we stand under its freckled shade, waiting for the fourth coracle man to turn up. Two of the men were smoking and wearing collarless shirts of Welsh flannel; one had a Navy pullover and another a Navy twill coat which he laughingly told me he had bought second-hand. Their trousers were dark, probably utility, with shoes or boots on their feet, neither wearing Wellington nor rubber shoes, as their fathers had done.

The coracle, for those who have not seen it at work, is supported on the man's back by a leather strap. This runs across his chest and is attached at either end to the centre seat. On the river, the catch is kept under the recess of this bench, a second board having been nailed at right angles to the seat to form this recess. This enables the fish to be thrown behind the coracle man under the seat, leaving the front clear to manoeuvre the net or take in a fresh load. When the coracle is carried, the salmon can either remain in this recess, which in an upright position becomes a ledge, or be thread on a strip of willow and carried in the hand, a matter rather of whether you want to show off your catch or conceal it.

The damp net, when carried, is placed in a bundle on the top of the coracle, like a 'mat' of seaweed. The staff, used for 'knocking out' the fish, is also fastened to the seat and lies at the extreme right-hand side. The paddle, carried with the rest of the pack, is threaded through the right armpit and slopes down between the craft and coracle man behind his back, the blade appearing on the left side at the level of his hand, and being altogether about 5ft in length. They travelled in this fashion towards the quay of Carmarthen, down the cemented slope and hard steps of riverstone, through Jolly Tar lane, under washing lines and past caged birds, to the fresh breeze and green river banks. The turn of the tide was favourable, the red silt coming down from the Sawdde tributary, twenty miles away, mixing angrily with the gravel tones of the river bed. Only one net could be used, as the fourth man to complete a pair of nets had failed to turn up.

There were three things that astounded me. The swiftness with which they entered the coracles: the second leg entering the bottom of the boat almost before the first; the lack of interest from passers-by; and the winning way in which William Evans, with all the excitement and intensity which is felt at the start of a race, paddled out with his right hand and held in his left, high above his head, the leading line or head-rope of the net. This stretched across the width of the Towy like a finishing tape.

Meanwhile his father, David Evans, shook out the remaining net and stemmed his craft almost to a standstill by working his paddle in a figure of eight. If a salmon swims into the net, say, one similar to that caught on the Wye a few days ago weighing 48½lb, it remains in the stronger mesh first, and is quickly drawn up by the coracle men to form the first pocket or bag. Later, if the salmon has not already escaped, it is encouraged to enter the lighter mesh and second bag, from where it is deftly drawn into the coracle, despatched with a staff and stored under the wooden seat. 'Funny if we caught one straight away,' one of them said, as they levelled up with each other. And, with the net subsiding into position, they travelled downstream rapidly out of sight.

And what had we left? Pastoral meadows on the one bank grazing cattle and sheep; butterflies flitting among the agrimony and soft rush at the water's edge; the hard line of the Roman Hills; further distant, the limestone ridge of Llangyndeyrn, with its square-boxed chapel resting like a full-stop on the horizon. But near? What changes break before us. The Cow and Gate milk factory, railway signals. Harries' Towy works, galvanised sheds, Joseph Rank, flour merchants, the new Carmarthen bridge. Perhaps, soon, a new coracle: lighter and tougher than the pair now floating downstream, one nearer to that fashioned by Jochebed, a coracle covered with synthetic textile made from the cellulose of reeds, and machine-sprayed with ICI plastics.

Craft and Upkeep

The number of coracles in use is counted by the number of nets. The River Towy, having eight to ten nets, has sixteen to twenty coracles. Other coracles are also in use on the River Teifi, at Cenarth, near the site of a salmon leap; at Carreg Cenen, not far from Llandilo; on the River Tâf at St Clears; and one at Laugharne, owned by Richard Hughes, the author. But, as David Evans who made it said, 'I doubt if he goes out in it.'

When in constant use these craft last two seasons, about the same time as a net. This does not include repair. Holes are often seen deliberately cut out of the upper rims of the boat, so that the material can be used for patching the lower parts of the coracle which are in contact with the water. The reason for this is that the calico is already prepared and seasoned, and therefore quicker and firmer to use. The whole operation consists of melting down the patch with the flame of a match, when it immediately adheres to its original cloth, and fills the gap.

It is during the winter months that new coracles are made and nets are breathed. The yard used for storing coracles and drying nets is also used for the preparation of hazel strippings, slats of ash and the black job of covering the calico with pitch and whatever other ingredients particular coracle men wish to use. The calico is cut to shape inside the cottages and, when possible, in one whole piece. War has interfered with this possibility. Scarcely any cotton is available and, when it is, it is often too narrow and requires many coupons. If white calico is unobtainable, then flowered cotton or gingham is used; and the amount required today is about 5½ yards.

The slats are of ash and are curved to the traditional shape; they are tacked together and lie at a distance of about 6in. from each other. The whole wickerwork is strengthened and bound at the top with thin strippings of hazel, which are as hard to find as the ash, and sometimes willow is substituted. They are either plaited, eight to ten strippings, such as I saw the Evans family make, or twisted in much the same way as wheat is bound into sheaves. It is when this frame or skeleton of wood is completed that the calico is cut to its size; and the tighter and more skilled the fitting, the more riverworthy the coracle will be. This is often the women's job, as it is also the greater part of her contribution which helps to breathe a net. A coracle, if it is well made, should be up to 120lb in weight, and, if William Evans is right, 'should never sink, even if water reaches right up to within a few inches of the rail'.

Either from coracle men or in snatches of conversation at the 'Sloop Inn' and 'The Jolly Tar', I have come across quite a lot of information which might have otherwise been withheld.

These details are characteristic of the Towy coracle men. I remember one day, the water was not dark enough for the nets. The coracle fishermen went for a drink and left the coracles standing in the lane, resting on their sides. It seemed inconceivable to me that some child or other did not tear the calico or even want to take the coracle on the river and try it out for himself. 'No, they won't touch it; they're used to seeing them around.' But I was thinking of the natural curiosity of the evacuees.

It is not always wise, I was told, to land with the first catch of salmon or sewin. 'Better stay along, otherwise you're giving up the pitch to the next man coming downstream, and he no doubt would sooner run over your pitch than stay for an escape out of the net.' Quite often there are fights between the young and old as a result of these pitches. Their fishing hours are limited, for many of them have been conscripted into factories. They can fish at night, and, provided the tide, weather and month are favourable, this is exactly what they do. They drift down the river, sacrificing their hours of sleep, and remain until the early hours of the morning. The only sound in this drift of darkness is the sound of their voices. 'By them I know whether 'tis a good catch or no.'

As for their instinct in finding the new shifts of sand in the river bed, treacherous quicksands, small whirlpools large enough to upset the coracle, strong tidal currents, no scientific training could teach them this. J.G. Frazer in the *Golden Bough* has noted this: 'Now they tell the depth of river or sea bed by the smell. By the smell of the sea bed found on the lead; or by a strip of seaweed caught in the hemp. They will tell you whether the water is shallow or deep.' Another quality these coracle men have retained is certain idioms and old Welsh words which are forgotten today. In the official guide of Carmarthen, which I suspect was written by the late George Eyre Evans (founder of the Carmarthen museum), a reference is made to this effect, which runs: *Gwar bach y gored. Gored* means a weir for taking fish, and is a very early Welsh word, found in one of the poems in the "M.S. Black Book of Carmarthen", *circa* 1159 '

I have left the bread or breathing of the net until the last, as well as the coracle man's homestead. This is usually of stone, limed white outside, and consisting of two rooms, sometimes containing a loft or one room above, with the staircase running from one of the lower rooms. Victorian settings, with King Edward or Her Majesty still on the columned walls; a rack of underclothes airing from the ceiling; plush curtains and table cover; hearth black as the coracle; mantel shining with a strip of metal; a dresser of many jugs and plates; and, a great pride, just now I am thinking of one home in particular, a pincushion in the shape of a heart, studded in design with glass coloured beads, and set in a glass box. In such rooms, on winter evenings, families sit preparing the twine for their nets.

The first mesh, shaping the bag or pocket, is made from cow-hair. This is either bought by the pound or is given by farmers who have a soft spot for salmon and are willing to diminish the tails of their herd in part exchange. About 5lb of cow-hair is needed for the breathing of one net. Horse-hair was once used, but preference is given to cow-hair, as it weighs lighter when it lies wet in the coracle, and scarcely holds any water, drying very rapidly. The length of each cow-hair varies, the best are 12in. long, or more. They are twisted into strands with a wooden winder, and then about three to five strands are again twisted to form the finished twine, which is then knotted. The second bag or pocket is made from hemp, when obtainable (if not, from cotton), and is white in colour. The two are joined in such a way that, if spread out flat on the floor, they would form one large circle, the headrope threading through the outer edge of the net and running on eight or twelve rings of horn.

In conclusion, I should like to give two reasons for my article on the coracle. The first and least important is, because most information about coracles is out of date. Take the 14th edition of the *Encyclopaedia Britannica*: 'Coracle, a leather-covered wicker boat used in Wales.' That is all. The latest edition of a South Wales guide book refers to coracles of canvas, and the few postcards of coracles are over a hundred years old. And the second reason is, to complain about the scarcity of calico for the coracle trade, and the injustice of the men having to give up eight coupons for every coracle made. Should not we encourage rather than stint this balanced craft? Cannot the Ministry of Fisheries or Board of Trade be their bene-factors?

The Welsh Dragon

Queen Elizabeth sent out a royal command in the sixteenth century to correct what was then a 'gullimaufry' of the high standard of literature demanded by her Court. Her dissatisfaction was not with the talented Welshmen about her Court, but with those Bards and Minstrels of North Wales who called themselves poets. They were little more than tramps and caused havoc when canvassing their verse. She granted twenty licences to those successful in the Bardic Laws and metrics of their time, with the right to sell their poems from door to door if they wished.

Today the situation is reversed. It was not long ago that a mother whose son had died young, went round with a large wicker basket selling his slender book of poems like a gypsy queen. Villagers bought her wares because of her pride; or because they knew the young man. A year later a minstrel walked down the middle of a mud road singing his 'penillion'. Later, in the Black Horse, his dramatic powers brought those present to tears, for this was a minstrel who lived solely by his songs and so they had to be good. But the general trend among the younger Welsh poets is to play safe. It is, then, with Celtic sorrow that the bell must be tolled. But chiefly as a warning. The true fire and the religious zeal have gone, and it is nowhere more apparent than in the derivative work of the younger Welsh writers – more apparent among those writing in English than those writing in Welsh.

In the poetry of the last year or so, it is the sweet rural voice that is raised, but by poets who have never carted manure. They are pastoral poets, romantically set on their object like the Elizabethans, but without their technical skill. They are inclined as well to dip into the Bardic Cauldron instead of preparing their own 'cawl'[1] and learn the metric ingredients. Mr Dylan Thomas, Mr Vernon Watkins, and one or two others save the situation. Mr Dylan Thomas's *Collected Poems, 1934–52*, are to appear shortly with ten new poems, and Mr Vernon Watkins, a poet of integrity, has just had his Heine translations published in America. He continues to

The Times Literary Supplement, 29 August, 1952.

write poems, he says, but at 'glacier speed'. Among the others, Miss Lynette Roberts published her second book of poetry last year. Mr Roland Mathias[2] published a second book of verse likewise, and Mr R.S. Thomas issued his own book of poems *An Acre of Land* at the reasonable sum of 3s. 6d. The critics have given his work considerable support. He is a poet who knows his limitations and wisely keeps to his own field. His first book of poems, *The Stones of the Field*, was published by the Druid Press.

In the magazine world, *Wales*, edited by Mr Keidrych Rhys, whose simpler lyrics are not unlike those of Mr Thomas, ceased with the Druid Press. *The Welsh Review*, edited by Professor Gwyn Jones,[3] no longer exists. *Dock Leaves* has struggled up, and is proving a wholesome contrast to the dying magazines strewn over the arterial roads of Great Britain. The editor is Raymond Garlick.[4] If any literary magazines survive it is usually because the editors have changed their character from monthly or quarterly publication to that of an annual. This has happened to *Y Fflam* and *Llen Cymru*. *Y Llenor*, a Welsh magazine which is similar in academic approach to *Scrutiny*, is to reappear under a new editor. In Wales the majority of publications are in Welsh. Besides the Welsh Digest, *Y Crynhoad*, there are also quite a few children's books, and even a comic, *Hwyl*. Then there are two newspapers, *Y Cymro* and *Y Faner*, which must also be mentioned as they carry so much creative work in their pages. They can be said to be the source and pulse of current Welsh literature. Incidentally, the Welsh community in Patagonia have their own newspaper, *Y Ddraig Goch*, and publish most of their books in Argentina. They hold as well their own Eisteddfod.

If current Welsh literature is cheaper than it is in England, this is because the Welshmen refuse to pay more. Bookshops are badly hit by this fact; but even more through the vast organisation of the County and National Libraries reaching far out into every desolate hamlet. At the opposite end of the scale, however, the Gregynog books must not be forgotten. These were never cheap because they were published as works of art in themselves; the death of Miss Gwendoline Elizabeth Davies, one of the two sisters who founded this world-famous press,[5] has revived imperishable memories of its great days.

Among the younger Welsh novelists, many books have been published in the last twelve months. It is possible to recognise a certain ability in their work, but not yet to pass a final verdict. It will be interesting to see whether they are caught in a flood tide of easy success, or prove their resolution by hard and original work. Messrs Rhys Davies, Geraint Dyfnallt Owen, and Rowland Hughes, author of *O Law i Law* (now in translation), are some of the few who write out of their own hearts.[6] Mr Rhys Davies's novel *Marianne*, based on a Welsh theme, came out last year and was recently transferred to America between the shiny covers of the Popular Library. Professor Gwyn Jones has assimilated in his prose what Mr Graham Sutherland described, when he painted in Wales, as a 'quality of light that is magical and transforming'. His novel, *The Flowers Beneath the Scythe*, *The Prospect of Wales*, and the cheaper edition of his part-translation of *Mabinogion*, all contain that transparency of vision. Mrs Marion Roberts has contributed a wholesome autobiography about the struggles of a Welsh farm, and though she cannot be considered as a young writer, this is her first book. Mr Gwyn Thomas has varied the mood by writing a humorous novel, *Now Lead Us Home*.[7] Mr Richard Vaughan, Carmarthenshire-born, followed his first novel, *Moulded in Earth*, with a swift second, *Who Rideth So Wild*. He and Mr Islwyn Williams provide fresh blood. And of the two, Mr Islwyn Williams is the one to stretch and apply that Celtic imagination which is a heritage of the medieval tradition. His novel *Dangerous Waters* takes us not off the planet but under the ocean. The prose style is fearless and direct. It does not succumb to any temptation to create a self-conscious literary style. Another novelist who has helped to bring in fresh vitality from an outside source is Mr Norman Lewis.[8] His book on Indo-China, *The Dragon Apparent*, was highly successful last year. Another travel book of his is shortly to appear, on Burma. He is a talented writer whose novels are his best work. Mr Emyr Humphreys's third novel, *A Change of Heart*, is also vigorous and well-written.[9] Among some of the best younger novelists writing in Welsh should be named Mr T. Rowland Hughes (until his recent death), Messrs Geraint Dyfnallt Owen, J. Gwilym Jones, G.E. Breeze, Miss Elizabeth Watkin Jones and Mr Tom Hughes Jones.[10] Geraint Dyfnallt Owen is a scholar, so that his novels always have a traditional and historic sense; *Dyddiau'r Gofid* is a sequel to *Nest*.

Among the flood of topographical books which fill the bookshops Wales is strongly represented; but not at the level of Geraldus Cambrensis, Pennant or Borrow. Mr Tudor Edwards's book on Wales is authoritative by right of his position as surveyor of historic towns and buildings in Wales. The two volumes on *Wales* by Miss Maxwell Fraser are also excellent and the result of many years of research and travel. Professor David Williams's *Modern Wales* is reprinting. A book on Cardigan, by Mr T.I. Ellis, the first of a series of thirteen books in Welsh, is just out.

To take us out of our insular selves there are Professor Mansell Jones, who has brought out serious studies on *The Background of Modern French Poetry* and *Baudelaire*, and Dr Pennar Davies, whose recent article on 'The Dilemma of the Welsh University' should be compared with Mr Ivor Lewis's article 'Welsh University Intelligence'. Mr Aneirin Talfan's critical work has also attracted much attention.[11] Some 80 plays have been written in the last year, but these again are mediocre.

Many Welsh writers have not been mentioned, but however wide the net is stretched it is unlikely to include a higher proportion of the forceful and the unexpected. For what the Welsh dragon lacks at present is fire; and before the people of Wales can rest content with their literature – excellent though it be – the younger generation must rediscover the source of that fire before the particularities of the Celtic imagination are once again submerged in an Anglicised culture.

LITERARY MEMOIRS

Wyndham Lewis 1948

Portrait of Lynette Roberts by Wyndham Lewis, 1948. By permission of Walter Michel and the Wyndham Lewis Memorial Trust (a registered charity). Original drawing on long term loan to the Courtauld Institute of Art Gallery.

Tea with the Sitwells

Sept 2nd. '43

Yesterday, a wretched day of my life. A day which has worried into today and still leaves me without peace, or any clear definement of what I think on simplicity with regard to verse. We were to meet Edith Sitwell for the first time. For a small tea-party: the invitation itself was out of order with these times. However having washed Keidrych's 1943 shirt, I had no facilities in this boarding house with which to press it. Neither was I able to iron my own lawn blouse, I therefore rushed off to Barnsdale Road and did it there. Keidrych wore his only second suit pressed by me [illegible], his only pair of shoes and strange and very beautiful red/bottle-green tie which, with the surface texture of the wool and the thin interwoven thread of deep red, a mellow shade was acquired which is to be found in old winebottles when the red of wine still remains to the sides of the bottle. I wore a black dress which I had two years before this idiotic war and a riding hat which I had decorated myself with the breast feathers and tail of a pheasant. The navy blue tail feathers were caught at the back of the brim and around the whole I drew a navy blue veil. I was as pleased with my hat as I was with Keidrych's tie. In clothes I had no alternative but a black costume which was tailored [for] my sister in 1938 and was still rather too large for me. My cotton dress which I had made myself was at the laundry, the rest at Tygwyn, Llanybri.

Normally I would not care a damn what I wore, but with this fashion for bohemian dressing, velveteen jackets, dirt and beery flesh – I was determined not to look poverty stricken, wretched to the discomfort of many. My hair was straight to the shoulders and we arrived too early. Early enough at the Sesame club 49 Grosvenor Street for Edith Sitwell to be there. She was not downstairs. We were sent up past a corridor of two slab cakes resting on a ledge and through huge mahogany doors where 'reserved' in large letters made what I knew would terrify me appear more precious than ever. We were announced, to find no one. There were many small

Unpublished typescript.

tables dotted and laid with white cloth about the room. No doubt cut-ups of some large Victorian damask. We walked over to the cool and ornate marble piece to find spread over the whole surface Edith Sitwell. Madame Tussaud. Wax. Out of the past, out of a picture. I was shaken more than I had expected to be. And it was some considerable time before I could register all that I saw.

A huge crucifixion is always a barrier. Hers seemed 6 inches wide and was on old ivory to match heavier bracelets on either arm, and a huge mulatto ring of the same tone. All this weight of carving resting against a tremendous billowing of thick taffeta, which was not of today. The sleeves raising into huge mutton chops and meeting on either side around a gathered shirring of black velvet sufficiently raised to give the suggestion of an Elizabethan ruffle. One glazed and shining shoe tipped beneath her skirt. Her voice was melodious, distant and remote. Her pale eyes and silvered shading glittering over them, as she had a habit of half closing them to penetrate the object of her sight. If it were not for her folds of tender white flesh which surrounded her chin I should say she were inhuman, but her voice, flesh, warm and comfortable handshake in [contrast] to the spiritual length of her hands helped to withdraw this horror with which I was confronted. Her hat – also a riding hat but higher and of the white of death (could this be ghost of Beau Geste?). The whole outfit, which no doubt many others than myself have seen, would consider it to be a beau geste and no doubt Edith S. and her brother [would] be the first to admit it. The mouse hair drawn back behind her ears, white, but under the hat white-mauve face with its small mouse eyes and corresponding slit of a mouth. This may appear a cruel detail, but if I say of myself that I was so nervous, that in my opinion I looked like a near tart perhaps the exaggeration of both will place the whole into a vivid picture to which it belongs.

She thanked me for the *Ladies' Magazine* which I had sent her, 1784. Silence. Awkwardness. And silence. One person came in, Mrs Macpherson, the purse of *Life and Letters*.[1] Then Osbert Sitwell who I had already seen before wearing a sweat rag when he came off the Queen Mary, with my sister and brother-in-law, travelling on the same liner. Mr S. was slimmer and thank God this time looked no different to anyone else.

We spoke of the next war … I suggested that during that no doubt people would attend films of poetry with unseen voice as opposed to the poetry reading which was to take place in aid of the Chinese at the Wigmore Hall, and in which I knew Edith and Osbert S. were taking part. I said I hoped poetry would soon be filmed.[2] Edith remained silent. Osbert agreed that it would be a good thing. Keidrych suggested Dante. Edith bowed to his opinion and thought that was a good suggestion (what might Eliot have thought!). Osbert had just returned from a studio – he was arranging about one of his stories which is going to be filmed. Inquiries were made about Keidrych's work, he spoke of the government racket and we all stood for someone else had come in.

We stood up and cut up the conversation and sat down and stood up for the next two hours. Mrs Kilyham Roberts, editor of twentieth-century poetry Penguins. Old I thought, and probably not unlike what Mrs Reg Moore and Val Baker will look like in the future. Mrs Harding, society and cultural belle. A small young man who went and came within ten minutes. Constant Lambert with a stick. Robert Herring,[3] very much changed after seeing him five years ago. His face was swollen on one side, no doubt a result of this new neurosis which we all seem to be victims of one way and another. A silly woman, another woman; anyway, not many yet too many. Apart from Edith and Osbert there was no one to talk to at all. Neither was there any conversation worth remembering. The whole fashion of the afternoon was dated and fell a victim to convention – as guests we had to conform to this, as guests to distinguished literary people I should say, otherwise we would not have strained ourselves to conform. The second meeting *cannot* be the same, if there is to be any survival of freedom of thought and manner.

For one moment only there was a possibility of any interesting conversation or discussion, but this broke up with the standing and sitting process. And it was this: Edith said she was going to give a lecture on the 15th to a whole lot of schoolmasters. I said what a pity there will be no one there to disagree with you and you will hate that they will all say 'yes, yes of course'. And she had already pointed out that she was going to say that there had been no good writing of poetry since 1920 and speak of the great need of simplicity and that she was going to attack me [illegible]. I felt her judgement, also she should not remain as an opponent of our generation and I resented this, which left me quiet for some time. Constant Lambert bent forward and said I quite agree with what you say. Here then were two distinguished persons, a poet and composer, demanding a return to simplicity, and perhaps we can say of both that they are the most complicated examples of that art than we have ever had. (Of Lambert I speak with a little reserve as I do not know all of his work.)

Lambert spoke of Aragon, of his internal rhyme as they were

new. Edith told him they were not, that Marianne Moore had used them for some time. I told them both that they were very old form of metre used in the medieval period and one of the 25 codes belonging the to cynghanedd.[4] I continued and asked them if either of them knew if the Welsh or Roman used this metre first. There was no answer. I reminded Edith of the book I had sent her of Welsh poetry and hope she will now read it with more interest. Lambert then spoke of repeating the first letter twice. Again Edith said this was an old practice. Dear dear. So this frustration went on. This futility of manner and custom which was and is a barrier to all of today, for we cannot continue with it, and something else better I hope will come instead. We said goodbye. Edith said we shall meet again, and Keidrych and I raced back in the rain to enable him to get back to work as he was on duty that night in the decoding room from 6p.m. until 4 in the morning.

And so after many hours of quietness and racing mind I come to the sinister barrier of this surrealist lady of our land, whose exterior pattern I could hardly accept and were it not for the inner heart of humanity and great critical capacity for experiment with our prosody and adding to our culture I should alleviate from my brain. But now the only problem was to accept this contortion of exterior appearance, this burlesque of pattern, and dwell on the problem which arose and still worries me, at this very moment, as I proceed along the page. Simplicity. I know that the simplicity which Lambert wants is not that which Edith Sitwell means. He has made the same mistake as her reviewers. Today simplicity cannot be taken apart from its age, must be *part of it*. It is the lack of this acceptance which makes the application of the word so impossible for most people to accept. Pastoral ding dong is OUT.

Visit to T.S. Eliot

Appointment with Mr Eliot at 3 'o clock Thursday June 31st 1948
I took the two children as Prydein was his godson and this was to be
the first time that he had ever seen them. We were late, and they
were both miserable as they had failed to have their short sleep
during the day. As we hurried up Guildford Street it seemed to me
strange that the only person I should see that I knew on this four-
day visit to London should be no other than that near landlord and
owner of 'Court Henry', Lieut. Col. Audley Lloyd. I could not stop
to speak with him as we were already so late and as he hadn't
noticed us we passed on. As we reached Russell Square the Council
Borough of Holborn was busy serving up various drinks and snacks
to the odd strollers or pleasure-sitters listening to what the man in
charge termed highbrow music.

As we turned into Faber and Faber something told me Mr Eliot
was not in, but somewhere outside on the street. I looked out for
him and thought I saw a back-figure similar to his. That is tall,
stooping, and with clothes that draped casually around him. The
smiling fat and buxom receptionist said when I queried his being out
that on the contrary he was in. Almost before she had finished her
remark Mr Eliot came in. He had been out he said, but no one
knew that he was out. He was wearing a navy blue garbardine mac
and what appeared to be a new black foreign office hat. He was
thinner, younger of face and lighter in the mind. In other words in
that flash of seconds I felt he did not ponder on much of any particular thought but rather that the cloud of doubt had lifted so that he
was able to see fairly directly on any subject he wished to apply
himself too. Would we wait while he went upstairs and prepared for
us. I was astonished to see an odd collection of magazines in the
waiting room and apart from tourist leaflets to Belgium and France
what astonished me most was a booklet on *What is Communism?*
Another gentlemen waiting in the same room suggested that they
had been left there by some feller or other ... propagandist ... They
did that in the restaurants, popped them under plates and all that ...
We saw a mouse running up and down the jasmine, I picked a piece

Unpublished typescript.

each for the children, and we then went up.

Mr Eliot met us outside his lift. Angharad and Prydein were both impossible. They spat on the floor and tore up the jasmine and pamphlets of paper, they cried and fought. Mr Eliot's approach to them was maternal and apart from one or two considerations which prove this we spoke above their heads and through this frightful din. I told him as an introduction that they could both say Mr Eliot and Eliot respectively and he asked when would they be able to say Tom. He had been ill and recently recovered from an operation of hernia. I asked him if he had to wear one of those fearful instruments and he said yes. He had been recuperating for six weeks after this and stayed with friends in the country where he was given breakfast in bed and allowed to remain alone and undisturbed until lunch time. He was interested to know if I had written any more poetry and concluded quite correctly that I had not the time. He told me that though he knew I could write prose that poetry was my métier. That that was my way forward. He also knew that after such a lapse of non creative work I should find difficulty in starting again that I would become panicky ... nervous ... and that really ... one should never stop for any length of time from continuing with one's work. I asked him how he knew this and he replied that he had experienced it himself. I told him that I hoped to put aside two or three hours for myself a day and in that time start by either reading, drawing or studying. I also told him of the additional handicap which was a conflicting issue of crossroads and a decision which only I could decide; that of returning to the elemental words and simple voices of living – i.e. basic rural cultures, earth rhythms ... what we will be forced back to if that atom war arises. A cleansing purity and rebirth of sound, recreation refolding of the world such as we had the refolding of the various strata, Icelandic stone and bronze age etc. And ... hitting against that view which is one of isolation, severe pruning. The whole discordant universe, the cutting of teeth, one rhythm grating against another, the metallic convergence of words, heavy, colourful rich and unexplored. Both I feel have not been properly attempted since the concern of both projects cannot be related to one poem but requires the exploration of the respective poet's lifetime. Both would be valuable and of the two the first is probably of greater value in its relation to literature for future years.

To go back as so many of our contemporary composers have done to the seventeenth century is to escape or lean on someone else's leg. What is needed is a courageous fresh voice springing out of a fount of new fields of research. The research and experimental work has therefore to be attempted first. Now I mentioned none of these points to Mr Eliot but merely pointed out the two roads. He agreed with me that there was no standard of poetry today that the poets were concerned very often with writing a poem but not with the greater influence of poetry on a future generation. He doubted whether either Auden or Spender cared. I said of the two I thought Auden was better in this respect but that Spender had written some good poems. I suggested that it might be a good thing if we had a sound and objective analysis of contemporary poetry and Mr Eliot wisely said that he thought this should be written by a man who was not a poet himself ... but there was no one to be found. I thought that if a scientific research were made, filed, etc. that the answer would be found in the statistics themselves. He did not disagree with this suggestion.

We lightly touched on his recent lecture on Milton. I told him how it took me five months to get hold of a copy. He told me he was going to Princeton University in the autumn; but that he could only manage to get away for two months. Einstein of course had a permanent position there. He was not compelled to follow any routine but was merely invited to study on the premises using a small house put aside for such distinguished visitors when much to my amazement Eliot said he would make his own breakfast! Then work in the library, eat on the premises and retire for the night. We should of course be doing something like it in our Universities. I told Eliot not to leave it too late but to give up the work at the publishing house soon. I pointed out (which of course I realised he already knew) that it was in this way that he could best influence others and apply himself to his own work. Which I thought he must have a lot to do. He told me that he now only came in three afternoons a week, but that during the war when I last saw him three years ago he was then coming in from the country for three whole days a week. (I then noticed that he was wearing the tie that I gave him.) I then told Mr Eliot that I did not think that there was anything particular that I had to say to him except for the anxiety I felt for Mr Wyndham Lewis. I had seen him a few days previously and what had really disturbed me was a very bad drawing (chalk on what I believe was brown paper). I told Mr Lewis that I did not like it and he hurriedly explained that it was a bread and butter portrait. Well for Mr Lewis to stoop to that level was sufficient evidence of the precarious financial situation in which he was supposed to be. I asked Mr Eliot if he could do anything about it. I told him I was willing to help; but in this matter a person of authority was best. I reminded him of the help he gave Arthur Machen. He said some-

thing about Herbert Read being the person. I said I had no faith in
Herbert Read ... then mentioned Sir Kenneth Clark. And so we
came round to the British Council, CEMA[1] and Arts Council,
which led me up to the David Jones Exhibition. There was an
example of State buying. Here nearly 50 per cent of his paintings
had been bought by various State grants. Mr Eliot quite rightly
stepped in and said he was very glad to hear it for David's sake. I
agreed but said the distribution of buying should be more even and
what where they going to do with these paintings anyway ... send
them abroad? Mr Lewis of course really wanted State security and
yet would kick it away with his other leg. Say £2,000 I suggested. I
told Mr Eliot that he had had £500 advance from Nicholson and
Watson. I asked Mr Eliot if he thought it would be any good if
Keidrych wrote any stern letters to the press. But Mr Eliot said
Wyndham Lewis was difficult and that might do more harm than
good. He asked me if I had been treated well ... which amused me.

As David Jones was very anxious that Mr Eliot should see his
show I rang up his secretary and asked her to tell Mr Eliot how good
it was ... as a form of promoting. But unfortunately he was unable
to go, the Exhibition closing on the day before Mr Eliot returned
from Oxford. I told him why David was interested and that he had
thought about using the portrait of the prince in his book which
Faber were publishing. On inquiry I told him David was still at
Harrow on the Hill where he had pretty well fully recovered and
that I was sure he would like to see Mr Eliot. Mr Eliot having said
'Can he be seen?' I said 'I shall go now.' Angharad was crying
behind me on the armchair ... when Mr Eliot got up and gave her
the handcarved elephant with the broken tusk to play with. He said
that he thought children today weren't taught enough about fairies
but that he was sure mine were. They were not, so I did not reply.
He added that the children's books were so bad or some such adjec-
tive. I asked if he would like me to clear his floor of all the pieces of
jasmine and torn paper ... and as I bent down in an attempt to pick
them up with Prydein hanging from my lap ... he quickly replied,
no, that he would like them left to remind him of our visit. He took
us down in the lift when Angharad howled. It was her first lift-trip
on the down scale. He told her she was very brave. We went like
a gathering into the waiting room where Mr Eliot scanned the
magazines and said they were rather a poor assortment but that
the Communist pamphlet was all right as it was really an anti-
Communist article. I said Why have any? He said as we again
gathered around the closed door that he would like to see me more
often. And somewhere in the confusion, as I had now rapidly

become a hen collecting up her chicks, he said the name Lynette very distinctly. I did not reply Tom! Neither did I kiss his falling cheek. I did not want to make him into a grandfather. Detachment is good in the literary field.

Federico García Lorca[1]

It was at nine in the morning that I set off to see Lorca's birthplace, travelling the way that he must have travelled backwards and forwards to Granada; the dust had been sprayed with water, and nimble men in faded blue cotton kept lifting their baskets of sweets arranged with kaleidoscopic precision. One or two sweets would be bought for a peseta or two. As no one bought any, I wondered as the glassy baskets were thrust in front of me, how it was that they did not melt. Meanwhile other people waiting for the tram were pestered by shoe boys. I was waiting at the via 3 for Fuente Vaqueros, and because I had waited for three-quarters of an hour, I was convinced that we should travel by one of the less frequent blue and white streamlined tramcars.

Behind me stood Plaza de Toros, where Lorca's friend Ignacio Sánchez Mejías[2] had killed many a bull but had died in another arena. As all Spain is reflected at a good bullfight, so is all Spain caught up like a storm, consumed, and laid on paper like a corpse, in Lorca's Lament for his Matador friend. (I remembered as I waited, that sometime before leaving England for Spain, there was a cutting in one of the newspapers about another poet, Roy Campbell,[3] who was to become Domingo Ortega's picador in Madrid.) Then someone nudged me. It was one of the small neat peasant women holding a large striped bag full of her belongings which bulged against her black apron. She wore *alpargatas*, but they were no longer soled with coiled hemp, instead the factories had substituted thin layers of rubber. She pointed to the tram as it rattled and pitched towards us with Fuente Vacqueros written across the front as its terminus. The tram filled, everyone entering methodically from the same side, and taking a ticket from the conductor who perched on something high, probably an iron rod. He handed each of us some change from a heaped tray of grey centavos. My ticket cost 5 pesetas and 5 centavos. As previous rides, within walking distance of the Sacromonte gypsy caves, or as far as the River Daro at the base of the Alhambra, only cost 40 centavos, I knew this would be a very long ride and take about one hour and a half.

Unpublished typescript.

The tram as I had wrongly thought was small, shrivelled, mazy in colour and motion, so much so that the glass windows leapt to and fro, in and out of their rickety frames. Four windows had already cracked, and the molten sun poured through the glass with the strength of a lens so that at any moment a smouldering of smoke or spark might appear on someone's clothing; together with the images of the dark corridors of the houses as they flickered on the pane. Everywhere a plainness prevailed, grilled windows and a scarcity of water. Large earthenware jars over-brimming with water stood before the doors, enamel basins, and jars carried on the head. There was a drought, there had been for many months, so all the water mains were cut off from two in the afternoon until sunrise the next day. Since the time of Lorca's death in 1936, the problem of water, which reoccurs symbolically and as a vital need in most of his plays, has not changed. As the last few houses in the street deteriorate and rot the window pane darkens, there is no sun, and a strange damp-ness enters the soul.

Then suddenly, as the last remaining house bumps out of sight with the jerk of the tram, a flood of colour and free space of land and hills stretch in every direction. Plains of varied greens, containing fields of white flowering cotton plants, low unstaked vineyards; but most luxuriant and elegant of all, the tall splendour of the tobacco leaves, some of the fragrant spikes starting to flower, and the heavy harvesting of their leaves which strain each file of oxen as they sway ponderously along. The men walked slowly beside the sledge carts. Here and there, men and women dressed in orange, lilac, and indigo appeared like tropical flowers in the green setting, each with wide shaded straw hats. Some of the curing factories and store sheds were poorly equipped, having only a thatched roof supported by tree poles, with runs of wire on which to hang the leaves: other factories had developed an entirely new style of archi-tecture. For the cemented buildings were perforated with large scroll patterns with elaborate pierced carving in order to give the correct circulation of air. Beyond this rich growth of green lay a purple haze of mountains with the snow-white peaks of Sierra Nevada. Nearby, in the foreground, running sometimes to within a few inches of the tramlines, spread the ploughed red soil tilled by an occasional *puestero*, his mangy dog, or the donkey shading among the sugar canes. Then for leagues and leagues the dry desert soil would stretch unrelieved except for large boulders, when the tram became a toy and one careered wildly and disjointedly over it.

Inside the tram there was one of the civil guards singing flamencos. Then he started up with two others the current popular *estrillo 'Doce e cascabillos lleva mi caballo por la carretera, y un par de claveles al cuelo prendido lleva mi romería'*... A vineyard holder at my side, embroidered with words the face of a town solicitor as he sat splay-tailored to deliver a legal document. 'Did the vineyard holder know where the Sanchez lived?' Women got in and out at various stops, which could either be said to resemble nothing, a cluster of Moorish houses, or white square dwellings. These were stops where the peasants waited in circular groups for the tram to arrive. They would stand on the tramlines, then as the tram bore down on them they would disperse like bees, then swarm together arriving from all directions, entering in a wild scramble through every entry, crawling even over the driver as he bent for protection over the iron wheel, as though the tram itself were the Queen bee. This was particularly noticeable to me, as I had been checked in Granada for not obeying the civic rule of entering only on one side of the tram and through only one of the four entrances. It was also at such a congested stop as this that I noticed a dramatised version of an American film nailed into a whitewashed wall.

Following these scenes, a long stretch of thorns and thicket coiled like rusty barbed wire over the landscape, occasionally scattered with coloured rags hung to dry over the bare thorns. There were the strong twist of the lemon trees with their few remaining leaves, the yellow fruit fastened with strong green sap onto the heavily-laden boughs. Pumpkins like setting suns dried on the red tiled roofs. The white, then mauve-white washes on a cluster of houses with a strip of canvas or sacking serving as a door, hens and dogs with flying wings and paws scattering as the tram now reaching its terminus takes a narrow bend with added speed which leads right into the thick core of this scene. This was Fuente Vacqueros. We had stopped short of the village *paseo* where two Hobbema rows of trees extended to a point in the horizon, the dust beneath them shifted to and fro as our *alpargatas* slipped over the surface of the road. It was as though the village was built on a hard concave of sandstone, and the powder from it had been worn off the rock by the inhabitants themselves. It reminded me of some of the outlandish places in Buenos Aires where I had once lived, where trams were drawn by horses, and horses were tethered to some *boliche* post waiting saddled in the shade, where one shop sold every-thing and bartered with exchanged articles.

I was guided with much pleasure and exhilaration to the white one-floor house about fifty yards from the tram. The house with its hard uneven texture faced the *boliche*. A group had followed me and stood concerned as I tried to get an answer at the door, then they became agitated that I could get no reply. '*Pero si señorita está en casa*', I knocked again and thought of Masefield's 'listeners'. Women on either side leant out of their windows and called down to the linked patios at the back of the houses. At last someone came, it was a heavily built man of about fifty. As I turned he seemed to rise out of the sandstone rock. He bowed beaming, then took a weighted iron key from his pocket and opened the door. The house belonged or was rented to him. He had been fetched from the *boliche* where he was having a drink. As I walked down the passage over the plain red tiles, with the charcoal burner bordered in the kitchen with the same tile, I could see the sunlight falling into a passage from the patio. A tall peach tree bent over the whitewashed wall from a neighbouring garden. And I concluded, with perhaps a certain sense of reality, that more than one peach had been taken by Lorca from this large overbearing tree. The stone patio was crowded with washing tubs, mangles, buckets and cans. I neither heard nor saw any romantic nightingale as some writers have told us to believe. Apart from this stone yard – the word 'patio' really misinterprets what is meant – I saw one other room, the front room which I was told was just as Lorca had left it. It was only then that I found that this whitewashed house was where Lorca had lived, and not where he was born.

The room had a honey coloured glow, created by an all-over ochre distemper, a mellowed print and lace curtains through which the sun's rays were fused. It was bare and sparsely furnished as most peasant rooms are, containing an occasional hard chair and plain wooden table, no more. And I thought as I stood for some time in this quiet atmosphere, that here was a setting, and perhaps one like it in every house in the village, where the future mother-in-law in *Bodas de Sangre*[4] would have sat when making inquiries about her daughter-in-law's dowry.

I came out of the house to find many of the people still there. For no one from abroad had ever travelled to Fuente Vacqueros by tram. I was taken – though *snatched, drawn, pulled* – would describe my memory of the time more aptly, across the *paseo* to visit a relation of Lorca's, which to this day I cannot define. It was to see Lorca's *prima hermana*.[5] For this we had to only cross the *paseo*, and wait for a herd of oxen belling their way with harvested tobacco leaves. I noticed as I went a group of men, women and children, all sitting on top of a huge heap of maize. The *prima hermana* told me to sit outside on the chairs, which were already placed on the dusty road in front of the house. So I sat and watched. After some time, another woman was fetched. As she held one of those wicker brooms in her hand I took her to be one of the family. Lorca's *prima hermana*, not without some authority, told her to take me across the *paseo* to see Lorca's birthplace. So back I went, across the paseo, under the sunspeckled trees, again accompanied by five or six strangers. This whitewashed house was the same as the first house that I had visited. A young couple lived in it where their own children had been born. And the room which they showed us, where Lorca was born, was still used as their bedroom. It was a bedroom, meaning that it had distempered walls and a bed in it. When I returned to speak with the *prima hermana*, who was a woman of prestige with a strong personality, I asked her if she had any photos of Lorca's house. She said that Americans sometimes came in their large cars, took a photo then motored straight back. But that if I wanted to know more about Lorca I should get in touch with her brother in Granada, who had letters from Lorca, and as far as I could understand manuscripts of his as well, but I could not be sure. 'Yes, that was a photo of Lorca on her dining room table.' 'They talk a lot of nonsense about him,' was her most emphatic summing up. 'And he was not interested in politics.' 'He prepared his plays in the village, they were performed by the villagers themselves, here in Fuente Vacqueros, later they were performed in Granada.' 'He had many friends.'

As we talked, the woman who had taken me across the *paseo* to see the house in which Lorca was born, stood all this time against the kitchen door which led out into the patio, leaning always on her wicker broom. While the *prima hermana* swayed to and from as she spoke in her rocking chair. We were sitting all this time inside the house in the corner of the tiled hall with the dining room door open so that we could look directly into it, just as one might look through a window into a garden. That is how I saw Lorca's photo in its silver frame, and the silver tureen of fruit standing on a lace mat. Though we had only been together a little under an hour, I left them, as a friend might leave with many messages passing between us.

I now wandered to the pile of orange maize which spread about twelve yards over the road. Perhaps I should explain that the middle walk with the avenue of trees was the *paseo*, and the two outer stretches, *carretas* for passing oxen or donkeys laden with saddled baskets of charcoal. It was over one of these dusty tracks that the people were busy working. The incessant chatter, cries from children, and continual flight of the empty cob as it was thrown over their heads, was an annual occupation which Lorca himself must have tried. An iron wedge was held between the knees and the laden cob drawn swiftly over the blade and twisted so that in one quick movement the golden grain fell and rippled down the rising heap. As this stripping process took place, there was another person continually filling a large wooden box with grain, which held roughly half a cwt of grain. For this measure, they told me, they received one peseta and twenty-five centavos. And to give some idea of prices in this summer of 1953, they are coffee $25 a kilo, cooking oil $2 a litre, *vino corriente* $4 a litre, washing soap the crudest quality $2. And the woman at the Torre de la Vela at the Alhambra told me she received 8 pesetas a day for cleaning and attendance.

Soon the clanking of the return tram could be heard in the distance. I walked towards the tram rails as it appeared round the corner through the boughs of the lemon trees, tickets and worn white dwellings. I made one or two *passos* of one of the Bailes Sevillanas '*Mi novio tiene una novia que es mâs bonita que yo*', playing the castanets which I always carried with me for practice. '*Es una ballerina*', and they dropped their cob stripping and ran towards me. Their love of dancing, sense of rhythm is so great, that even when an imperfect movement was made, such as mine, for them there was no particular distinction, it was someone dancing, dancing because they felt gay and wanted to. And in many places in Southern Spain I saw such spontaneous steps or well known dances, sung and turned with exact timing, such as a group of children half in the gutter in Seville and gypsy children, who were waiting for their turn to play some hopscotch game danced vigorously under the river bridge. There were as well servants on the Plaza Nueva who repeatedly kept the guard busy as he circulated from one section to another to try and stop them dancing. So dancing and with one or two others, I jumped up into the tram, and with many joyous shouts, waves and signs, the tram rattled off.

On the return journey I practised the castanets or '*palillos*' as they are called in Granada, both the Sevillian and Granada rhythms because I had a lesson with Carmen de Granada. I was due for the second lesson, which I had each day in the late afternoon, but the tram came to one of those rail circles which are essential to one line tramways so that we had to stop until the second tram came along. And it was a stop. Now too late to turn up at Calle San Isidro, I decided to get off at the Gypsy Caves of Sacromonte, for after all they were Lorca's friends, and his volume of gypsy ballads *Romancero Gitano*[6] had been entirely inspired by their struggles and beliefs. From this moment onwards I became more relaxed, and saw on the return journey the wide stretch of the plateau edged with unfolding mountains as they rose out of the earth's crust. The fertile crater of another planet. When suddenly without any conscious transference I found I was out of the tram standing on top of the Sacromonte mountain with nothing but the Gypsy Church of San Miguel in sight and one white dwelling. I watched two soldiers in the distance guarding the boundary stones standing on the mountain's ridge. An old woman, the owner of the white dwelling, came out and invited me in her home. I stayed half an hour and then left. Within a short while I found I kept slipping in the dust as I tried to zig-zag through prickly cactus and in as difficult a descent as I had ever made. This was close to the old peach coloured Moorish wall which curved like a dinosaur's spine – I hope the wretched animals had spines – down and up towards the Alhambra hill. It was not the height that both-ered me, but the ways. These had only appeared because gypsies had repeatedly used the same winding treads. The whole mountainside scattered with tall cactus made it even more troublesome, as the spines are poisonous, but the slipperiness of the tread path was worse. At times it followed the very edge of the hill, sloping always out towards the bowl of a cliff face where 600 gypsy caves were built. This required an enormous strain on the leg muscles to try and keep the correct sense of gravity to stand. Anyway down this goat leap I went, sometimes on all fours, passing every now and then in a twist or leap down, the entrance to one of the caves.

These hovels are holes worked out of the earth and it occurred to me, that perhaps these gypsies were the reborn souls of all those men and women who were tortured and cast over the tall Alhambra walls. Around each of these hovels was a broad wash of lime, used I felt not for cleanliness, but in order that the gypsies might find their cave late at night. As I wound, slip, fell, slowly down the dusty face of the hill, some of the lower cave openings glittered and blazed with tourist contamination. In these few, their whitewashed walls inside the caves were covered with minute utensils in copper and brass forged by the gypsies themselves. I was not pestered. I was not followed. And anyway some of the gypsies I had already spoken to, either on the road or up at the Alhambra, where they wandered round selling castanets in elaborate gypsy costumes. When they saw that you realised that they were doing this because they had to do it to keep alive, but that they would prefer to stay on the hill and do some washing, or just be among themselves, they respected this judge-ment. Even the gypsy boys who I had passed under the shadow of the Moorish wall, played with little or no concern that a stranger was passing by. A pet bird in a cage hung from the branches of a solitary tree, and they continued and succeeded to throw stones at lizards and kill them at some distance with one swift aim. This I saw.

I had almost reached 'the moment of truth', when a gypsy came out of her cave entrance as I passed. 'Come in,' she said. I shook my head. '*No puedo señora.*' I said this, though I had intended not only to go in but to sleep in one of these caves. I then told her that I had no money on me, which was true. She said she did not want any, and repeated the offer and was very persuasive. '*Pero entra.*' I spoke to her with Spanish I could remember from my native South American country, the Argentine. This she understood. And anyway her own idiom was not purely Spanish. After a long time of mutual liking, a deep sympathy developed between us. She asked me if I would like her to dance, then and there. I said no, that I would dance for her. She liked this inverted twist and laughed so freely, that she would have enjoyed anything that I did. Within a few seconds, she was up dancing with me. Tired, she came forward and touched my clothes, she wanted my bolero. This was made, as was also the dress, in Egyptian cotton. The dress which was a Dior model had been given to me by a friend. She wanted it badly, and the colouring and design were certainly magnificent. For exchange she offered me her tribal red scarf with the fringe, which is of much significance among them. Then would I take her earrings which she was wearing for the handkerchief I had on my head to keep off the rays of the sun? I said no. So she took off her earrings and struggled hard to put them through my ears. But only one would go in. She went off stage, or so it seemed at that time to me. She went deeper into the tunnelled earth and came back with an unusually long darning needle with white thread still running through it. She took my ear lobe in her hand and proceeded to puncture a new hole. Alarmed that she had not sterilised the needle I said I would have it done elsewhere. That I knew someone who would do it. She stripped off all the clothing she was wearing except for a full skirt which hung loosely at the waist. She tried on the bolero and drew the front together over her sagging breasts. She fretted and fussed because her flesh was showing all around her waist beneath the bolero. I told her that it was meant to do this and that the effect would be very good for the tourists when they danced in the caves at night. Or, I added, as she still seemed unhappy, she could wear a blouse underneath it or a wide *faja* of another colour. This immediately said, no doubt indirectly through my suggestion, 'Could she have my blouse to put under it?' Then what would I go home in I wondered? I told her, as I now stripped a second time and handed her my blouse that this was impossible, because the police had already turned me out of Seville Cathedral for wearing this same fashionable outfit. In other words the Dior dress with the white nylon blouse under it, for the arms had been too exposed. I had been careful about the neckline but apparently no flesh must be seen above the elbow. 'Oh I could put her tribal scarf over my breasts,' was my gypsy friend's reply. That would do to get home, and she would keep the blouse and bolero. Knowing well that trouble with the police might occur in the streets of Granada I remained firm. She then understood as I did that they might accuse her of having stolen my clothes. They would not see that it was a privilege. But she loved the bolero, its clear hard blues, citrine, chestnut and grenadine red. She stroked it but troubled again about her falling breasts. So I hoisted them up and secured the front of the bolero as tightly as I could, but not without several previous attempts for like kneading bread they kept altering their shape. During this, to us a hilarious performance, with the cave dwelling always open looking out onto other mountains, where any passing gypsy could see us if they wished, a conversation arose between us about 'teaties' her word not mine, which went on for some time as it can between two women. She kept on her bolero, patting it and twirling round, then put my handkerchief, a white one, over her shoulders instead of her red tribal scarf. I carried one earring in my hand, and wore the other in my ear which she had managed to secure, thanks to her skilled efforts. And with this gold coined glitter in my ear and red tribal scarf I walked out of her cave. I recall with great happiness her mischevious smile, just one of those smiles that are there simply because they can never be hidden and the rhythmic swing of her walk charged with electricity as she waved down at me, and climbed, leaping up the rock face on to the next strata towards other caves to show all her friends. To any other person but myself, this was not an important incident, but it may prove that money among them is not everything; which is the customary belief. And I had found this to be so with gypsies in Wales for whom I had made gypsy shirts to dance in, with nomads in the Chilean lakes, and with shepherds on the Hortybagy Plain in Hungary.

Some children were dancing on a plateau before a cave using stones as clappers to beat out a rhythm. They sang and used the customary hand beats, but they had not seen me. A woman high above me, about three stratas up, stood outside her cave and looked down as she shook water out of her newly washed clothes. She threw them up so that they opened like flags, then lowered them quietly onto the thorns of the cactus plants. I noticed that her hair, and that of two other women I had passed when making those Leucadian leaps down the mountain was plastered flat with metal curlers. These would be in preparation for their *sactas*, when they would glue curls on their cheekbones and foreheads with such precision that they looked like tendrils of iron. Or a cluster of snakes that leapt and curled up out of their hair as they danced.

And so I spent the last three hours until the time had come for my lesson when I felt, that though I had deprived myself of learning another Sevillian dance – I learnt so quickly – I had instead a deeper and more natural understanding of Lorca's work:

> Oh city of gypsies,
> Who could see you and forget?
> Let them seek you on my brow
> The play of moon and sand.
>
> (Trans. by A.L. Lloyd)[7]

I realised, as I had not realised before, that *Blood Wedding* was not an intensified highly symbolic play, but just a natural event, one out of so many, recorded with absolute truth and perception, naked as the knife which flashes through the play. Having that same stark quality that Synge's plays have. His work, as I see it, has nothing to do with politics, but everything to do with the sense of justice and rich environment of the native people.

As the Alhambra fades, the colour, thought, music, and poetry fade into the surrounding landscape and into the minds of the people as they receive the vibrations. The strong Moorish influence, the cruelty, passion, and spirit of blood permeates them.

And just as we might advise a Spanish friend who wants to assimulate Hardy, to live in his forest village, walk about the fields, see his stone house, the diver bird in its streams, hear the dialect, legends still spoken with a modern slant, and see those same men covered in the red soil as they wind down from the quarry hills; so equally more satisfying by using this same method can we understand Lorca. But with how many does he still remain an exotic poet. Or a political thug or political idol, it depending entirely on which party is examining his 'entrails'. I say 'entrails', because with their limitations this is all that they see, for the natural man the poet remains unchanged.

So after the dance, high up from a minaret, with the setting sun around me falling with a sediment like fluid sandstone, red over the Sierra Nevada, catching the toothed edges of the Torre de la Vela, the gypsy caves of Guadiz rising out of the plateau like early beehive dwellings, to the gypsy caves of Sacromonte out behind this mountain over the green stretches of tobacco plants, extending always out over the dry red soil towards Fuente Vacqueros, the poet's birth-

place and where Lorca grew up. With the *Lament* which he wrote
to his matador friend, I sent his words out into the air at five in the
afternoon, it was exactly five in the afternoon: ...

There was no prince in Seville
Who could compare to him,
Nor any sword like his sword
Nor any heart so earnest.
Like a river of lions
His marvellous strength.
Like a marble torso
His fine drawn caution.
The air of Andalusian Rome
Gilded his head.
Where his smile was a nard
Of wit and of skill.
What a great *poet* in the ring.
What a splendid mountaineer in the mountains.
How soft with the wheat ears
How hard with the spurs.
How tender with the dew.
How dazzling with the feria.
How tremendous with the last
Banderillas of darkness. ...
But now he sleeps endlessly ...
Stone is a forehead where dreams moan.
Where is no curving watercourse, nor frozen cypresses.
Stone is a shoulder to carry time
With its trees of tears and ribbons and planets ...
For the stone traps seedlings and cloudy skies,
Skeletons of larks and wolves of darkness ...

Lorca (trans: A.L. Lloyd)

LETTERS TO ROBERT GRAVES

Publicity portrait by Ida Kar, taken in 1953 for the publication of Roberts's book *The Endeavour: Captain Cook's First Voyage to Australia.*

1943

8, Guilford Place, Flat 6, London WC1
December 13th '43

Dear Robert Graves,

Thank you v. much for your letter. Thank God I am at last some-what free. The article on 'village dialect' has gone to the *Wales* publishers; & now I have only to type out a few of the stories which have constantly been rejected by the rheum-eyed editors. The stories based on *genuine dialect* are good – the article I don't know? I should like to hear your opinion as it would help immensely. Anyway I had to do it to correct all the false misinterpretations found in short stories written by foolish pimps such as Henry Treece[1] & other [...] girls belonging to that rugger editor John Atkins of *Tribune* (now George Orwell).

I did not thank you for your contribution of five poems to *Wales* because I have nothing to do with it. – Keidrych is the editor – I merely enthuse him & help send out bills & enter subscribers when I can. But I did ask K. to let you know how much I liked them – some more than others. 'The Door': the simplicity of treatment & the symbol of the *door* is grave & masterful. The uncertain cadence of the rhythm: emphases on she – she – I find this poem deep in the order of symbols & very moving. I prefer this to all the five poems. 'Through nightmare' has magic & the strangeness of speech acquired by all disorientated syntax. It takes me back to some of Laura Riding's poems which I value: But it has an inner flow & peace which hers did not have. I believe Lucia[2] will bring you great happiness. Greater than you realise.

About the notes I had for you. Since I last heard from you, the [handing] off from Apollo to the White Cow & the distance trav-elled is so immense that I cannot see that anything I have will be of much use.[3] K. returned with Rolleston & Squire the other evening & they are so, (to *me*) frightful that I am not sure it is quite what you want. Of the two, the Rolleston is preferable. Perhaps you have them; if you haven't seen them they are the legends for the public with hot sensuous Celtic twilight plates & quite obscene – not in its literal meaning – but worse merely vulgarised settings (e.g.: What Layamon did to poor Mr Wace llc!). If you care to borrow these let me know & I'll strip them from K.'s shelf. I admit they would be useful for tracing any particular myth, symbol, or legend. (I am fascinated by your White Cow's circular route. There is a ref: if it is of any use in *The Welsh People* by Sir John Rhys & David Brynmor Jones – to a White Bull with red ears p. 229 (T. Fisher Unwin. London. 1900. 2 ed.) I expect you remember the story in the Mabinogion of the *white* greyhound with *red ears*: there should be some parallel here 'the hounds ... were of a brilliant shining white, & their ears were red; & as the whiteness of their bodies shone, so did their ears glisten ... (Mabinogion *Pwyll Prince of Dyfed*). And if again this is any help: in *Wales today* I've always noticed that they call all burnt sienna shades *red*. A cow's normal hide say Hereford would be *red & white*. The farms which they have (in S. Wales) – white with red doors & yard gates – are the rich brown of a cow's hide & not the colour red as we know it. There is in this same book, which I recommend to you as a *permanent reference book,* a chapter on the early laws of the *gweli gwelys beds* possessions of the bards etc.

[...]

When I was at Bedford Place June July Aug I can't quite remember when, I made a rough draft of a poem ten stanzas nearing the Englyn so that the break of the voice – lowering of tone – fell *before & not after* the line: I have yet to work hard on it – unlike Keidrych I suffer v. much when I write. Anyway the theme is the birth of words & the brief stanza breaks up into the alphabet all of which is based on the true symbols – letters & psychological mean-ings transferred & *brought up to date without* checking the *original symbol or meaning from the text.* (E. Davies.) I took the key from our friend *Rev. Mr Davies & an* eg is Y – Yew man eating his hat – isola-tion. I think this is *funny*!! The Ego or *super ego man* & then the *madness tailing off.* Hope you like this. My only respectable draft is with T. S. Eliot as are all my other poems. God knows what he will think but I am determined to put up a fight to get it accepted among all the others which he is *recommending* to the Board (this was about a month ago). [...]Now that I am free – I shall no doubt work on this poem – & will send you a copy as soon as it is finished. I even feel *if* you were a contemp: the alphabet should be done together. But as it is your knowledge & ability far outreaches mine so that in the end I should feel I had no right to sign my name.

[...]

I think your suggestion for a basic understanding of symbols & prosody v. important. It is the one thing most poets *all lack today.* They are too blown up by their own exotic ego's & too great – (i.e. Tambi, Treece, Comfort,[4] Vernon Watkins) so much so that they

would not attempt to study or progress in their own capacities.
There are many factors against the suggestion – but here at this stage
– & I'm sure Keidrych would agree with me – the answer must be
positive – we can always thrash out the disadvantages at a later
interval. The danger must only be judged at its final issue i.e. *the
work & output of the poets. If* there is any breeding or stink of group
gatherings – the whole idea is useless. I do not believe in group,
collective gatherings – this sort of thing is acceptable to craftsmen –
but not to poets.

[...]

With best wishes
Yours v. sincerely
Lynette Roberts

[...]

Yes please send me a book for my square white room: any book you
choose. If you wish a 3 & 6 second hand one. And let me know if
you want to borrow K's Rolleston or Charles Squire.

1944

8, Guilford Place, Flat 6, London WC1
January 14th 1944

Dear Robert Graves,
It is so trusting of you to send me part of one of your charts &
current information on the progress of your work. I *can be relied upon*
in this matter you will find no disillusion. I have not shown the
letter to Keidrych because I think this is better: neither did I discuss
the subject with Alan Hodge[5] – though naturally Keidrych & I
inquired after you. I think your work will be most invaluable & no
doubt through enthusiasm exaggerated – parts of your theory totally
wrong etc. etc: But encouragement *you must have* for the *impression*
that you will make on the minds of the people who will 'strike', no
doubt oppose or foolishly swallow all; can only at a later period, ten
years perhaps, mature when the whole thesis will fall into its correct
place in relation to our literature. Today we need myth more than
ever: *but not blindly,* only in relation to its scientific handling· in relation to today. You will help us here – just as David Jones is helping
us with his paintings: so damn sight better than those surrealist

writers' & painters' montage & pastiche. – I have been interrupted by a letter. A strange pleading little from one of the villagers of 'Black Anchor' Llanybri. 'Would I do a good turn would I meet his son Vernon at Paddington who has been called up & put him safely on the Gravesend line' – The child – for he is – never having left the village & the pathetic strain behind his father's demand.

And to go back to your letter – I think the difference shown between Duir Robin & Tinne Wren is most important. The Welsh as you know have the wren myths: they must find & see a *wren* on Christmas or N. Year's Day I forget which – there are I believe sayings still in existence & we certainly have looked for them in our village.

[…]

The Yew man: Your interpretation of the saying gives him a new aspect. My definition was to bring about the death image (poison) & the philosophy it entails superman super ego – in one sentence I therefore made him eat his (hat) i.e.: hat as symbol of false person-ality of head that which heightened his mind to such an extent that he ate his own self up exploded with superego & ended up in isola-tion (the equivalent to death).

About the book – I should so appreciate one written by yourself *on poetry*. The only one I have *read* by you & have on my shelf is *On English Poetry* Heinemann 1922 –

And now I am going to ask you a favour like that old villager friend of mine. I wrote *within a month* direct on the typewriter a novel with two clear cut purposes. (1) as a test of will to see if I could finish the damn thing in a given interval (I did not consider it a good thing to spend more than a month's energy on a pot boiler.)

(2) to make money for Keidrych & I so that we could continue to write *seriously & study* for the rest of our lives without the need of financial aid.

Keidrych thinks as I do that *it will sell* v. well. Not because of the book – but because of the conditions – there is a demand & a literary vacuum waiting for a Welsh novel. The period is chosen for two reasons: because I was brought up in a French & Spanish convent & therefore knew I had the atmosphere & RC conditions & secondly because rural villages in Wales are still so medieval in craft & manner. It was observations I had made on thatching etc.: lining – I do my own for the cottage – that enabled me to write of these again & probably correctly (since the custom has not changed & because in the method there might be some distinction from that of the Engl. Med.) – There are terrible passages of slop but these I could cut alter or restrain. Would you look at this for me – & if you think it printable perhaps you would be so kind as to recommend it to a publisher!! Keidrych as you know has been ill again.

[...]

I have or shall have I believe a book of poems out by Fabers: though I am still waiting to hear the final decision of the Faber Board. I had previously been approached by two publishers for my poems but rejected them because I didn't like the gang (Fortune Press & Phillip & Unwin). Tambi also made vague hints about a pamphlet of poems. I may too collect & reuse my Llanybri fragments of which K. is printing three in the next no. of *Wales* & send these out to a publisher – *I'm not sure* – anyway these two projects are my serious work as opposed to the *Rank'ian Novel.*[6]

The photo of Nesta[7] is beautiful isn't it? [...] She is not Nesta – but the only woman I could find suitable of the period. The strange thing is her crown with its then fleur dy lys & now appearing to us P. of Wales feathers & the brooch with the Cathedral symbol of Christianity of S. Davids the Rose – single petalled rose –

Must see to other domestic duties.

I will write again sometime.

With best wishes
Yours sincerely
Lynette Roberts

8, Guilford Place, Flat 6, London WC1
Feb 10th 1944

Dear Robert,

What a wonderful surprise but what a hard gift to offer me.[8] To thank you I shall apply it as best I can to my own tortured prose; & I am thinking in particular of my effort on 'Village Dialect'. The book arrived yesterday, & because of this I resented keeping a dinner engagement when I would have preferred to read quietly by the fire. So I can only make a few comments. The beginning is so well written & defined – clearly stated – that I can follow judgement & criticism on Eng. Lit. when in *Epilogue*[9] I often find the prose horrible (in margin: This is a personal judgement & not critical. I shall have to find out why I find this trouble over a number of the articles in Epilogue.): as horrible to me as the prose of 'Dialectical Materialism' so that unless I can overcome the obstacle of the particular style, either by understanding or submitting to its structures, I can never hope to appreciate the ideas or argument

which it carries. Another e.g.: of what I mean is this. I bought I.A.
Richards' book sometime last year it cost me a hell of a lot of
money at the time I brought it home to read & found it so foul in
style – *foul to me* – that I couldn't understand a word of it.[10] So I
took it back [...] within twelve hours & asked if I might change the
book as the prose was so unreadable. I know this book of yours can
help me a great deal. I know further that it will give much enjoy-
ment, fury & stimulation. The 'Fair Copies & Comments', the few
I have read, are covered with human & penetrating satire. These no
doubt permit them to exist on the page, because if I am to be
truthful to you, there are many many occasions when I would
prefer the obscurity, ambiguity & all the wrongs of the original
paragraphs. For me, too many resemble those paraphrases of poetry
which are made in school – & in which the original poetry is so
much better however vague or secondrate than the extended &
scriptified prose. Such exactness & rule for prose is good for a
fundamental knowledge & for extended knowledge into criticism,
clerical work, reviews, journalism but in *no way* should it be
allowed to arrest the unlimited ways of using prose, anymore than
poetry, which has fundamental rules, should be *bound* to them. And
I believe this is what you & Alan imply.

[...]

There is so much thought & study behind most of the prose
writing in Epilogue that I shall have to read the articles & poetry
occasionally & v. slowly. I am so happy to think they can remain on
my shelf, as they are obviously something to read & enjoy more
than once. We need such criticism today – more than ever – but
unfortunately chaos has penetrated our minds, all writing & art.
(This is a wicked generalisation & to some extent is more applicable
to the younger generations only.) How long will it be before reaction sets in? I see John Betjeman (the new 'Priest' of the middles[11])
is making an effort. The Devonshire parsons of the nineteenth
century have given him a tip. Did you see his poem in *Cornhill* or
even his book reviews in the *Daily Express*. They (the Tory
stooges) are going backwards to go forwards, because they have no
courage, creative, or staying powers. They will even YET bow to
the middle-class mind before they are rejected. And we, God knows
what will happen to the young writers who feel in anyway independent. Your judgement on Politics in your letter & further the
article on Poetry & Politics in Epilogue gave me much courage & a
realisation to some extent that I was right – even though friends
succeeded in making me quaver by saying I was escapist, not socially

conscious, etc. etc. For these are almost the last things which I want to be.

[…]

Everybody is mad here in London. And the last thing permitted to any writer is that he should be allowed to sit quietly & study his own job. Tambi: goes round quoting Paul Potts[12] whom he is going to publish in book form … or as at Empson's party recently for the Chinese Legation he waved his arms & having made his usual declaration '*I am the Great Tambimuttu*' he went up to these & told them 'that emotionally he much preferred the Japs'. – No one has a job – Keidrych, George Barker, Tom Scott, Julian Symons, Ruthen Todd (has but he wants something better than selling books to customers.) Glyn Jones, Neville Penroy Thomas (previously assist Editor of *Woodgreen Observer*). All are registered at M.F.L. but for weeks nothing has happened. O yes there is also that sad dejected Maclaren Ross out of a job. […] They are v. miserable – dogmad.[13]

Nesta is mostly v. bad prose. I have plenty of patience – plenty of will – but I'm not quite sure that the damn book's worth it. I tried to keep it transparent, simple, & clear, & *I am afraid* that it may become laboured, heavy, awkward in patches, if I try to alter or improve it too much – I think cut – cut – cut – might be better. Take out the slop. If I *had mastery over my prose,* which I haven't, I might attempt a complete rewriting. I see progress in my work probably three or four years' study & practice will be necessary before I can put any statement I have clearly on paper.

[…]

I gather that you would like to have all Edward Davies' translations of Taliesin. I'll inquire for you. What puzzles me is what does he mean by I was born 'Under the region of the summer stars'. As the legend carries the tale in various versions that he was shipwrecked & found in a coracle, or like Moses cradled in reeds, I have often wondered if it may have meant under the Southern Hemisphere or tropical stars.

I do thank you again for the gift of books. They are, & will be, most treasured under my care. I feel too, that not only I, but all young writers would do well to read Epilogue again. With me, I read it for the first time. For as much as I tried I could never procure a second hand copy. K. of course had some copies but they were stolen with many other of his books by the socialists!! I wish to God you had analysed that bête noir of mine Hugh MacDiarmid or is it a pity to give him publicity! The sun is beautiful in this room & I must now do some work.

Lynette

N.B. I am especially proud of the American edition of *The Reader over your shoulder.*

8, Guilford Place, Flat 6, London WC1
[wrongly dated] Jan 26th '44

Dear Robert,

With all your own work, rush & concentration of it, I somehow feel v. ashamed that I should have bothered you at all with the wretched Novel.[14] But with Keidrych out of a job – no health insurance, or pension, & not much hope of the ulcer healing, I thought perhaps I could make some money to cover our financial insecurity. Your just criticism & judgement will help. I shall no doubt exclude my modern voice. Revise *Nesta* ruthlessly, & the *time* situation which drives Nesta & her lover apart. Potatoes! I had no idea that they were not introduced until the sixteenth century. There are so many other wild plants belonging to this same family that I thought they existed before the Britons. Fuchsia – it grows wild in Tresco Scilly Isles. There is the ruin of a monastary there, & at a time when the monks travelled so much thought I might accept the idea that a cutting had been raised from one foreign bed & sent to S. Wales. I especially wanted to stress the warmer climate ... the vineyards which S. David's possessed, the excitement in growing a flower which the monks had never seen before. With your help I now realise I must either pull this plant out or define *why* it is there. Simnel cake – this was a favourite with the Brothers of S. Francis of Assisi & as the Eng. trans. was taken from a ms of circa 1250 thought this entry of diet not only characteristic but also probable of the time. There is I *believe* also a ref. to simnel cake by one of W. Bards when attacking the monks.

Did I tell you Keidrych has started a publishing firm, he has found someone who is willing to put up £200 – a young farmer in Cardiff. The firm is registered 'The Druid Press'.[15] K. intends to bring out a book of his own poems, about six essays on Wales by J. Cowper Powys who has already sent the MSS, & given his consent & various other projects. He is much happier organising this though I have pointed out that he may have less time in which to write – *or will it give him the incentive.*

I have read more of your prose book & think it should be established in every school here & in B. Council Culture Centres abroad. That publication by Otes Ferguson interested me a lot. There are quite a number of poets contributing to jazz which I get ... Nicholas Moore[16] ... Ruthven Todd. You write a poem & you call it Blues – the rhythm doesn't matter in fact it often has flat feet.

[...]

Epilogue: I did not mention Laura Riding.[17] And would never isolate her prose from the various other representations in *Epilogue*. I have discovered my personal prejudice. It is that the rather dry & heavy verbal phrases used to convey ideas & thought. This isolation of words from the human & emotional element of man, *for me*, only conjures up one thing – the Law – solicitors – & their fearful cryptic world.

[...]

I do hope these poems please you as much as they have me – if only in re-reading them. The cattle passing over the dawn. The sun rising on the water like a herd of collected cattle. This image is so good if you have seen it as I have when the outline of thousands of heads stretch over a dull wet plain.

Let me know about *Lit. of the Kymry* if you want it. Otherwise don't trouble to write.

With best wishes & thanking you very gratefully for all your trouble, time, & thought in giving me help.

Yours Lynette.

8, Guilford Place, Flat 6, London WC1
March 28th '44

Dear Robert,

Keidrych thank God is better. Consequently I am too. He has been v. difficult. He is at Cardiff at present making contact for his Druid Press. I miss him v. much, three days' separation seems v. long. David Jones[18] is writing (has almost written) an intensive article on Welsh Visual Art. And you I hope will also graciously send us something. The reaction to *Wales* 3 is that *serious articles* are more appreciated just now than any story or poem.

[...]

Churchill's speech sounded like a Tory losing fast – fancy letting the world know of his fear of Aneurin Bevan & his gang. Why not give him a job to absorb this restless energy.

I miss my cat & I hate my poems.

I heard C. Day Lewis read the other night. He is like a temperate book on a shelf. We dined tog. previously with the organiser [...] His fear (I think I am right in saying) of being bombed is *so great* that he has withered away – submitted to death like Alun Lewis before his time. I mean by this during his living life. He wondered to me – if he shouldn't stay at the M.O.I. instead of Kensington. His poems – a great many of them harp on death in *Word Over All* – Have lots of work to do for Keidrych – general correspondence –

Hope the enclosed pleases you,

Lynette

8, Guilford Place, Flat 6, London WC1
Saturday [c. 7 May] – '44

My dear Robert,

Thank you so much for writing to me. Yes of course keep those books a while longer. I had written to you about a fortnight ago thanking you for being so generous to allow us to publish your article in *Wales*. But somehow the letter became knotted & remained unfinished. I did not read Part 1, & was away when the proofs passed through London previous to their being sent on to you so, I cannot discuss them yet. Personally I think you have done a damn useful bit of work. And even if certain old professors refuse to agree to your answers & the solving of these symbols – at least you will have provoked them. In fact they will stimulate the whole complacent face of Wales including Charles Williams's 3rd rate knowledge on Taliesin! I understand your fury at the barrier all those people of authority put up. They *refuse* to help, & are even reticent in allowing you to see the *original documents*. Idris Bell was like this when I inquired to see early books of 1606 at the BM. I disturbed him in his iron cage, no doubt he locked the gate *twice* after I had left him. As I have said before, the authentic documents should be photographed & printed off, & be available to every person interested in studying them. To have the only rare document say in the BM, fails in my opinion when those living outside the area cannot see it, and Christ, the jitterbugging of poems of even established poets has had me astray quite recently. I thought the Golden Treasury & Ox. Bk. of poetry pretty reliable and from it quoted Sir P. Sidney 'My true heart' which *is* printed as a rondel – only to find that it is a sonnet the last four lines omitted in the two former anthologies. Now which of these is right. Anyway the rondel & sonnet were so interlaced as far as I can *see* that the misquote is not so serious as it first appears.

[...]

I have lent David Jones two books on Celtic Inscriptions in Gaul by Sir John Rhys: one is the thesis, the second the corrections on his first statement. It is in these that there is a photo of Apollo's thigh with the inscription & acknow. to him as their god. David will forward this to you at my request as soon as he has finished with it. (He has your address)

DEOAPOL
LONUS XV
X CABFUN

Would you be interested in a thesis on the *Thorn Tree* by Vaughan Cornish D.Sc. This tree doesn't come into your symbols or is it part of gorse spindle O for sun for pain Christ on Cross.

I envy your son going to Wales. Hope he gets that tile.[19] What to do about it? Write about it – connect up all the legends (have it photographed if you can't get hold of it ... to study). A reading into the probable poetry from which it came & please hack that idiotic & sentimental story about Gelert ... with which Cabel is connected – I refer to the dog that was shot for killing the child when it really killed the fox & saved the child – as opposed to that of the Mabin. It could no doubt be brought into your part Section on the Dog. I suggest if Sam can get hold of it you keep it in the house in your study & eventually give it to the Cardiff Museum when you can no longer look after it (i.e. say if you go abroad). The Museum is cool, spacious, & well tabulated: the Poets section being particularly good: (i.e. med. folklore) & has a better situation & background for Welsh objects. I believe there is mention of paw tile found in Strata Florida or thereabouts in a book on Welsh Cathedrals published by G.W.R.!! I have it in Llanybri – but not here.

Sweet of you to send Keidrych a book on T. it hasn't arrived yet but no doubt will this afternoon. (It has just arrived May 8th.) He is the person to do it, & has as well a damn high standard to compete with (I refer to Giraldus Cambrensis & John Pennant) (Borrow I *loathe*). But he cannot write it here: i.e. within one room, we shall have to find a larger flat. I wish K. would consider living peacefully in Wales: in a larger house say near the Aberystwyth Library but he won't. I cannot say I am happy in London

[Page missing]

see from his last air mail. [Alun Lewis[20]] believes the poems of his new book to be not v. good. – He above all people resented deeply being called the Rupert Brooke of this war & in my opinion intensified the lack of action in his physical & spiritual life (especially through military period) (For he never saw action, not even as much as K. on the Dover E. Coast.) by using […] cuts & visualising himself dead – half dead – about to be – In analysing only ¾ of his poems in *R. Dawn* I find fifteen contained references to the death wish. Tributes to him are [ornated] & out of all proportion to all the other poets which we have lost. This to me shows our degradation of literary standard more than anything else: & though I knew him, perhaps better than those who have spoken of his loss – I prefer to remain silent rather than add to this disfigurement of false praise.

Keidrych has just come back. And as neither of us have had lunch (it being about 3.40) we must eat.

We both send our love to you.

Lynette

P.S. It may interest you to know that it was I who chided Keidrych & Alun (by letter) concerning this publication of poems with Fortune Press. Both had even got so far as having delivered their MSS with Crooked Caxton. But with my persistance both managed to get their poems back. Caxton wrote to me asking to publish my poems but I *never* answered his letter.

8 Guilford Place, Flat 6, London, WC1

October 5th 1944

Dear Robert,

Thank you v. much for your letter. Your MSS on bardic mythology was left in Llanybri. I believe I wrote & told you this, that I felt it too uncertain at the time to bring it up to London owing to the flying bombs. I doubt if I shall be returning to Llanybri for a month or two: could I leave it till then, or shall I try & make one of the peasants understand where it is & get them to send it up.

[…]

I have no idea of what arrangement he [Keidrych] has made with you. But I doubt if *any* can be made until he has either more paper or money. At the moment we haven't even enough money to consume all the paper ration that is given to us: & what is *over would not* be sufficient in my opinion to publish anything except pamphlets. *By this morning's post* Keidrych received a letter from Kemsley House suggesting an interview for *next week*. If he is lucky then he may get both more money & paper, anyway he will let you know. Keidrych is better, but not fit [...] No, our problems are *soluble*, & I believe quite different from Laura's & yours. I think little, or nothing of my work at present, & Keidrych thinks even less of it. But I have the guts & faith in myself to continue: & this more than half solves our problem. The second half will be solved either when Keidrych gets down to writing regularly (as you do) or when or if he gets enough money to carry on easily with *Wales* without the restriction of limited shillings & financial worry.

[...]

I have kept an entry for you from the Lit. Supplement which no doubt you have seen. You will have to excuse the grease & food on it. I threw it away & then remembered I needed it. My book of poetry'[21] should be out soon: it has already been advertised by Faber. I now want to do some experimental work *(not necessarily for publication)* & will in the next few months get a room to work in, either here or in Wales.

[...]

I heard at the Polytechnic Spender, Day Lewis, Barker, Roy Fuller, Macneice, Lehman all give readings of their poetry. Day Lewis & Macneice excelled. Day Lewis safe & traditional with a quiet rendering – Macneice bastard-looking: excellent delivery of sinewy & satirical verse. *The general image*: Kisses, kiss, bluey sky: general impression: lack of rhythm & form.

Let me know about your MSS whether to have it sent up or wait until I go to Llanybri.

With best wishes to you & your wife.
Lynette

8, Guilford Place, Flat 6, London WC1
Nov 1st 1944

Dear Robert,

[...]

Keidrych & I saw David Jones last night. He has just returned to London, looked v. thin, & has been ill again – too ill staying while at the Pigotts to write or paint. He mentioned that he had had a letter from you which he had neglected & not yet answered. T.S. Eliot gave a lecture on classicism at the Virgil Society: also two others in Wales Bangor & later one on Minor Poets at Swansea. Eliot says: 'nothing can be done with Wales for another 50 years!' He too looks – grey & pained. Then from David's, after speaking about T.S.E. we visited the Glass's[22] – There Jane was ill in bed recovering from – what the doctor, thinks might have been flu. Douglas looks distracted with too many orders which he cannot cope with. Jane needs a good rest. In fact Robert there seems to be a general bout of neurosis springing out of the most unusual people.

[...]

I hope your MSS on bardic mythology is published soon. I should like to read it in print. *That is read it as a whole.* Read in sections, when it is published in *Wales*, I find it hard to understand ... but that is probably because I know so little about mythology.

[...]

Shall pack & post off your parcel now.

I should like to send my best wishes to Beryl if she will accept them. In fact I hope to meet you both someday.

Good luck to the publication of *The Roebuck in the Thicket* (a wholesome title). & see the publishers state in the contract *how many* they will bring out & whether they will reprint if necessary *if not* give you the right to hand it over to another publisher. There is a lot of that going on now.

Best wishes,
Lynette

8, Guilford Place, Flat 6, London WC1
Dec 18th 1944

Dear Robert,

Forgive this long delay; but I have been waiting to hear from Fabers in relation to the comment you so kindly sent. So far nothing has turned up – but I have no doubt that they will both accept & print your praise. It is good & generous of you to have offered to have done this for me; & coming from you who are not easily hedged into praising or giving criticism which you do not believe – I would thank you Robert most gratefully. *Concerning what you say about 'Orarium',*[22] the poem was written straight off – almost subconsciously; though that which I expressed in its final phrase is something which I had accepted & believed it *intuitively*: not through my study of mythology or penetration into science. I did know however that sorrel hair was a characteristic of most prophets so instead of using that same image I introduced sorrel chest to imply the same. The rhythm & syntax was influenced by a reading of Anglo-Saxon writings which I had been studying the previous week in order to try & find out what *were* the first Saxon rhythms to be used: that is Saxon as opposed to the early Celtic schools. [...] I was glad to hear you found pleasure in my Llanybri poems. I especially wanted to write well on the *curlew* & had admitted my failure to Eliot before publication. I think the idea is good & result quite appalling. I shall attempt this again but how I don't know. I *did* want to get the feeling of frustration in relation to the bird's imprisonment & lack of wholesome environment *in relation* to all peoples living in this world today. I tried to use the exact [qualities] of a curlew's call which so often breaks with those four shrill notes — — — — Shagreen-bleat is *bad* as you point out. I had in mind the shagreen quality of its legs – the greezing gooseflesh ring of its voice. When writing simply I see that it is better to get the correct word *once* than use compounds. In poetry which is rhetoric & largely consists of metaphors – I believe this adulteration is permission: it is also correct in the poetry based on the technical Cynghanedd schools.

Cwmcelyn – I don't know? I have given Alan the whole 175 stanzas to read. It is a long heroic poem. I cannot change it; but I believe a stricter technique would have reduced the poem & clarified what I wanted to say. On the other hand it would have been less pliable & adventurous & may have constrained that which I had purposely set out to do: which was to use words in relation to today – both with regard to sound (i.e.: discords ugly grating words) & meaning.

I think this third section of 'Dog Lapwing & Roebuck' will clarify the issue for a whole lot of readers who are perhaps wondering what you are up to!! It is I believe the easiest to understand. Having finished *The Golden Fleece* & without *any* classical education I do find it much easier to now follow your 'Roebuck' thesis. It enables me to see the world pattern of mythology with a slight modification in each country. As an ordinary reader

[Remainder of letter missing]

1945

8, Guilford Place, Flat 6, London WC1
January 5th 1945

Dear Beryl & Robert,
– This is a letter from both Keidrych & I to congratulate you both on your newborn son.[24]

[...]

Edith & Osbert[25] are still up in town. Keidrych & I have seen them both alone & at one of their tea parties – a larger one than usual this time. Edith spoke well of you, & she wants to be friends with you(!) She said she – 'never quite understood why we stopped being friends.' – She further asked us when writing to mention this fact to you. She has been v. human & good to Keidrych & I in a quiet way & we appreciate this v. much. There is much stress in their family. A law suit to be shortly called which may mean the loss or gain of their Lord father's fortune. Osbert is thin & looks v. worried. The tea party at the 'Sesame Imperial & Pioneer Club' was overflow from a private show of John Piper's work at the Leicester Galleries. He has been painting [Renishaw] environs with a view to illustrating O. Sitwell's new autobiography *Lefthand Righthand*. I do not like his work ... though it has been explained that his dramatic qualities & black sky are suited to [Renishaw] since it is surrounded by mines & industrial soot.

Yesterday I had (*at last*) an amusing letter from Eliot. He first spoke of the quotation you so generously gave me –

'This (i.e. quotation) must have given you great pleasure & is also, considering its sources, very gratifying to me. What I mean is that I think Graves knows what he is talking about' –

He then continued to tell me a tale about Francis Thompson & the ghost of Chatterton in relation to a rather worrying & peculiar p.card we sent him for Christmas.

Excuse writing – p. office pen – haste to catch post – have been addressing envelopes most of the day.

About your poem[26] Robert – It reads well & easily with a natural cadence & I especially like the stanzas 2-3-4-7 – & naturally the connecting links between the first stanza, & end of sixth.

I do hope Beryl will regain her strength quickly – will you give her my love & take this letter along for her to decipher when you visit her in Hospital.

What I should like to know is *what flowers?* did the great boar trample down in ivy time.

Forgive this scrawl – Keidrych & I both send you & Beryl our best wishes for 1945.

Lynette

Tygwyn, Llanybri, Near Carmarthen

My dear Robert,

This is to thank you for your serious & kind acceptance to be Angharad's godfather. And I feel quite sure you will have plenty of opportunity, with Beryl, to help her through various crossroads & emotional crises.

[...]

A young minister & poet has been here. A gloomy sort of person – who like most intelligent ministers today doesn't believe in the church that he preaches. It is the people far more than 'they' who have the conviction – & wish to join in communative praise, or prayer – But *not 'them'* – the yg ministers, who have the courage – guts to alter &set the old time stage of religion to modern conditions. They are bastards & I am 4 square behind you in this matter. He is *R.S. Thomas* & has gone to St Davids with Keidrych with the idea of rambling & enjoying the countryside of Pembroke which he does not know.[27]

The Christening was as it should be – for me – it was in

[Remainder of letter missing]

1947

Llanybri thawing out March 17th 1947

My dear Robert,

I've got to that pathetic stage where I can't remember if I have written thanking you for the pound note you so kindly sent Angharad for Christmas or not? I know I have attempted to write several times but more than once have been frustrated by some domestic routine.

[...]

Yes I know that Pryderi in the M. was not the same. But I do think that the spelling and magical application which the name and story has been given is founded on one of the original great leaders of Britain ... I did read your reference about P. in one of your essays printed in *Wales*.

I also enclose a snap of Angharad taken previous to the great white blizzard. She is holding a proof copy of Keidrych's NEW FORMAT for the next number of WALES. We had a tough time for a few days. We were snowbound and Keidrych with the CC's consent organised a gang of amateur roadmen to shovel a way out. These were to be paid, and men and women (in all fifteen) came along. They opened up one road with drifts (the highest twelve feet high) and by the third day the milk was able to get through driven by tractors. We were out of coal one day but that was more a nervous discomfort for the mother rather than a cold interval. I should stay where you are for a while as most things are hard and getting worse. A visit in the summer is not so bad as you would not feel the lack of fuel ... only the lack of a QUICK hot meal. We are luckier than most in that respect and Eliot, from whom I have recently received a letter, thinks 'just at present a hard rural life, once one is used to it, seems preferable and at least more dignified,

'Photo of Angharad aged two, now at Ivy Cottage as we had notice to leave Tygwyn owing to it being sold to another buyer while we were in it. Here she is holding her father's new cover for *Wales* magazine. And this is the time when the "bullcows" as she termed them continually seemed to get loose.' (See pp. 80–1.)

than a decayed metropolis accustomed to amenities which are
ceasing to be possible. But apart from the lack of heat and deteriora-
tion of diet, we have no water in my flat at all at the moment, and I
wish I could go out with a pail to break the ice on some wee burn
and boil a kettle over a peat fire.' Of course one doesn't take a pail
one takes a heavy 4 gallon churn or two galvanised buckets (as you
know). As for getting water the damn thing is naturally frozen up
and we all wait at home until we are quite desperate hoping that
some other farmer will be more desperate than us and go out before
us to light a fire and thaw out the water. To use a boiling kettle is a
waste of time.

In the way of writing I have done nothing. But I still have an
ardent PASSION for *penillion*.[28] I want to write *penillion*. I should
like *penillion* sung at my son's Christening. As I cannot write it
myself ... I cannot even attempt it owing to pressure of work ... I
am trying to persuade others to write it for me. Last night I coaxed
Keidrych. I believe it is the most authentic and most wholesome
material from which to build up any rural poetry. It is never sentimental in its original state... and there is far too much of this sappy
quality in the Welshman today. His singing is BAD and not good. It
is far too emotional and lacks both restraint and dignity.

I do read your poems and a few others occasionally. Your poem
'To Sleep' I cannot help comparing with Sidney's; then too 'Theseus
and Ariadne' and 'Lament for Pasiphae' recall for me some echo of
the Elizabethan poetry. 'Twelve Days of Christmas' is daring and
fresh. I think your poetry is exceptionally valuable because it stiffens
up the too journalistic and limp defects of most modern poetry
today. I like the strength and direct statement, of your poems: the
mastery of line and word. I mean by this that there is pleasure, wit,
and meat to be found in a single line of your verse, and not a pulp of
ersatz with one anaemic idea thrown in at the end 'And the worms
ranged and ravaged in between' ... 'Their groans and whispers down
the village street ... Soon soured his nature, which was never sweet.'
I like the staunchness, grit and biting power of your poetry as I said
before. The concentration of time and meaning ... compression of
thought. APT. To the point like the old Bardic men. Their minds
were weapons and they used them as such.

My son who refused his feed at 6 a.m. is now impatiently waiting
for me to attend to him. The time is 10.5 and another day March 18.

My love to all your family and especially to Beryl. This is a miserable disappointed letter but at least it is completed, do share this with
her if you wish.

                                                                Lynette

1948

Ivy Cottage, Llanybri, Near Carmarthen
18-1-48

My dear Beryl & Robert,
A Happy New Year to you both & to all your children. First & most urgently, I *do* hope no MSS of yours Robert have been affected by the Hamish Hamilton fire.

[...]

I have one *tremendous longing* & it is certainly NOT FOR HEAVEN it is to get back to my poetry: to leisure & to peace of mind intervals of 4 & 5 hours, away from the children, husband & all domestic cares.

I was interested in your judgement of R. S. Thomas.[29] I look upon him as a rival 'on the field'. (Not seriously though, as fortunately I have never felt envious of other poets.) He is too much the vicar musing on the what he terms boorish farmer. I think too you sensed a real failing when you say his poems do not stir you. He is so DEAD. The embers after a fire has extinguished. The embers in a vicarage grate. He requires mountains to move him. But I have many dislikes in poetry but none are personal. I find other poets v. admirable *perfect* because of their limitations.

I had a letter from Rhys Davies & he says a friend of his saw a lot of you both in Majorca but doesn't mention any name. I have never written so freely as when I stayed in Madeira. I think it is the sun, perhaps partly v. partly the wine, – *& detachment* from all other countries & culture. The Island enigma.

[...]

K. & I. both failed to get an A[rts Council] Award. I have no idea who has succeeded.

[...]

With love from us all here. The sky has been transparent blue cold, the trees bare hard rather brittle, the ploughed land is *red* silurian when we all walked *today* along the Chapel Road.

Lynette

Ivy Cottage, Llanybri, Near Carmarthen
July 30th 1948

Dear Robert,

I have been foul in not writing sooner. However much I try I could never recapture the enthusiasm and draw I felt towards your book. Of course it has taken me a long time to read through *once*; and before I can really understand it, I will have to reread and look into it on several occasions more. Thank you very much for this book. I thank you also for being so generous as to mention my name in the Foreword. The opinions at the end of the book on poetry so provocative. Your challenge and discovery are wholesome, and no doubt the bald-brained bards will rail at your 'encroachments' this coming week. (The N.[ational] Eistedd.[fod] Keidrych is holding a tent there 12 foot x 12 foot.) I like the return of the gleemen. The book is so full of wit. Something which we have neglected seriously in poetry.

[...]

I took the two children with me up to London. I was there only five days but managed to see David Jones' Exhibition of paintings. Wyndham Lewis in his studio, and Eliot. Eliot told me he was fascinated by your book. He is going to Princetown for two months. (he can't spare more time) to sit like Einstein as a superior beast. He told me he would have to make his own breakfast in the cottage or shack allotted to him. Wyndham Lewis, who I spoke to for two solid hours, or rather he spoke to me, was not rude – as everyone seemed to expect. He is bringing out three books shortly. On the Americans (god help them). On himself in relation to certain reviews and critics; and a small book on liberty and freedom.

I must catch this post if the letter is to go off today. I now have leisure. Every afternoon off since I returned from London four or five weeks ago. I have written much ... pent up lines and images which have been locked away. The unfortunate part is that because of this they follow their own pattern. This I cannot alter. I have tried. Even though I have determined in my mind to keep an eye on form. But I think after a month or so I shall relax and then set about what I want to do with both my conscious and unconscious mind. I'm sending you two or three poems to read. I have about ten. In my opinion I am not sending you all the best. I'm glad you are bringing out a critical work on Poetry. I have one of your earlier books on this subject. Bought it second-hand for a bob.

My love to you both, Beryl and Robert, and all your family,

Lynette

1949

as from Ivy Cottage,
Jan 2nd 49

My dear Beryl & Robert,

[...]

I find the cultural standard of London appalling. With the exception of one or two good Italian & French films there is nothing to see or digest. Most of the Painting Exhibitions are put up boys. The established Lit. papers disgraceful. The prose heavy & three times as roundabout & involved as T.S. Eliot's which is saying a lot. *Horizon* has been on the market but it is true that C. Connolly has been on the continent five mths & a friend of mine Sonia Brownell (their sec.) carries on singlehanded.

Jan 12th 49 A Happy New Year to you all from us now at Llanybri. Last night I read some of Siegfried Sassoon's Collected Poems & found them v. good. I enjoyed one I noticed which was written to you using your Christian name.

We saw Alan. I for a short while. I think Keidrych more than twice. He has married happily I think & seems to have matured, though I detect, perhaps quite wrongly a frustrated streak to his nature with regard to writing. I think his work may shut it out. I saw Eliot, & called round at Faber's about 6.05 p.m. after putting the children to bed. The medal & illuminated parchment had just arrived & apart from Faber the chairman & one or two late staff stayers I was the only person to see it.[30] As it was going to the bank I concluded that I would be one of the *few*. He is undoubtedly proud about this recognition. He has consented to *consider* another collection of my poems, which I hope to send him in the near future – but its so damn hard to get a moment – good if I get it! He – Eliot – as far as I could gather did little or no writing in Princeton but he found it stimulating.

[...]

I wish K. wasn't tied to *Wales* & the Druid Press. I wish he would sell the Press & keep *Wales* the magazine. It only seems to bring in the most terrible debts [...]

Love Lynette

APPENDIX
NOTES FOR AN AUTOBIOGRAPHY

Lynette Roberts's passport photograph, c. 1935.

Notes for an Autobiography
Selections from an unpublished typescript[1]

[…]

From England my mother sent a cable to father for money. He sent some straightaway. Then we wrote letters, Win and I, confirming Mother's statement about Mrs Barwell and Miss McClachlan's drunkenness and irresponsibility.[2] He wrote by return telling us all to go back to him in Buenos Aires except Dymock who was to stay at Wykeham Boarding School [Winchester] and go for his holidays to Mr and Mrs Hitch in Worthing. This news about Dymock grieved us all but our father would see him during his vacation every two years on his return to England.

Our mother had nothing suitable to wear. Mrs Hitch had some model dresses she no longer wanted. 'Would your mother like them?' My mother tried on a beige striped velvet dress. The stripe was 3 inches wide with some stripes of silk lying upwards and others lying downwards. The neck was scalloped with three-quarter sleeves, tight fitting with a hobbled skirt. Of course it was out of fashion. I told my mother she looked wonderful in it, and she did. So she bought it. She also bought a black taffeta and chiffon model dress. But what I liked best was to see her in an emerald taffeta evening dress. It was bouffant and draped. The black dress she would wear with her jade necklace and earrings.

Mother was excited end nervous. She hadn't seen our father for several years. I was eleven years old, Win ten, Dymock eight and Rosemary five. […]

We arrived and were all hugged and kissed except Mother. Father just said Hello to her! We felt it after all she had done to save us.

Our first house was comfortable but too far out from Buenos Aires. My father had to take a tram journey pulled by horses to the nearest railway station. One night a panting servant arrived from an estancia: 'Would Señor come immediately the lady says two gauchos are fighting with knives trying to kill each other!' These gauchos were more ferocious than the peons. They would fight to death using their left arm with a poncho wound round it as a shield. My father took a light carriage and horse and went immediately. He stopped the fight.

We were in this house only a few months when we found some-thing vastly superior. Ramos Mejia was out on the railway and had its own station. The house had a hedge all round it like Mechita. The gate and side panels were high, made of strapped and scrolled ironwork. On the left was a small dwelling for the gardener and his wife. They were making tomato purée on huge hair screens and drying the tomatoes in the sun. On the right a tennis court. In the middle was an avenue of fir trees leading up to the verandah of the bungalow. Left of the bungalow was a windmill and well to the right lay a green wooden hut where the servants slept. In the front of the house leading to another road was the most beautiful acacia tree, or Wattle as mother called it, we had ever seen. The fluffy catkins were as large as marbles and covered in pollen, the grey leaves feathery and soft. Everybody remarked on it especially Alfredo the gardener. Here mother had her same old treadle sewing machine as in Mechita. Father had his double bed, and we had our upright piano, with the pianola fitted to it. Mother had in a separate room, her single bed with the silver backed brushes and comb. The kitchen had charcoal fires until mother bought a paraffin oven as well.

Soon we were to go to Boarding School, to the English school in Buenos Aires. Meanwhile I had a talk with my father. We walked together under the avenue of fir trees. Did he know what Mummy had done for us in saving our lives?[3] I told him. 'I never realised' he said. Would he please take down the photo of the lady on his bedroom wall – it upset her? It was an old love of his called Nora Sloan from Glasgow. He was moved. I asked him to forgive me for talking to him like this. He added 'We'll see what we can do.' A few days later my mother called me 'He loves me,' she confirmed. 'And he has taken down that photo of his first love.' 'How do you know?' I asked. He invited me to his room she said happily.

Mother was a different person. She didn't care that she couldn't wear the hobbled dress there was always the black one. We went around the garden together and stayed by the acacia tree. My mother told me about her relatives the Williamses in South Wales. About the *Geelong Advertiser*, how a relation started it, and how Harrison founded the Ballarat Grammar School for Boys and Major Williams of South Wales, Narberth, who was in the Grenadier Guards or Queens Guards, and there were Davies in South Wales related to us. 'It's so hot, I'd love a cold drink from that well. Ask Alfredo to bring us some.' She drank it and said it was most refreshing. 'Would I have some?' 'No thanks Mummy' I replied. I was not 12 years old.[4] The well had never been used. My mother got ill. She lay in bed and said she knew what she had. I made her some scones on the paraffin stove, she loved them but would eat nothing else and only drink coffee. The doctor ordered her to the British Hospital in Buenos Aires. How would she get there? She was too ill to go by train so she would have to travel for about four hours journey in an open Victoria coach and horse with Mrs Dudbridge, a friend of mother's from Mechita. She was coaxed down to Ramos Mejia by my mother. Rosemary was away at the time. Only Win and I remained. To show you my sister's courage she kissed my mother goodbye. But I couldn't. I just stood back and said 'Goodbye'. She had typhoid.

★

While Mother was in hospital I had two days in which to get us ready for the Convent. While we had to wait for our vacancy in the English School our father had put us in the Convent of the Sacred Heart. Nine bed sheets were required. With a small flat iron on the charcoal fire and chromium shield I ironed nine sheets. I shall never forget it and told all the nuns I came in contact with. They put up their hands as the old lady who made mud bricks did in Mechita and as the gardener put up his hands again in Mechita when he found I had bitten into the tomatoes. They were all surprised.

We wore silk navy blue blouses with Peter Pan collars edged with white lace and white mother of pearl buttons with navy pleated skirts and black strap shoes. White stockings. On Sundays we wore white silk dresses with veils and white gloves. We had to bath in long cotton garments so as not to see our naked bodies.

I didn't learn much at the Convent but won a gold medal for the piano and did some elaborate hemstitching. Win was always ahead of me in lessons. Rosemary was consoled. A strange thing would happen – the nuns kept asking us to go into the chapel and pray for our mother. Of course we prayed for our mother and I couldn't understand it. Then my father called to see us. He was greyhaired and shaken. He told us mother was dead. He was shocked and told us we must be brave. We were silent and cried alone.

He didn't send us to the English School in Buenos Aires because they had an outbreak of typhoid and he was afraid. He would have to send us to boarding school in England and this for him meant extreme loneliness.

To England we went and joined our two cousins Fiona and Alison. We went to Bournemouth High School for Girls, and there we wore vests, liberty bodices, navy bloomers with pockets, navy gymslips with white blouses and navy braid sash. Alison and Fiona were both very intelligent and well ahead of us in class. I learnt nothing except Botany, English Literature and History. When I had my first book of poems published I sent Miss Rowe, the literature teacher, a copy. She had done so much to put life into Shakespeare's poetry and prose. She was an inspired teacher.

As a relaxation I journeyed with my father in his touring Bentley. It was a beautiful green, with long strapped bonnet, cupped seats and wire wheels. From Bournemouth I found myself in the Lake District there he took me to the home of 'Peter Rabbit', 'The Tailor of Gloucester' etc. It was a dark panelled house, and the illustrators were small and lively. We drove North West to Plas Newydd and Betws-y-coed and to Ruthin on the River Clwyd. It was a small town made up of painted black wood and white plaster similar to Elizabethan times. 'Your grandfather was here,' my father remarked 'and so was I for a time. I stayed with Col. Cornwallis at the ruins of the Castle.' I said to my father nearly every butcher is a Roberts. My maiden name and the name under which I wrote was Roberts. Then picking up three new fishing rods we drove on to Scotland, to Gleneagles golf course. We left the Bentley outside the golf course and went in.

When we came out everything in the car had been stolen. All his new fishing gear. On to Glasgow. In Coatbridge my father said 'Stay by me and you'll get a surprise.' I waited. Who should turn up but Nora Sloan. Not expecting us she didn't blush but turned red. My father knew that every Tuesday she'd take the tram into Coatbridge to see if there were any letters from him at the AA club. She was married and had a young daughter who had fits and who needed a lot of her mother's attention. We parted.

When we got back to Buenos Aires as a relief from mother's death we all went to the Chilean lakes. We took a long train journey then went by car, taking another long journey to the Lake NAHWEL HUAPI. There in the bowl of the mountains were two signs of humanity. A plain wooden rectangular house where we were to live, near to it on a slope a wooden hut with one white horse. Facing the house the glacier lake was to the left. Mrs Dawson had three girls all young up to the age of thirteen. None of them had gone to school. They had never seen a train and would ask us what a cinema was like. They were barefoot.

My father went down to the Lake to fish so I went with him. There he pointed out to me, like peering through glass, a huge fish. It was a salmon. Neither of us had seen so great a fish. He tried coaxing it with spoon and red wool. But it was asleep.

Later Win and I joined the young ones to ride bareback down to the lake. We used lassoos and bolas. I managed to catch a calf. As in polo the direction of the horse is maintained by the pressing in of the leg with a slight movement of the body to the right or left. As for the long manes which the ponies had you just grabbed it.

The sides of these mountains had caves and Mrs Dawson when she had time had explored them. On her mantelpiece were the results of her work, worked beads, golden necklaces, earrings, a rib with an arrow through it and many other things I cannot remember. One day I went out by myself. I wandered through the tamarisk and green bushes and over the thick grass to the tributary of the Glacier. I saw a man bending down over the water shaking a sieve, panning for gold. He was looking for more gold. I spoke to him and told him he would find a greater quantity in the caves.

'An Inca, the last,' said Mrs Dawson, 'lived in that hut with his white horse. He comes over every few months with something he has made and exchanges it for 4 kilos of maize flour. I saw him once at the door, his face was like the outside of a walnut shell. He had in his hand a beautiful pair of magenta and pink moccasins with elaborate design of leather and gold relief.' 'Where did he get the gold?' I asked Mrs Dawson: she was silent. Then I said 'How old is he?' 'He's been here since I can remember, but we can't speak to each other – he knows some ancient tongue.' One night it snowed lightly. So we went out to trace the prints. Soon we traced the puma print right up to the house. 'They don't hurt man,' Mrs Dawson said.

I collected stones from the Lake, they were various in colour and could be seen clearly through the pure Glacier water. There were purple amethyst, orange quartz, turquoise, green copper and several pyrites.

I read that the Incas if they shot a white man buried him upside down and that is how Mrs Dawson found the skeleton. Then I was inspired by the expression where 'the sun tied up' 'lion grass', and Haravec the tribal poet, so wrote the poem 'Xaquixaguana'[5] [...]

For one holiday Fiona and I hired a cottage in the country and went bird watching. I illustrated the book and wrote most of the comments. When we returned it was handed in by one of the Girl Guides and I received 1st prize out of 500 people, for the most original presentation. It was highly commended by the Headmistress, a Miss Stocks MA. My father heard about it and gave me two signed copies of W.H. Hudson's *Birds of The River Plate* to encourage me.

Win spent her holidays on a walking tour with Alison, the eldest of our cousins. Sometimes for holidays we went to my godmother Aunt Lyn or we would go and be with Dymock at the Hitch's in Worthing. They were tomato growers and liked Dymock to help them in the glasshouses. But my brother though young had the makings of an engineer or electrician. He wanted to finish the wireless set he was making. He was thirteen years old. My grandfather became blind and I would sit at his feet when he explained that he found there was a God because of the glorious structure of the body.

He also told me how we must all get to the top. Herbert his son was now Harbourmaster of Sydney Harbour. 'Your Dad is doing fine, he'll get to the top.' Then how he had travelled from Wales to Australia. How my father was born there and how long it took to travel and what endurance it required. He continued my motto should be *Nil Desperandum, Never Despair*. He died and left me his grand piano. No one remembered this, so it was forgotten and put up for auction. Then they remembered and it went for £12. I gave my godmother the piano as I had nowhere to put it in school, and she gave me the £12.

Win and I each had a boyfriend. During the holiday at the Worthing we would motor, the four of us, in a Morris coupé. Win kissed freely with her partner but I did nothing. We went to the Worthing Pier where they had a swinging dance floor. This was made especially for the Charleston. We could stay out until 9.30 but had to be back at 10.00 p.m. ... One day Win's boyfriend said to me: 'Why don't you kiss him? Give him a kiss.' So I tiptoed up. He was taller than me, and kissed him on the lips. 'That's nice,' he said, 'do it again,' but I didn't. His name was Harry Leades from Sandhurst and today he is the Queen's Prize Rifle Shooter. We wore short evening dresses above the knees and used curling tongs on our short bobs leaving the back shingled. We wore makeup too and silk stockings and strapped semi high heeled shoes.

★

Dymock my brother was happy, he said at Wykeham. And liked by his rugger team for his courageous and swift play. He played Wing. He was also very keen on Test Cricket. One day he was found breathing in from a gas jet. It was disturbing. No one could find out why. We did know that he had seen a girl on the beach who he fell in love with. A pretty girl, daughter of a vicar, called Gwen. He managed to say a few words to her but that was all. Then at the

Christmas holiday at my grandmothers, he told me he wanted to learn the piano to play hymns, would I teach him? He wanted to be like Jesus. He wouldn't go to see Pavlova, but preferred to go to Midnight Mass. He came to me. I could sense my brother's urgency. It wasn't a crime, but he was adamant. I told him it was too far to go. He relented. I was worried about him. Win and I went off to our cousins the Sankeys. Geoffrey Baldwin Sankey was a barrister at the Inner Temple who had a twin brother. We were to stay just for the Hunt Ball. When we returned, everyone was silent. Then Doctor Charles Cowie, my godmother's husband, said quietly, 'Your brother is in the asylum.' When I questioned him he said Dymock had torn the sheets and 'thrown a record at your father'. 'That wasn't very serious,' I said, or words to that effect, then he added there was no hope – he was a schizophrenic. Our lovely brother. At the end of my heroic poem I wrote:

Mourn murmuring – remembering my brother
His cathedral mind in Bedlam …
Distrained – mallowfrail – turned to where
But today which is tomorrow[6]

After lots of persuasion from my godmother, Alison and I went to Queen Alexandra's Hostel, London. She studied music and I studied Interior Decorating at the London Central School of Arts and Crafts. The Hostel was situated next door to the Albert Hall and each Sunday we could get in free and hear the first performances ever played in London. No boyfriends were permitted without a description of the person and if approved certain powers were granted to meet him if it were allowed. This didn't bother either Alison or myself. At the Central I enjoyed it, designed and made printed textiles, carved two wooden panels, did a wood sculpture of two bears I had sketched in the Zoo which I gave to Rosemary. In carpentery I made a traditional table of my own design and had it french polished. For my father I made a cedar lined cigar box, finished in natural figured walnut veneer with a thin edge of ebony, it was very successful. I also learnt gesso work and gold leaf application.

[…]

Although I did not speak much about my brother I never forgot him. I was his favourite sister. He was moved from the asylum in Bournemouth to Manor House, Salisbury Although forbidden by Doctor Charles Cowie to see him at the asylum I was determined to try the Manor. I went from London by train. I was apprehensive. He had made me a metal box which I thought hideous. It was of silver metal, hammered out in small blows leaving an indentation all over the box. The box was lined and has as decoration a turquoise blue plastic lozenge across the top. The Manor was like any other large house with a heavy hedge at the entrance. I was now very nervous. I did not know what to say. The chairs were odd and varnished dark brown, the walls red. I waited. When he came in he was smiling. He was tall and slim in a navy blue suit. Yes he knew who I was. Had I received the metal box? 'I did not like it much,' he said. I was so relieved, even he didn't like it. Would he like to go out for a walk with me? 'Yes,' he answered. 'But I will have to get permission.' We talked about the family. Suddenly he said 'I must go' and disappeared. On another occasion I called to see him, this time a man in charge told me he didn't want me to come any more. 'Who was that screaming and screaming?' I said 'Was that my brother?' Not but it could have been. That was the end. Now Win took over and saw him with Eric Waldron her husband each time she visited England, that was once every two years. He has now moved elsewhere but I cannot get his address.[7]

After some objection I managed to get the consent of the Manageress of the Queen Alexandra Hostel to take out a Mr Maurice Shillington, who I had met at the Central, to Barkers for a Tea Dance. I bought a silk bois de rose dress with low sash and waist and fine pleating, silk stockings and high heels. I was very nervous and eager for success. But when he arrived all kind and smiling, the spacious Tea Room was empty. The dance floor bare! Through the painful conversation the dance band played 'Jeepers Creepers', 'O Lady be Good' and many other contemporary tunes of that time. I apologised.

After a year I went with Rosemary and stayed with Maurice Shillington at Glenmachan Towers, Belfast. He had become BBC's radio news reader and fallen for someone on another island. He had a distinguished home not unlike my grandmother's with silver tureens for breakfast on the sideboard. From these you would get up from the table and help yourself. The furniture was mostly Victorian. The curtains still laced. The maid in three-quarter length black dress with long white apron, collar and bows. The golf course lay to the left of the front door. And it was theirs.

A few months later I went to Germany with Rosemary and got to know her better then I went on to Italy, Venice and wrote my first poem. 'In these melodious hills'. I wrote it in the train crossing the Dolomites.

★

I returned to my father in Buenos Aires. He had a flat with three bedrooms in Calle Juncal. I redesigned the sitting room three piece and had it upholstered in graded grey 'rodeo' tweed. This was imported from France. The curtains and cushions were pale grey velvet. A hand embroidered long tapestry stool and Italian quilted cushions were all completed by Win and I. The carpet a deeper shade of grey. The whole effect was a quiet grey room with a rectangular glass jar of one coloured block of flowers.

Win took a secretarial job which she partly enjoyed. Rosemary was helped by Aunt Lyn. My godmother had trained and mothered her. Rosemary in turn had absorbed her teachings and become a loving perfectionist.

I had taken my mother's position and would go out with my father to the British Embassy, out to dinners and out to open, as I did once the Western Railways Sports Club, and cut the ribbons. What I enjoyed most as I loved and was proud of my father, was at a journey's end to walk along the train to the engine driver and shake his hand.

My father went on an expedition. It was to be virgin country. He was to look at the land with a view to extending the railway line. During his trip he took a geologist and water diviner. They found huge areas of petroleum bubbling up from the ground. Salt lakes and other finds. This my father filmed and sent the results to London. I saw this film and it was most exciting. He used to help everyone to improve their position. Eric Lawrence was one who he helped. Then his secretary had been with him 40 years starting his work with my father in Mechita, now he was still with him when my father was Director. A person he helped was Aristotle Onassis. He encouraged him to buy Argentine ships for transferring his oil.

It was about this time that I celebrated my twenty-first birthday. I took on responsibilities and gave instructions for the menu for the day, selecting a maid and training her. She didn't know how to place a knife and fork. She was Carmen and there is no other. The cook became ill and died. Her name was Selina.

We entertained the Directors of the Railway when they visited us. Sometimes taking the special coach to see whatever they wanted to inspect. These coaches were very luxurious. My father had springs to his bed and a bathroom alongside. One trip went nearly as far as Patagonia, right through Rio Negro, and took five days' journey. It was a new line, new fruit industry and new people and homes. It was very successful. My father as General Manager of the Western Railway and later Director was responsible for this. The cases of fruit would come to the flat to be tested. Yes, apples could grow on the soil, it was fertile, so could peaches, oranges, grapes and melons.

Only once there was an attack on my father. He had sacked a particular man. The man in revenge said he would take the lives of one of his daughters, presumably the eldest. My father called the police and they advised us, him and I to be kept in the flat and not go out. We did this for some time and were then liberated.

My father relaxed by sailing. He kept winning sailing prizes – he used the Gamecock Series III. These were from Harland and Wolfe of Belfast. From them he also ordered a large diesel engine to go in his new project, a comfortable motor vessel. With the interior design Rosemary gave him a lot of help. She had joined us now in Buenos Aires. I did not go yachting always. Sometimes I would sketch at the Buenos Aires Zoo. Thinking about this time I wrote the rondel 'River Plate' which was followed by the 'Voyage Home' and 'Royal Mail'.[8] We had on board Doreen Smiles and her husband Roderick Gregg. Noel Drabble, Phyllis and Freddie Neild, Kathleen Bellamy and many others. Once we had a Director, Lord Congleton. Win and I thought we would teach him something. So we suggested he should fish while sun bathing and I attached a line between his toes. Knowing we could regulate the fishing by the depth of the line we set the lead for rock bottom. He got a twinge in the toe and pulled up the line. Then to his astonishment heard a fish barking all over the deck. It was a barking fish.

I received a letter proposing marriage. About this time we went to English Balls. Win and I would buy second-hand models imported from France. Then later we had an excellent dressmaker who sewed in the flat. Gloves were required for men and women, and for the women a programme card and small pencil attached to the arm by a silken thread. We got over this uneasiness of not filling our cards by inviting four young men to cocktails and dinner. They soon filled our dancing cards and we were secure.

Besides travelling on the railway lines I was often taken to estancias right out in the Pampas. I would see the gauchos dwelling with their 'chines'. Their home was often thatched and looked exclusive half buried in the Pampas grass, with horses sheep-saddled tethered to a pole and fierce dogs baying. But a law was passed about this and galvanised iron became the roof of their dwelling. It was too hot. I quote the poem about this, one of my best: 'The New World'.

The New World

Memory widens our senses, folds them open:
Ancient seas slip back like iguanas and reveal
Plains of space, free, sky-free, lifting a green tree
        on to a great plain.

Heard legend whistling through the waiting jabirú,
Knew the two-fold saying spinning before their eyes
Breaking life like superstition, they too
        might become half-crazed.

Staring sitting under the shade of Ombú tree,
Living from the dust: kettles simmer on sticks,
Maté strengthens their day's work like dew
        on hot dry grass.

So the people baking too close fulfilled time,
Bricks became mud walls and the legend flared high,
Shadows broke, flames frowned and bent the sky
        proclaiming Indian omens.

Roofs fell clattering in on man and child,
Black framed their faces, from fire not from sun:
While before them land divided announcing
        stake peggers' loud claim.

Death ate their hearts like locusts over a croaking plain,
Fell tears red as fireflies on the rising dust;
Barbed wire fenced them in or fenced them out,
        these outcasts of the land.

So the people fled unwanted further on into the land,
On to the Plain of White Ashes where thorns spread
Like the wreath of Christ. Further out on to
        the ancient Sea of Rhea.

Ombú turned hollow as it stood alone:
Spiders lifted the lids of their homes and slammed them back
Sorrow set the plovers screaming at the falling
    hoofs and feet:

Cinchas bound their eaten hearts: leather sealed their lips;
Ponchos warmed their pumpkin pride: as insects floated,
As windmills grew. Ventevéo! Ventevéo! And further they
    strove, the harder not to be seen.

Lost now. No sound or care can revive their ways:
La Plata gambles on their courage, spends too flippantly,
Mocks beauty from the shading tree, mounts a corrugated roof
    over their cultured hut.[9]

About the birds. Some I saw were plenty of caranchos, oven birds, the burnt sienna ones my father pointed out to me with their remarkable oven nests. I saw red breasted blackbirds in Uruguay; also a flock of emerald parakeets. Hummingbirds are in the Argentine. Tinamon partridges which we eat, the common Rhea of the Pampas and the Jabiru. The spiders on the ground which I saw slamming down the lid of their burrows. This I mentioned in my poem 'The New World'. As I was taken along in a 'Tin Lizzie' Ford a small owl flew and fell on my lap clacking its bill to denote its anger. It soon flew away.

Mariusa Fernandez Beyro was my best friend. She had a studio and would paint still life. We would attempt to have soirées and skilled discussions. No English just Argentines were invited – philosophers, psychologists, journalists. It was very exciting. Then I went and stayed four–six weeks on her estancia. I learnt a lot about Argentine food, their cleanliness and good manners. I valued her friendship. She gave me a young leopard skin fur coat. I also had another worked in strips like mink. We had two cars and two chauffeurs but neither Win nor Rosemary nor I were spoilt.

Before leaving for England I must mention my very dear friend Robin Roberts. When I asked him to send one record from the Argentine to England he sent six by airmail. One was very successful as a background to my long Patagonian ballad 'El Dorado'.[10] It contains 120 verses and I cannot get it published thought it was recorded on Radio 3 twice. He also sent a large book of national Gaucho implements which has been very useful.

Nora Sloan decided to marry my father and came over first to get

her divorce. This was granted but it meant that neither her or my
father could go to England. I decided to leave but shortly before my
sister Win was married to Eric Waldron. My father was talking of
retiring and going to start an estancia in La Plata. I wrote for him the
sonnet 'Argentine Railways'.[11]

★

I went with Kathleen Bellamy (she is now Lady White – her
husband worked for M15)[12] on the Continent. She had fair hair,
black eyebrows and eyelashes. She was very lively and generous. We
each had £5 per week. She would write articles for *La Nacion*,
Buenos Aires, and I would illustrate them when suitable. It was
some years before the War but in Munich the baiting of the Jews
had started. The Nazis would search for them out of their homes
and take them jeering into the middle of the road. Other shops with
Jewish names would be broken down, the glass falling everywhere.
In the Pension where we were the owner was Jewish. Her name
was Frau Hostrup. She was very frightened and nervous. One day in
innocence I brought in a magazine which was the Nazi propaganda.
I think it was called *Stern*, anyway Frau Hostrup found it and was
horrified. She took it away. In the pension was also a young Jew, a
brilliant flautist. He too was shaking in fear. He would practise his
flute by the cadence using variety of speed and light and shade. Bach
is what he practised. His name, for he was a performer, was
Demetrius Callimahos. In the park there was a Nazi gathering. They
played the National Anthem but I remained seated. 'You could be
put in prison for that,' someone said.

   We left for Austria, then on to Buda and Pest. The train to Buda
and Pest was pretty stiff in the third class. The usual chickens and
geese hanging down from the luggage rack. We both talked and no
one understood. Outside the window were black pigs running
everywhere. The dark brown rectangular wooden houses were one
storied with a sky light in the roof. It seemed quite poor. At a night
club in Pest across the river we learnt the czardas. Callimahos joined
us in both Austria and Buda but when we introduced him to Johann
Strauss, a relative of Richard Strauss he vanished.

   We came back to London and found a Mews flat on short lease. I
started learning flower decoration at Constance Spry's in South
Audley Street. I passed when only two succeeded out of twenty
applicants. I also passed the horticultural written and practical work,
so now had two diplomas. Constance Spry asked me if I would take
over the Head of her artificial flower department after a lapse of two

years, but I refused. About this time I was photographed by Norman
Parkinson and Lenare.[13] During this time in secret I had to decorate
two vases for the sitting room in Mrs Wallis Simpson's flat in
Bryanston Square. The Prince of Wales was visiting her at the time.
Later I made a friend of Ineke Van den Berg. We kept giggling
together. She thought I was witty so she asked me to stay with her
in Holland, Wassenaar. I enjoyed myself until I went out riding and
fell head first on concrete. I had to lay in the dark for days.

Another friend I had was Louisa Hagaar, a German. She was
studying for her thesis on Remenscheider. I was studying for the
Quattrocento painter Lorenzo da Monaco. Regrettably she was
killed by a bomb in Germany during the War.

[…]

In London I met Merlin Minshall. He was like Tarzan only with a
slightly upturned nose, or was he like the bulldog type, the latter I
believe. He was an architect and had taken his Dutch barge
throughout the canals in France. He had also done a lot of car
racing. He was amusing and I liked him. He talked about his digs
and how they had an architectural flavour. 'Would he,' I wondered,
'know of a place for me?' Yes I am leaving my old digs you could
have them. We went round in his Singer car and called at 68
Newman Street W1. On the top floor one large room with two
reasonable windows, another was a largish room then a kitchenette
and sitting bath. 'Yes please, I will take it.' I moved in straight away
and started my flower business. I called it BRUSKA. I knew
nothing about business but just added 100 per cent to everything I
sold or decorated. It was simple, I could not go wrong. I had been
to dinner and lunch a few times with Robert Adeane and his wife.
He was in Buenos Aires and met us in connection with the Railways. 'I want to talk to you about your firm.' He took me to 68 in
an Alfa Romeo – nice. When we got there he asked me, 'What are
your overheads each week?' I did not know what he was talking
about. 'I decorate the Hyde Park Hotel Buttery each week, do two
vases and occasional weddings that's all.' 'Well I wondered if you
wanted a van or something to carry your flowers in when you go to
the market at 6 in the morning.' 'No, I take a taxi if there are a lot
of flowers, otherwise I take the bus.' That was the end of the
conversation.

What I hadn't told him was that two crates of flowers came to me
each week from Tresco Abbey Gardens in the Scilly Isles. These
extraordinary perfumed and original flowers made my firm. They
were tropical and reminded me of Buenos Aires. Where did I get

my flowers the people asked at the Buttery? I would not tell them. What are they called?

I did the flower decorations for a Maharajah in the West End. I was invited to the Press Show. He brought his dancing troupe of musicians. They played and we danced. We danced several times, the entrepreneur having asked me for the Maharajah if I would consent to dance with him. 'Will you come to the Grosvenor Hotel for tea?' I said I would. I had to wear the same dress, a classical black with wide gold kid belt and large black straw hat with a huge French rose in the front. I was introduced to his wife and relatives then he clapped his hands and we danced. 'Will you stay to dinner?' 'I cannot,' I said. 'Will you come to the horse races at Ascot?' 'No.' 'Will you be my orange flower and come to India with me?' I said, 'I will think about it' and left.

[…]

★

I am recommended Celia Buckmaster to work for me.[14] She lived with her mother at 2 Kings Bench Walk. Her father was a Barrister. Celia is quiet and beautiful. We work well for a time and then decide to go to Tresco in the Scilly Isles. I decide on different flowers to be sent to No. 68. We find we both write. I had written some poems and showed them to her, also some stories. She had started a diary about a White Russian. We would go away again and write and paint. To Madeira. It would cost us if we slept on the deck and found our own food £5 return. Yes, we would do this. The ship *Hilary* was small and taking first class passengers on a shooting trip down the Amazon. We were to catch the steamer on its return trip. We had six weeks. I wrote more poems and Celia wrote more prose. Our house and studio and garden cost us £1 per week. I did a self portrait in oils and Celia did abstracts, we looked forward to hearing from London and Wales.

I had met Keidrych Rhys the Welshman and become attached to him. He was charming and spoke like a prince. He was a writer and poet and just starting his magazine *Wales*. I met him one evening when it was dark. We were both going to the same poetry reading in Soho. Tambimuttu the editor of *Poetry London* said 'May I introduce one poet, Keidrych Rhys, to another, Lynette Roberts, even if it is so dark!' It was not until after the reading that I dared take a look at him. He was 27 years old and good looking. I invited him and his friend back to coffee. 'You have a Welsh name, are you

Welsh?' he asked. 'I don't know,' I replied. 'Can I have some of
your poems for *Wales*?' 'I'm going away to Madeira, I'll send you
some poems then you can send yours to me. I will let you know my
address.' I had written and sent my poems, he criticised them and
sent me some of his. Mine were to be published in *Wales* as were
also 'Lorenzo de Monaco' in *Life and Letters*, with some of my
poetry and short stories. His poems to me were very good. One,
'Boxing Day' and another about Molly with him in the field.[15] I was
a little jealous of Molly as I thought I only filled his thoughts. Then
he wrote and said Molly was his pony! We returned home on the
Hilary just before Christmas. At one point, when entering Liverpool
no pilot had arrived so the Captain proceeded forward without one.
In the early morning there was a huge crunch and shudder and we
were on the rocks. A lifeboat was called and we went aboard. Alas,
we lost everything except my canary.

Merlin Minshall had asked me to marry him and I said yes. We used
to have exciting meals together. Merlin would cook Chinese food
and serve it up in Chinese bowls on plates with Chinese spoons. We
often had Sauterne or Barsac served in handcut glasses. On Sundays
we would go for trips in his car. He liked reading Trollope,
Dickens, Stern, Smollett and *Winnie the Pooh*. He always enjoyed
the part about messing about in his boat. He said I had improved
No. 68 by taking out the two cupboard doors and putting in flower
decorations and adding indirect lighting. He had one drawback, he
could get irritated easily, especially with the car. His wife was
divorcing him and he brought her to meet me. She was charming
and beautiful. I went to his hotel one day and saw a walking cane on
the dressing table. He said 'Someone's found out about it.' He
showed me. The manservant had left the catch between the stick
and sword undone. Merlin pulled out the sword. 'What ever are
you frightened of?' I queried. 'What was this terrible thing for?'
    The message reached his father that he was engaged and I was
invited down to his residence in the country. His former wife,
Merlin's mother, had committed suicide. Merlin took me into her
bedroom which had remained untouched. Then I saw her Bible full
of notes and references. He offered it to me but I would not take it.
Strange, his father was a Director of the Railways similar to my
father.
    Merlin smiled easily. Would I go to Suresnes in France with him.
'Yes I would love to go.' For an overcoat he wore a woollen scarf
and high pullover jumper. The car troubled him, he was going in
for another cross country rally but it [was] not fit enough. The

country of Surenes was unspoilt, it had slight undulations and streams, rich green grass, bushes and the occasional poplar. We came to a small tavern. 'Had Monsieur a room?' 'No, two rooms,' I added. But one is enough. No, two separate rooms. We had the only two separate rooms they had. The meal of steak and salad was delicious. We slept in separate rooms.

[...]

★

Celia became engaged and left. Sonia Brownell like a young shepherdess became my companion. She had no job and I could not give her one. She was intelligent and spoke fluent French. Eventually she found a job with Cyril Connolly, the editor of *Horizon*. He too spoke fluent French. During some of her time she would wander up to the Portobello Road and go to see the two very good painters, Victor Pasmore and Coldstream.[16] They had heard about me and invited me to go up, but I refused. Sonia married George Orwell and lived in the country.[17] I knew Pasmore's work, at the time it was French Impressionist. Later he developed the abstract style. I lunched usually at Bertorelli's on soup or spaghetti parmesan grated cheese and sauce. I knew Pasmore sometimes went there, he too would have a plate of soup. My hair was to the shoulders and curly. I flipped it up on top of my head now it was Edwardian. I put on a white silk blouse with a yoke of small frills and then added a black velvet tie around my neck. I went and sat at Bertorelli's. Pasmore was there. He kept looking at me, then staring. I took no notice. Eventually he came over to my table and apologised for staring so much. I smiled and said I didn't mind at all.

Sonia had left and I was going out with Keidrych. He would invite me to the Wheatsheaf, Fitzroy Pub, Marquis of Granby and other pubs nearby. There he introduced me to various writers and painters. I met Augustus John at his studio. George Orwell at two different pubs on separate occasions. I had heard that once someone talked against Wales and Keidrych biffed him. He supported the Welsh Nationalists but was not one of their party.

Before going to Madeira I had made myself some gorgeous skirts. They were fully gathered around the waist into a tight belt and reached down to my ankles. One was finely french pleated as they are among the peasants in Hungary. Another was patchwork in different textures with pieces of mirror embroidered on. The choice of material was important. This coming evening I had put on one

made of Japanese hand blocked print in brick and puce with wisteria
design and colour. It was my favourite. I went alone to the Wheatsheaf to meet Keidrych. [...]

Keidrych sometimes went to Hampstead for the night but if he
missed the Tube he would go elsewhere. One day he showed me
where this was. He took me to a large room full of single beds. They
were beautifully clean and each had a white counterpane. Keidrych
usually 'kipped' with Pat Barton. The cost was 1/6 per night.

[...]

It was 1939. War was imminent, and we knew Keidrych and I that
he would be called up. We loved each other and had mutual inter-
ests. He asked me to marry him. I said I wouldn't give a direct
answer and must tell Merlin first. I told Merlin and we were both
relieved, it was over between us. Keidrych and I decided to go
straight to Wales. On the train I told Keidrych I would marry him.
We decided to live in a cottage in the country. Keidrych told me
that his parents treated him like a boy and that his mother nagged
him. When we arrive at their farm the two pet lambs leapt up at
him. He points out the salmon river and a few of the fields. We go
into the farm house. His mother thinks I am marrying him because
I am pregnant. I feel insulted. They speak Welsh all of them. I look
forward to leaving. The next day we go to Laugharne to visit Dylan
Thomas. This was in connection with the *Wales* magazine.

   We went high up Gosport Street and knocked. Both Dylan and
Caitlin were in. They came to the door together. They were not yet
in Sea View nor did they know at the time they had the prospect of
going there. They had a year ago married at Mousehole, Cornwall.
Yes, Keidrych could have a poem, he had already printed a section
of prose for *Wales*. Dylan had strong curly hair, a fleshy snub nose, a
full mouth and large brown eyes. Caitlin had fair curly hair but the
curls were smaller and finer and often on their own persuasion
turned into tendrils., She wore no makeup and looked like a shepherdess with blue smiling eyes. They were both warm and generous
to speak to and were very happy.

   A short while later we called on Dylan at Sea View. He stood
there in high navy blue sweater and cordoroy trousers looking like a
deep sea fisherman. He had no fire. He spoke of Caitlin being in
hospital to have her child. That he was fed up about the cancellation
of the broadcast on Welsh poetry that he was to have broadcast with
Keidrych. That he was working on a poem for Caitlin and had
nearly completed it.

I went straight back to London to get my furniture and clothes ready to move. Keidrych stayed in Wales with his parents. During this time a postcard arrived from a soldier who had been called up in France and in it he said he was going to kill me and that he could always trace my address. This was because he had fallen in love with me and his father was from a branch of the Embassy. I was shaken at the time but then tore it up.

★

One day who should turn up at the flat of 68 Newman St but Dylan Thomas. He was smiling and generous of speech. He loved the flat and commented on how he would like he and Caitlin to stay in the other room when they were in London. I said 'You're welcome but I will soon be moving down to Wales.' What Dylan had seen and liked so much was a royal blue suede distempered room with fine flesh coloured netting at the windows, and a flesh coloured Indian carpet. The double bed had a white candlewick bedspread which I still have. The box of white daisies growing at the base of the window pleased him. Following this he sent me two-paged very long letters which repeatedly someone stole. They may turn up. Anyway he invited me to his new home at Sea View, Laugharne, and said they had free electric light. 'Would I come?' 'Yes,' I said, 'I would.'

I took some clothes down to Wales and went to spend the weekend with Dylan and Caitlin. I took for Dylan Everyman's Rabelais Vols 1 and 2 and another book the title of which I forget but it had a number of forms for writing poetry – circular, triangular, octangular, square and many other shapes. These he used. We talked together, Caitlin, Dylan and I. I gave Dylan some of my poems and told him Tambimuttu had said T.S. Eliot liked them. He said he wished he had written 'The long nosed god of rain'.[18] He read all my poems I gave him and said that I must work hard and persevere. Keidrych he said was not a poet but I could not agree. Dylan was writing a poem himself at the time and gave three lines from one poem and asked, which was best? Neither Caitlin nor I could decide. He took me up and showed me my bedroom then he said 'If you are here I can reach you whenever I feel like it.' I was apprehensive. I was fond of Dylan but not attracted to him physically. Fortunately nothing happened. When I left I asked Dylan what he would like. And he said beer for breakfast. So I had a crate of beer sent to him.

I had a friend Betty who I called Bettore who polished the black linoleum floor for me. She was sad to leave me and worked in the basement at Lyons – about this time I met my Argentine friend Mariusa. I showed her the ring I had designed and had made up for my little finger. It was very modern in white and red gold set with a black intaglio stone.

I visited Sir Granville Bantock[19] at Mead Cottage, Buckinghamshire. He found out I was a poet and gave me an assignment to write verses for Richard Strauss waltzes. He showed me how I had to get the up stresses and down stresses in accordance with the music. He also sponsored me for a reading ticket at the British Museum. I visited him again this time with my published book of *Poems*. He had previously written to say he accepted my work. I met his wife Helen Bantock who was a poet and we had tea together. Their house was full of gifts from Sir Granville's travels to the East. He had the distinction of introducing Sibelius to this country and of being a Judge at the Welsh Eisteddfod, in fact he was called a bard. He himself was a distinguished creative musician.

★

It was late Summer 1939, Keidrych was still in Wales. I also went to Wales to look for a cottage. We both fancied Llanstephan. I stayed at the Cottage Hotel, Llanstephan. We decided to get married there. I wrote and told my father who sent me one hundred pounds. Keidrych's next move was to go and see Dylan to see if he would care to be best man. Yes, said Dylan but I've never heard the service and don't have anything suitable to wear. Who could help him? Finally it was decided to write to Vernon Watkins so the letter was sent.

We called again at Dylan's to ask if all was well. And he said 'Yes'. They gave us a pottery breakfast set which lasted a long time. For the wedding I did not buy anything new. I carried wild flowers and gave Dylan a bunchful of wild flowers for his lapel. Vernon Watkins' trousers were draped around his shoes. Caitlin looked outstanding in pink with a rose pinned to her breast. I was alone and late and I hesitated going into the church. I wasn't sufficiently confident. The wedding march was played three times before I entered and then as I drew up to the altar I found myself next to Dylan Thomas. After a pause the vicar switched Dylan to the side and put Keidrych in his place. Afterwards Dylan told me how impressed he was with the words of the service but he also added that he had never seen such a bevy of beauties as the bridesmaids.[20] They were Kathleen Bellamy the journalist from Buenos Aires and Celia Buckmaster who used to help me with the flowers and then had a book *The Village* published. The two of them, Caitlin and Dylan, together with friends went to the pub for free drinks. Meanwhile I had to be with Keidrych's mother and father and have high tea at the Cottage Hotel. Keidrych and I took the Post Office van to Carmarthen where we caught the train to Swansea. We had to sit inside the van where the parcels are usually carried to be hidden out of sight.

★

The honeymoon in Swansea was pleasurable. The Hotel was foul. We called at the Kardomah[21] to meet Keidrych's friends and met many whose names I am not sure of but one was Charles Fisher another American Talfan Davies possibly Dan Jones. Keidrych particularly wanted to see Vernon Watkins but it was not possible. We returned to a flat in the Cottage Hotel, Llanstephan at £3 a week. The Cottage Hotel was a white mansion that stood in its own field. This field had cows and it reached down to the sea. I have an entry in my diary 'Carmarthenshire Village':

> My sister's birthday and I have celebrated it by scrubbing the floor, cleaning the grate … Keidrych enjoyed his lunch; he looks very unpleasant today. Debauched with his four-day beard, he is busy scratching behind me writing to Kilham Roberts asking if the Literary Society will grant us some money to live on. There can be no dole for us. The Minister of Labour said we had no stamps. Even though we have both worked previously for two or three years. Neither can he give us a job. Then what are we to live on? There are fallen apples and onion soup, but how long will that last? Today Keidrych frequently finds cinders or grit in his stewed apples. I told him poets must always expect pieces of soot in their dishes that is their fate. He laughed and said what he usually does, 'You ought to be filmed.' His ears are scarlet and I hate him, he is always chewing humbugs.

I walk up to Llanybri and go to the grocery shop. I ask Mrs Davies if she knows of any cottage that is available. 'Oh Yes,' she said. 'There's one down the road opposite Rosie's.' I went and liked it very much. Keidrych and I went into Carmarthen to meet the owner. She said we could have the cottage for 3/6 per week. But first she would 'do' it out. So one room was papered pale pink and the other pale blue. All the woodwork was painted white. My furniture was brought down from London, 68 Newman Street, and we settled in.

Keidrych and I decided to make 'pele' instead of using coal. To do this he fetched a bucket of clay from Cwmcelyn and we had the coal dust to mix with it. Water is then used and all three materials trodden on until they are set, like syrup on a spoon. This is left until excess water drains off it and then it is picked up in the hands and formed into balls. Such fires are warm and peaceful to sit over, keeping up a consistent heat not unlike a brazier. The fires once lit seldom go out.

There was little money. Keidrych's mother sent one pound a week. We had whatever subscriptions came in. At any time Keidrych expected to be called up, meanwhile had had to join the LDVs.[22] He seemed to sit and do nothing. I started to get ill and began to nag him. This was unforgivable. In March 1940 I became pregnant and nagged even more then one day Keidrych said something about my father not giving us any money and I scratched him on the cheek. I immediately realised how wrong this was and apologised. He did not flinch but just forgave and kissed me.

The test about being an LDV meant that your poultry might be stolen and your wife might be molested. All the men joined in and night life became hectic.

Eventually I had a miscarriage through worry and lack of money.[23] I had continued headaches as well. I used this terrible experience in my heroic poem *Gods with Stainless Ears*.

How did we wash? The Diary has a note about it.

Well Keidrych and I wash once a week: we boil a bucket of water, strip exposing a small bare patch of flesh, we scrub the exposed part violently, then cover the part with wool, and immediately attack another part. Soon our whole body is cleansed from head to toe. We work thoroughly and methodically, each bending over his or her basin, sharing the soap which rests between us on the kitchen table.

My poem 'The Shadow Remains'[24] mentions this.

The two angels were given me by Sonia Brownell symbolising

Keidrych and myself who have not been acknowledged in the literary world for over 30 years.

Ernest Rhys the editor of Everyman calls. He is an old man and has a lot of literary things to say. He had a habit of coming up the Llanybri Hill, then halfway 'pressing' against the hedge and having a nap. As he walked he would gather various weeds for his tobacco and usually smoked them. On 10 May I met Ernest Rhys in the London ABC. There we had tea together and then went over to the office at Dents where he was to sign his name eighty times. It was sad watching him, his nerves were so shattered that he could only sign his name with the greatest of trouble, taking about five minutes over each signature.

Ernest Rhys told me a strange story about Ezra Pound. 'Once he Yeats and Ezra Pound were dining with a friend and his first wife, and that in the course of conversation Pound would occasionally bend forward and take a petal from one of the tulips centred in the middle of the table and then proceed to eat it. To the astonishment of all, he soon scoffed the whole lot. Followed by a large drink of iced water. He then took his hostess's animal rug, swirled this around him and curled up to sleep.'

Keidrych and I go to help turn the hay. On the way he remarks on my wooden rake and says he prefers the Llandeilo rake as its prongs lie vertically to the handle and so when in use it lies flat to the ground. My wooden rake had straight prongs. I am given the inner circle of the hay field as it is easier whilst Keidrych is given the outer circle. We cover several fields before we stop, having refreshment from time to time. The soft shade of green throughout the field vanishes and turns to grey. The farmers and their wives girls and boys who help are so jovial, they are full of fun. The wagons made by the local carpenter are all nasturtium orange and vivid blue. The hay is pitched and mounted up into a rick, some have a thatching threaded over the top.

I had been ill some time and they all came with their varied gifts.

Keidrych was offered a job about the time I was ill, that of cashier in Barclays Bank. But he had a Bankers Diploma or had passed a Bankers Guild so he was too proud to take it. As I explained, if he took it he wouldn't be cashier for long, he would be promoted.

After the miscarriage I stopped nagging and became reconciled to Keidrych. He would edit *Wales* in the sitting room. He had my walnut knee desk and his furniture was covered with work in progress, editorial, working on a poem, letters to subscribers and poets. Occasionally to my regret he would send my letters from Wyndham Lewis to me away. So we were very happy and content each writing in our own room. I never interfered with his editorship and he appreciated this.

Edith Sitwell wrote twice again and sent me £12 from the Royal Society of Authors. Her letters were warm and sympathetic. She also sent me some of her anthologies and books of poetry which I valued.

I was falsely accused of being a spy. Most of the village turned against me, and soldiers would be warned about me before I met them. A literary person coming from London was warned by Mr Mason the Minister of Education for Carmarthen not to see me. This person happened to be editing a Poetry Anthology. When I first saw him I told him about the false charges and he told me about the Minister for Education. I wrote a terse metric poem based on refuting their accusations.[25]

'Lorenzo Da Monaco' is published in *Life and Letters* and I have a lovely letter from Edith Sitwell.[26]

June 12 1940
The 10 o'clock news proclaims France has given in and I weep. By 12 July 1940 Keidrych is called up and we kiss lingeringly. Before this the recruiting officer didn't want him. He went as a gunman to the East Coast. Two villagers offered me their children to sleep with for company. One was a love child of six years old. 'Plasnewydd' is quoted re thought on war by some villagers.

1940–41
Evacuees turn up at Llanstephan. They kept all the girls and sent the boys up to Llanybri. They are strong and tough. They have no overcoats over their suits but wear their own knitted scarves and mittens. I borrow Rosie's harvest apron, a metallic print of mauve violets. I use it to put in my miniature paintings I am doing of the village. The one showing the estuary and Laugharne has my cottage Tygwyn in it. It also shows the methodical way the farmers distribute the lime.

I wrote notes on bird, flowers, butterflies and moths. I will quote one bird from my 'diary'. It is the moorhen. This observation helped to write the poem concerning its 'scarlet garters'.

Moorhen The dull slate ostrich texture of its breast feathers. The sheen of rust or parmel lichen on its back – the brown yellow gold of ginger-nuts. The two scarlet garters above the shining and rather large scaled legs whose vivid colouring was lime green, as fresh as the inner barks of trees. Enamelled or lacquered beak, scarlet with a bright yellow or orange tip. Brown eyes with a red purple sheen when caught in the sun's rays. The rest of the feathers are black.

★

Some time in May when Llewelyn[27] was about five months old we took the pastoral way to Laugharne. Down a narrow winding lane thick with blackberry bushes and budding wild roses down past the Pentowyn fields left to the Bell House and shrubs. At the gate we had looked over the estuary and seen that the tide was out so John Roberts would be there. We rang the bell and nobody heard. We rang it furiously and louder. Someone popped out of the white house and waved. John Roberts in his Breton suit was soon seen untying his ferry. It was lying in the River Taf Estuary. He rowed over, his trousers rolled above his burnished knees. This was because the river was deep at the two sides. He took us on his back and dropped us into the boat. We rowed across the narrow stretch and we were in Laugharne. We would return this way we explained. 'Oh you'll have to wait for the tide.' Dylan and Caitlin were pleased to see us. After discussing poems, particularly those in the making, we had 'cawl' for lunch. Then read poems and discussed the call-up for both Dylan and Keidrych. When would it be? We had seen Dylan alone, when he was composing a poem to Caitlin in her absence. I believe she was away waiting for her baby's birth. Keidrych asked if the poem was ready for publication in *Wales*. Dylan read Rabelais and a poem of Vernon Watkins. We had fish for high tea then went to Browns Hotel. Caitlin stayed with the baby. A steady conversation arose between Keidrych and Dylan. 'Had I got any money?' I gave them all I had. Hours passed, the tide was nearly right for crossing. Keidrych wasn't drunk only what I call sozzled. It was still fairly light, we found the ferry and returned home.

The next day we had a Dylanesque problem – no money. Keidrych had spent all the £3 he had. It was Monday, what were we going to live on. I said 'We musn't get like Dylan and get in debt, we'd better not go and see them again.' I went to the grocery shop and got food on tick.

After some time Keidrych went with Dylan to the Appeal Court in Carmarthen. Both were discouraged by what they heard the Conscientious Objectors say.

I am back in Tygwyn and happy. It is a beautiful spring day and that means the gardens which are the allotments are starting to get green. The shallots are up. I put on my red cloak lined with a Scottish tweed and wear underneath it a navy blue and white check gingham dress. I am so very happy I quicken my step. I reach the bottom of the hill parallel to the union hall. Someone in a white sports car passes by on his way to the 'sticks'. He looks up the hill and then smiles. I look down the hill and then smile. That was all.

Usually to get to Carmarthen from Llanybri we would take the van. This was run by the grocer. Besides taking about eight passengers, four on either side, he would accommodate lambs and calves. This van ran every market day, that is twice a week. The driver Mr Sid Davies was very unreliable and the return journey was frightening. His friends had filled him with beer and the only way he could drive was to go zig zag from one hedge to the other. 'I'd rather walk' I protested once when I had to endure this 'tacking'. But I sat on, sitting in the front with the door open, ready to fly out. Sid Davies was the head of LDVs in the village. If a bomb came or fire broke out anywhere we could not quench it, there was no water. We paid a water tax. At the bottom of the hill in the corner of a field there was a press button. This you had to push and keep exerting pressure forcibly without releasing the thumb until sufficient water came out. If the farmer was watering his cattle he still had to keep pressing the button and the thumb became painful with so much pushing. 'Its a bugger I'll break the damn thing,' said Jack Vaughan and someone did.

Letters fail to arrive from Keidrych. This was unusual as we have written to each other weekly. In the last he openly stated that he was taking a girl to the cinema and holding her hand. I was worried about the consequences, but admired his openness. I believed in being faithful to Keidrych and not kissing and taking hold of the hand of anyone else. He had been moved to the anti-aircraft guns in Dover. There they had shelling from the French coast as well as overhead bombing. I would go and see him.

I went up to London early November. I was nervous. The sirens started up at 6 p.m. I went to the basement of Lyons and found Bettore. I asked her to keep me company and spend a night at a hotel. I was at Hyde Park and she said 'all right then'. I booked in at a Hotel on the corner. Bettore and I lay in our respective beds, the bombs started to fall around us. 'That's near I can tell,' she quickly exclaimed. Two or three hours had passed. I took out my embroidery. I was rendering a 'whipping' stitch, joining silk georgette on to pure satin. It was the yoke of a petticoat and the whole of the front was in bands of zig zag.

Other bombs fell. 'That's next door' said Bettore. I could hear people screaming and the ambulances. That night I never slept. The all clear still had not gone. Robert Adeane was manning the ack-ack guns in Hyde Park. His home had a direct hit or someone very near. He lived at Cumberland Place. There was a direct hit on the shops in Oxford Street and many elsewhere. At 6 a.m. after the longest known raid the all clear went. I was exhausted. I had to go to the station and get my connection to Dover. I sat at the station. There were no trains, 'there might be some later on'. I sat on in a daze. I was shocked. 2 o'clock came. I entered a train. I looked forward to seeing Keidrych and to kissing him and having his arms around me.

We moved along very slowly. As we drew into Dover I saw Keidrych from the window. He looked angry and had half a cigarette sticking out of his mouth. We met and he didn't greet me but kept the cigarette in his mouth. He took me to a bar and introduced me to a butcher. He had to go on duty. The butcher told me I was to sleep in his house. That he had a butcher's shop on the front but was bombed out. 'This is where they put me – right under the ack-ack.' He said Keidrych had met four trains and was worried. I understood why he had been angry. I refused a drink. He took me to the ack-ack section. There under a tarpaulin I met a soldier. 'Who are you?' he asked. 'I'm Keidrych Rhys's wife.' 'That can't be, he has had three women already, I can't think how he does it. How do we know you are his wife?' 'Well I have two children by him.'[28] 'Two children?' There has been a big raid in London from 6 p.m. to 6 a.m. 'There's gerry coming over – so long.' He got up to pick up the bombs. Keidrych came along and did some calculations and then fired, 'Missed.'

I went to bed early. The next day Keidrych had some time off so we went for a walk. There was a dog fight on at the time and the sky was scrawled over with white lanes. He offered me his metal hat but I declined. We came to a little oasis, a few young trees and bank of rich green grass. How nice to sit down. I climbed up and began to sit. Keidrych quickly warned me off, 'You can't sit there they've hidden the bombs under that grass.' 'Oh dear.' We walked back for lunch – a butcher's lunch – huge side of pork, no shrinking ounces of meat. I sat down opposite a young woman. 'Who is this?' she added. 'Keidrych's wife,' answered the butcher's wife. 'His wife? Why didn't you tell me?' 'There was no need to, only a little kissing between us,' replied Keidrych. 'And much more, much much more.' She began to cry. 'You should have told me.' 'If you want your divorce,' she said to me, 'I'll give it to you, just come to my room.' 'So now you know,' was how it was summed up. I continued eating my lunch.

Something was wrong. Keidrych could not make love to me, he had got used to this other woman and their ways in the dark. I left it and I knew also who the other woman was who visited him. She spoke his language. I thought the best thing to do was to give him a tremendous kiss and I did this and he asked me to do it again. He was on duty so I went to the train on my own.

July 1941
Many of my poems are published and some are in anthologies. I have a backward glance at the Argentine my father and Mechita. I start a series of poems which were written here in Tygwyn but they are a South American group.

1942 we have notice to quit Tygwyn. The landlord will sell it for a hundred pounds.

I missed Keidrych dreadfully. I joined him in Yarmouth and had to pass through London so I went to Celia Buckmaster's home at Kings Bench Walk. I was astonished to find the results of a raid were still pending after days. The fireman were pinned to the bleached bricks trying to put out the fires. The library books were in heaps on the ground. The Round Church had had a direct hit. The coloured windows were blown out and in brilliant pieces on the ground. Pegasus had melted and fallen, there remained a plane tree, some lily of the valley. It was Celia's mother who executed such bravery. The gentlemen assigned to be there had missed duty.

On the east coast on the cliff at Yarmouth there was near death for both of us when a gerry plane merged into the cliff through the moist sea mist. It struck a bomb onto the pier. As it approached below cliff level it had suddenly to swerve to avoid a crash. Keidrych used to the bombs dropped to cover behind a concrete block. I saw a soldier standing alone and preferred to stand still with him. There was no room behind the concrete block for three. A few seconds later the plane exploded, brought down by a battery a few hundred yards away. The soldier unknown to us came over and asked

Keidrych if he might 'shake the lady by the hand'. I suppose he thought I had been brave. But I was not brave. I told him I would not dive down and leave him standing there alone. It was a miracle the plane didn't crash on the highly fortified beach.

From these two bombing experiences I wrote 'Crossed and Uncrossed' the title referring to the ways of burial of the crusaders. Their shock I point out in the poem causes the crusaders to uncross their legs and through burning they turn into tang shapes.[27]

Lynette Roberts's gravestone, Llanybri. Photograph © Jean Storey.

Notes

CP = Lynette Roberts, *Collected Poems*, ed. Patrick McGuinness (Carcanet Press, 2005)

A Carmarthenshire Diary

1 'Ty Gwyn', which in Welsh means 'White House', was not included in *Poems* (1944) and was not published until 1953, when it appeared in *Poetry* (Chicago), 82. It appears in *CP* on p. 89.
2 Douglas Glass (1901–78), photographer. Among his famous portraits are studies of Graham Greene and Giacometti. See also Roberts's letter to Robert Graves 1 November 1944 (p. 180).
3 *CP*, p. 12.
4 *CP*, pp. 24–5.
5 LDV: the Local Defence Volunteers, or Home Guard; BEF: the British Expeditionary Force.
6 From 'The Shadow Remains', *CP*, p. 4.
7 Ernest Rhys (1859–1946), London-born Welsh writer and founder-editor of J.M. Dent's Everyman library. He was a founder-member, in 1890, of the Rhymer's Club, which included Ernest Dowson, Lionel Johnson and Arthur Symons. His *Welsh Ballads* appeared in 1898. The title of his autobiography, *Wales England Wed*, is taken from his short poem the same name, and which begins 'Wales England wed, so I was bred ...'
8 W.H. Hudson (1861–1922), writer and naturalist with an interest in South America. His most famous novel, *Green Mansions*, appeared in 1904, and his autobiographical memoir, *Far Away and Long Ago* in 1917. The latter tells of his childhood in the South American *pampa*.
9 This poem, or the poem it is part of, was never published and was not among the manuscripts of Roberts's unpublished poems.
10 Rosie Davies's words recorded here form the basis of the poem 'Plasnewydd', *CP*, pp. 4–5.
11 *CP*, p. 19.
12 'Death that Monster' is among Roberts's unpublished poems.
13 *CP*, p. 26.
14 The poem did not appear in *Poems*, but was found in typescript among the poems submitted to Eliot for a third book of poems. The manuscript has a handwritten comment at the bottom by T.S. Eliot: 'Rough. But interesting'. It appears on *CP*, p. 91.
15 'Eiluned' or 'Eluned' (pronounced 'Elined'), is the Welsh name

'Lynette'.

16 *Gyda chofion caredicaf*: 'with loving wishes'.

17 *CP*, pp. 5–6.

18 *Hen wlad*: 'old country'.

19 *Calon cryf*: 'strong heart'. *Gyda chofion caredicaf*: see n. 16 above.

20 *CP*, pp. 4–5.

21 *Cofion Caredig I gyd*: 'love to all'; *cofiadur*: Ernest Rhys means a short biographical sketch; *dyn tlawd*: 'poor man'.

22 *CP*, p. 10.

23 The letters between Alun Lewis and Lynette Roberts and Keidrych Rhys can be found in *Wales* VIII/28 (February/March 1948). For an account of the friendship between Roberts and Lewis, see John Pikoulis, 'Lynette Roberts and Alun Lewis', *Poetry Wales* 19/2 (1983).

24 The poem that Roberts made from this connection is 'The Temple Road', *CP*, p. 98.

25 The painting to which Roberts refers is now lost, though a colour photograph exists. It is reproduced on p. 1.

26 The sequence of poems to which she refers are on pp. 27–31 of *CP*.

27 *CP*, pp. 14–17.

28 *CP*, p. 13.

29 'The Circle of C', *CP*, p. 7.

30 The poem 'Paulinus' is among those Roberts sent to Eliot for his consideration at Faber. It is unpublished.

31 *CP*, p. 20.

32 *CP*, pp. 8–9.

33 *CP*, pp. 6–7.

34 Mansel Thomas (1909–86), composer, conductor and radio broadcaster; later Head of Music at BBC Wales.

35 CEMA: the Council for the Encouragement of Music and the Arts.

36 Grace Williams (1906–77), composer and friend of Benjamin Britten. Her *Fantasia on Welsh Nursery Tunes* was composed in 1940. Arwel Hughes (1909–88), conductor and composer, succeeded Mansel Thomas as Head of Music at BBC Wales. Daniel Jones (1912–93), composer and friend of Dylan Thomas. Jones wrote the music for the 1954 radio production of *Under Milk Wood*, and his Fourth Symphony is an elegy to Dylan Thomas.

37 Vaughan Thomas (David Vaughan Thomas, 1873–1934), composer, best known for his settings of Welsh poetry and folksong arrangements. 'Canganyedd Ar nos ar brief': Roberts has mistranscribed the Welsh, and it has proved impossible to trace the work from the title she gives.

38 Roberts is thinking of 'The Love Song of J. Alfred Prufrock'.

39 Lewis's poem is collected in *Raiders' Dawn* (1941); Roberts's 'Poem from Llanybri' is the opening poem of *Poems* (*CP*, p. 3).

40 This paragraph is crossed out in the original text, with a handwritten annotation: 'Stupid. L.R.'.

41 *Maté*: a South American herbal drink. It is also mentioned in 'The

New World', *CP*, p. 28.

42 John Ormond Thomas (1923–90), better known as John Ormond, Welsh poet, journalist and documentary filmmaker. His *Selected Poems* (1987) are published by Seren.

43 There seems to be no poem by Roberts about the robin.

44 *Savorifach*: winter greens.

45 Among Roberts's unpublished poems is an unfinished poem entitled 'Sacred White Cattle'.

46 In her compact and suggestive poem 'Chapel Wrath', Roberts describes the changing tradition of grave-lettering, contrasting the 'machine-lettered century' with the 'deep set letters on shoulders of slate/ [which] announced their death with the pride/ Of a spirited horse' (*CP*, p. 93).

47 *CP*, p. 93.

Village Dialect: Seven Stories

1 *Cwtch* or *cwtsh*, South Wales Welsh for 'cuddle'.

2 *Pele* is a long-burning mix of coal dust, clay and water used for hearth fires. Roberts writes a poem called 'The *Pele* Fetched In' (*CP*, p. 89).

3 *Merchan fach*: West Wales dialect, meaning 'little girl'.

4 *Teulu*: Welsh for 'family'.

5 Mrs Jones, Parc-yr-Hendy: throughout her poems and prose, Roberts follows the Welsh custom of appending a person's profession or place of residence to their names.

6 *Tŷ bach*: Welsh for toilet; literally, 'little house'.

7 The devastating bombing raid on Swansea, known as the 'three-day blitz', took place over three nights on 19, 20 and 21 February 1941. Roberts mentions it in her diary, p. 47, as well as alluding to it in *Gods with Stainless Ears*. This story first appeared in *Life and Letters To-Day* in 1941 with the title 'From a New Perception of Colour: And I shall take as my example the Raid on Swansea'.

8 Xebo7011 is Lynette's wartime identity number; Xebn559162 that of her neighbour, Rosie Davies. Roberts also uses Keidrych Rhys's identity number for that of the unnamed gunner in *Gods with Stainless Ears*.

9 John Roberts, the fisherman, is transformed into a mythical boatman in *Gods with Stainless Ears*, and further described in the diary, p. 66.

An Introduction to Village Dialect

1 This article precedes the seven stories in *An Introduction to Village Dialect*, which were conceived originally as illustrations of the continuities between the living speech of Llanybri and the ancient forms of Welsh, and more generally of what Roberts perceives as the common

root between all 'languages of the soil'.

Since the article's interest lies less in its factual and scholarly accuracies than in the insights it gives into Roberts's ideas about spoken and literary language, between ancient forms and current dialect, and about the relationship between past and present, I have confined my editing to correcting misprints and silently rectifying errors in modern and old Welsh.

Welsh Essays

The Welsh Dragon

1   'Cawl', a Welsh broth of vegetables and meat.

2   Roland Mathias (1915–2007), Welsh poet, critic and short story writer. He edited, with Raymond Garlick (see n. 4 below) the seminal anthology *Anglo-Welsh Poetry 1480–1980* (1984).

3   Gwyn Jones (1907–99), the Welsh novelist and scholar. Jones edited *The Welsh Review* for ten years between 1939 and 1948. He also translated the *Mabinogion*.

4   *Dock Leaves* was founded in 1949, and in 1957 changed its name to *The Anglo-Welsh Review*. Raymond Garlick (b. 1926), Welsh poet, critic and editor. Garlick was born in England but moved to Wales and committed himself to Welsh culture.

5   Gwendoline and Margaret Davies dedicated their substantial inherited wealth to, among other things, the purchase of Gregynog Hall, a country house in mid-Wales bequeathed to Wales as a centre for the arts, and a large collection of modern art left to the National Gallery of Wales. The Gregynog Press, or Gwasg Gregynog, was founded in 1922 and continues to produce high-quality pamphlets and broadsheets.

6   Rhys Davies (1901–78), Welsh novelist and short story writer. Geraint Dyfnallt Owen (1908–93), historian, especially of Wales, and novelist. (T.) Rowland Hughes (1903–49), Welsh novelist, dramatist and poet. *O Law I Law*, his first novel, was published in 1943.

7   Gwyn Thomas (1913–81), Welsh novelist and short story writer. His best-known novel, *The Dark Philosophers*, appeared in 1946.

8   Norman Lewis ((1908–2003), travel writer and novelist. He and Roberts became close after Roberts's divorce. There is an unpublished poem dedicated to him among her papers.

9   Emyr Humphreys (b. 1919) is among Wales's foremost novelists, with more than twenty novels to his name. He is also a poet and the author of an important book on the Welsh poetic tradition, *The Taliesin Tradition* (1983).

10   John Gwilym Jones (1914–88), playwright, academic and author of two novels and a collection of short stories; Elizabeth Watkin Jones (1887–1966), a writer of novels and plays for children; Thomas (Tom) Hughes Jones (1895–1966), poet, teacher and short story writer. It has not been possible to find any material relating to G.E. Breeze.

11 Aneirin Talfan (Davies) (1909–80), poet, critic and broadcaster. He produced the broadcasts of Dylan Thomas's early works, as well as founding a Welsh publishing house and Welsh language magazine.

Literary Memoirs

Tea with the Sitwells

1 *Life and Letters*, a magazine of literature and current affairs, to which Lynette Roberts contributed, was edited by Robert Herring (see n. 3 below).

2 The idea of poetry and film is obviously important to Roberts. In the preface to *Gods with Stainless Ears* she writes that 'the poem was written for filming', and there are numerous filmic devices in the poem.

3 Robert Herring, the editor of *Life and Letters*, was also a notable film critic.

4 *Cynghanedd* is an ancient Welsh strict metre form still used today. Its intricate sound-patternings are approximated in English by poets such as Gerard Manley Hopkins and Dylan Thomas. Roberts herself uses *cynghanedd* and *englyn* techniques in some of her poems (see p. 5).

Visit to T.S. Eliot

1 CEMA: see n. 35, 'A Carmarthenshire Diary', above.

Federico García Lorca

1 Federico García Lorca (1898–1936), poet and playwright, was murdered by Nationalist partisans at the beginning of the Spanish Civil War.

2 Ignacio Sánchez Mejías (1891–1934), to whom Lorca dedicated his famous 'Llanto por Ignacio Sánchez Mejías ('Lament for Ignacio Sánchez Mejías') was a famous bullfighter who had retired but was persuaded to make a comeback on 11 August 1934. He was gored by a bull and died within two days.

3 Roy Campbell (1901–57), South African poet and translator. Campbell was, unusually for an intellectual of the period, a supporter of Franco and the Nationalists during the Spanish Civil War. He was also one of Lorca's most skilful English translators.

4 *Blood Wedding* (1933).

5 *Prima hermana*: first cousin.

6 *Gypsy Ballads* (1927).

7 Roberts is quoting from A.L. Lloyd's translation, *Lament for the Death of a Bullfighter and Other Poems* (1937).

Letters to Robert Graves

1 Henry Treece (1911–66), poet, novelist and editor associated with the 'New Apocalypse'; co-editor, with J.F. Hendry, of the 1939 *New*

Apocalypse anthology.

2   Lucia Graves, born in July 1943, the first of Graves's children with Beryl.

3   Graves at this time is working on *The White Goddess*.

4   Meary James Thurairajah Tambimuttu (1915–83) was born in Ceylon and played an important role in the English poetry scene of the 1940s. He founded *Poetry London* in 1938. Alex Comfort (1920–2000), poet, novelist and gerontologist. Later better known as the author of *The Joy of Sex* (1972), he was a noted poet and novelist in the 1940s.

5   Alan Hodge, Beryl Graves's first husband, collaborated with Graves on *The Reader Over Your Shoulder*, subtitled *A Handbook for Writers of English Prose* (1943).

6   Otto Rank (1884–1939), disciple and critic of Freud, was also reputed to be a feminist. His *The Trauma of Birth* was published in 1924.

7   *Nesta* was the working title of Roberts's medieval historical novel, of which no manuscript survives and which must now be considered lost. Most of what we know about it is in these letters between Roberts and Graves. Nesta, or Nêst in Welsh, was known as the 'Helen of Wales'. The grandmother of Gerald of Wales, she was the daughter of Rhys ap Tewdwr, the last independent prince of South Wales. In 1108 her kidnapping by Owain ap Cadwgan led to a war.

8   The gift Roberts refers to here is a copy of Graves and Hodge's *The Reader Over Your Shoulder*.

9   *Epilogue*: a magazine edited by Laura Riding and Robert Graves between 1935 and 1938.

10 It is not clear to what book by I.A. Richards Roberts is referring.

11 There is an unpublished poem by Roberts called 'The Priest of the Middles'.

12 Paul Potts (1911–90), poet, anarchist and friend of Orwell. Potts memorably called Dylan Thomas 'the biggest minor poet in the language'.

13 George Barker (1913–91), prodigious poet associated with the 'new romantic' and Apocalypse groups. Tom Scott (1918–95), Scottish poet and critic, one of the major writers of the post-MacDiarmid generation, best known for his poetry in Scots. Julian Symons (1912–1994), poet, novelist and historian. Ruthven Todd (1914–78), Scottish poet, novelist and scholar, influenced by the surrealists in France. Glyn Jones (1905–90), Welsh poet, novelist and short story writer. Jones was in touch with Lynette Roberts later in her life when she returned to Wales, and lived near her in Carmarthenshire. Julian MacLaren Ross (1912–64), writer, memoirist and dandy. His lively portraits of literary Fitzrovia give a unique insight into the artistic culture of the 1940s.

14 In a previous letter, dated 13 February 1944, Graves had written: 'Nesta back. She has great charm. The trouble is that you see her so much a part of yourself – of course, that is the charm of her, self-love is always the best egg to bind a story-cake together – that you can't make up your mind whether the story is called 'Nesta' or 'Lynette

Writing about Nesta', for Lynette is always breaking in with 'hoodoo', 'fou-frou', 'aluminium', 'Knossos', S. America, modern painters and so on ...' See *In Broken Images: Selected Letters of Robert Graves*, ed. Paul O'Prey (London: 1982).

15 Keidrych Rhys's Druid Press published Roberts's *Village Dialect* in 1944.

16 Nicholas Moore (1918–86), a poet associated with the New Apocalypse writers, and son of the philosopher G.E. Moore. His *Selected Poems* are published by Carcanet (ed. Peter Riley).

17 Laura (Riding) Jackson (1901–91), poet and literary critic, collaborated with Graves on, notably, *A Survey of Modernist Poetry* (1927) and the journal *Epilogue*.

18 David Jones (1895–1974), poet and artist who identified closely with Wales, author of two long poems *In Parenthesis* (1937) and *The Anathemata* (1952).

19 In his preceding letter, Graves writes that he has sent his son to North Wales to look for an ancient tile, believed by the farmer who found it to show the paw mark of a wolf 'but [which] I am pretty certain, now I have reread the relevant passage in the Mabinogion is a sacred paw mark of Arthur's hound Cabal... What shall we do if he succeeds?'

20 Alun Lewis (1915–55), Welsh poet and short story writer, was a friend of Keidrych and Lynette. She wrote 'Poem from Llanybri' for him, and he responded with his poem 'Peace' in *Raiders' Dawn* (the book to which Roberts refers as *R. Dawn*). His second book of poems, *Ha! Ha! Among the Trumpets* appeared in 1945. He died on 5 March 1944 in Burma.

21 *Poems* appeared in November 1944.

22 Douglas Glass (1901–78), photographer. See also n. 2, 'A Carmarthenshire Diary', above.

23 'Orarium': Roberts had sent a handful of poems to Graves, including 'Poem from Llanybri', 'The Shadow Remains', 'Earthbound' and 'Orarium', all of which Graves approved. He was less sure about 'Cwmcelyn', the final poem in *Poems* (which later becomes part of Part V of *Gods with Stainless Ears*). I discuss Graves's and Eliot's comments on Roberts's diction and vocabulary in *CP*, pp. xxxiii–xxxiv, and quote from their letters to her.

24 Juan Graves, born 22 December 1944.

25 Roberts received a lot of support from Edith Sitwell, to whom she dedicated *Gods with Stainless Ears*, but remained ambivalent both about her poetry and what she represented.

26 The poem is 'To Juan at the Winter Solstice'. The reference to the boar and the trampled flowers a few lines later is also to that poem.

27 Druid Press published R.S. Thomas's first book, *The Stones of the Field*, in 1946.

28 *Penillion*: a form of the Welsh *cynghanedd*. See also n. 1, 'Tea with the Sitwells', above.

29 The letter from Graves commenting on R.S. Thomas, to which

Roberts refers, is missing.

30 Eliot won the Nobel Prize for Literature in 1948.

Appendix: Notes for an Autobiography

1   Extracts from the typescript were first published as 'Parts of an Autobiography' in the *Poetry Wales* special issue on Lynette Roberts (1983,
19/2, pp. 30–50). The original runs to 55 pages of type, with handwritten alterations by the author. Parts of it have been omitted on the
grounds of factual inaccuracy or confused conception. The circumstances under which it was written – Roberts had just been sectioned
under the Mental Health Act for the third time – need to be kept in
mind when reading it. It is for this reason that it is placed as an
appendix to this book.

2   The previous notes had described the general neglect the Roberts children had suffered from their guardians, the Barwells, at a time of
displacement and confusion in their family life.

3   A reference to the mistreatment of Lynette and her sisters at the hands
of the Barwells.

4   Roberts's mother died in 1923, on the day before Lynette's fourteenth
birthday.

5   *CP*, p. 30.

6   The lines, which Roberts misquotes here, are in *CP*, p. 69.

7   Charles Dymock Roberts's death certificate states only that he was
born around 1913. He died in 1980, having spent his life in mental
institutions.

8   'River Plate', *CP*, pp. 30–1; 'Royal Mail', *CP*, p. 27. No poem exists
called 'Voyage Home', though Roberts may be misremembering one
of the South American poems that appear towards the end of *CP*.

9   *CP*, pp. 28–9.

10 *CP*, pp. 115–29.

11 *CP*, p. 29.

12 Kathleen Bellamy (1912–2003), novelist and journalist. She later
married Sir Dick White, head of M15 and M16.

13 Norman Parkinson's (1913–90) subjects included the Queen Mother,
Michael Foot and Margaret Thatcher. Lenare was a photographic
studio specialising in society photography between 1924 and 1977.

14 Celia Buckmaster (1914–2005), novelist and painter.

15 The poems by Keidrych Rhys to which Roberts refers are 'The
Prodigal Speaks' and 'Poem for a Neighbour', which appeared in *The
Van Pool and Other Poems* (1942).

16 Victor Pasmore (1908–98) and William Coldstream (1908–87).

17 Sonia Brownell became Orwell's second wife in 1949.

18 The poem Roberts refers to here is 'Song of Praise', found among her
unpublished poems and collected in *CP*, pp. 81–2.

19 Sir Granville Bantock (1868–1946), composer and conductor. Gran-

ville Bantock was Roberts's great-uncle. Lynette and her sisters remained in contact with Bantock's widow after his death.

20   This is confirmed in Thomas's letter to Vernon Watkins, claiming that the wedding was 'distinguished mostly by the beauty of the female attendants, the brown suit of the best man [he had borrowed it from Watkins], the savage displeasure of Keidrych's mother, and Keidrych's own extremely hangdog look and red-rimmed eyes' (*Collected Letters of Dylan Thomas*, ed. Paul Ferris, London, 1985, p. 419).

21   The Kardomah café in Swansea was the meeting place for a number of poets, artists and musicians, including Dylan Thomas, Vernon Watkins and Ceri Richards. It is still there.

22   LDVs: see n. 5, 'A Carmarthenshire Diary', above.

23   Roberts's miscarriage was in March 1940.

24   'The Shadow Remains', *CP*, p. 4.

25   'Raw Salt on Eye', *CP*, pp. 6–7.

26   The article, a mostly biographical essay on the artist, appeared in vol. 25, no. 34 (June 1940).

27   Llewelyn Thomas, son of Dylan and Caitlin.

28   Angharad and Prydein Rhys had not in fact been born at this time.

29   *CP*, 20–1.